CENTRE FOR CO-OPERATION WITH THE ECONOMIES IN TRANSITION

MASS PRIVATISATION

AN INITIAL ASSESSMENT

ORGANISATION FOR ECONOMIC CO-OPERATION AND DEVELOPMENT

ORGANISATION FOR ECONOMIC CO-OPERATION AND DEVELOPMENT

Pursuant to Article 1 of the Convention signed in Paris on 14th December 1960, and which came into force on 30th September 1961, the Organisation for Economic Co-operation and Development (OECD) shall promote policies designed:

— to achieve the highest sustainable economic growth and employment and a rising standard of living in Member countries, while maintaining financial stability, and thus to contribute to the development of the world economy;

— to contribute to sound economic expansion in Member as well as non-member countries in the process of economic development; and

— to contribute to the expansion of world trade on a multilateral, non-discriminatory basis in accordance with international obligations.

The original Member countries of the OECD are Austria, Belgium, Canada, Denmark, France, Germany, Greece, Iceland, Ireland, Italy, Luxembourg, the Netherlands, Norway, Portugal, Spain, Sweden, Switzerland, Turkey, the United Kingdom and the United States. The following countries became Members subsequently through accession at the dates indicated hereafter: Japan (28th April 1964), Finland (28th January 1969), Australia (7th June 1971), New Zealand (29th May 1973) and Mexico (18th May 1994). The Commission of the European Communities takes part in the work of the OECD (Article 13 of the OECD Convention).

THE CENTRE FOR CO-OPERATION WITH THE ECONOMIES IN TRANSITION

The Centre for Co-operation with the European Economies in Transition (CCEET), was created in March 1990, as the focal point for co-operation between the OECD and the countries of Central and Eastern Europe. In 1991, the activities of the Centre were expanded to include the New Independent States of the Former Soviet Union and, the following year, Mongolia. In 1993, the Centre was renamed Centre for Co-operation with the Economies in Transition (CCET) to reflect its wider geographic coverage. Since 1991, the Centre has operated a "Partners in Transition" Programme for the purpose of providing targeted assistance to the countries more advanced in introducing market-oriented reforms and which desire to become Members of OECD. The "Partners" are now the Czech Republic, Hungary, Poland and the Slovak Republic.

Publié en français sous le titre :

PRIVATISATION DE MASSE
UNE PREMIÈRE ÉVALUATION

Foreword

Policy makers in a number of economies in transition have espoused mass privatisation, i.e. the rapid large-scale transfer of state-owned assets to the private sector. Forcing through a rapid change of ownership in the enterprise sector has been identified as an effective way of creating a substantial private enterprise sector, which is an essential component of any free market economic system. Such programmes have posed policy makers in the transition economies with major challenges: identifying the most effective ways of transferring state assets, which account for more than 90 per cent of a country's total assets, into private hands and promoting the development of a viable private sector.

This report examines some of the different approaches that have been adopted by reforming economies to mass privatisation, including voucher schemes and state-owned investment funds, and some of the difficulties experienced in implementing the programmes. There is clear evidence that mass privatisation is by no means a sufficient condition to ensure the development of private firms: it is only a prerequisite. Enterprise restructuring must be another component of the process. It has proved more difficult to implement. While instances of voucher sales in combination with more traditional methods, such as trade sales, have often led to the necessary enterprise restructuring, they stand in contrast to examples where little incentive to impose rapid restructuring has resulted.

An important task thus facing those economies in transition that have embarked on mass privatisation programmes is to overcome the many weaknesses that characterise corporate governance and the existing difficulties in corporate financing, which are the result of inefficiencies in the banking system and the underdevelopment of financial markets and institutions. The expansion and strengthening of secondary markets for privatised enterprises' shares could offer an opportunity for a new wave of ownership change that could lead to the concentration of shares in the hands of capable investors and entrepreneurs.

With its focus on the experiences with mass privatisation of the Czech Republic, Poland, the Slovak Republic, Lithuania, Kazakhstan and the Russian Federation, this report aims at assessing the benefits and shortcomings of the main approaches followed so far. The various analytical contributions here included were presented at the fifth plenary session of the OECD Advisory Group on

3

Privatisation, which was held in Paris in March 1994. They are preceded by a Synthesis Note, drafted by the OECD Secretariat, outlining the main policy issues in the mass privatisation debate.

This report was prepared by Stilpon Nestor, Principal Administrator in the Directorate for Financial, Fiscal and Enterprise Affairs. It is issued on the responsibility of the Secretary-General of the OECD.

Salvatore Zecchini
OECD Assistant Secretary-General
Director of the CCET

Table of Contents

Introduction

The fifth plenary session of the OECD Advisory Group on Privatisation (AGP) took place in Paris on 2-4 March 1994. Its topic was "Mass Privatisation: A First Assessment of the Results". Participants examined the design, implementation and preliminary results of mass privatisation programmes from different countries in transition. Under these schemes, ownership rights to a broad range of enterprises are distributed to the population within a relatively short period of time by means of vouchers or, in certain cases, other means of exchange that favour small "investors" with little or no capital.

This report contains a number of the papers presented at the meeting. They were drafted on the basis of an OECD Secretariat questionnaire. The overview and issues paper, written by **Mr. Ira Lieberman** (the World Bank), describes the objectives of mass privatisation and examines the issues related to the implementation of such policies from a comparative perspective. Two papers are published on the Polish Mass Privatisation Programme: a descriptive paper by one of its architects, **Dr. Jerzy Thieme** (Polish Ministry of Privatisation), and a more critical commentary by **Prof. Jan Winiecki** (Warsaw University). There are two papers on the Czech Republic: the first, by **Dr. Jan Mladek** (Central European University, Prague), focuses on the process and results of the innovative mass privatisation approach in this country; the second, written by **Dr. Dusan Triska** (RM-S Exchange, Prague), describes the institutional framework and economic significance of the emerging post-privatisation secondary markets. Developments in Lithuania, which also followed a mass privatisation approach, are discussed in two papers: the first, by **Mr. Albertas Simenas** (Economics and Privatisation Institute, Vilnius), describes the programme and its implementation and results; the second, by **Mr. Algirdas Semeta** (Securities and Exchange Commission, Vilnius), focuses on the organisation of Lithuanian secondary equity markets and the problems faced by policy makers in the development of effective mechanism for the re-allocation of shares in privatised companies. A report by the KRP Project Management Group describes the Hungarian "small investor" scheme, which has some elements of a mass privatisation scheme, although it is primarily a mechanism for selling shares though public offerings in the stock exchange[1]. The paper by **Mr. Maxim Boycko** (Russian Privatisation Centre, Moscow),

Prof. Andrei Schleifer (Harvard University) and **Prof. Robert Vishny** (Harvard University) on the Russian mass privatisation, explains the reasons for its very rapid pace and discussing the benefits and problems related to such an approach. Finally, mass privatisation in Kazakhstan is the subject of the paper by **Mr. James Varanese** (White & Case, Prague); this country has developed its own approach and is at the first stages of its implementation.

A number of important issues emerged from the papers and discussions in the meeting:

-- **Political commitment and support** at the highest level are essential for the success of a mass privatisation programme (MPP). The implementation of a MPP should be preceded by an extensive campaign to inform the people of the contents and benefits of the programme.

-- The **credibility** of a MPP depends to a great extent on the steady supply of a "critical mass" of state-owned enterprises (SOEs) being offered to the public against vouchers or other preferential means of payment. The implementation of mass privatisation requires the establishment of powerful institution(s) that can enforce government policy on a large number of SOEs and proceed in a speedy and efficient way with their mass corporatisation and privatisation.

-- There are many alternative **structures of MPPs.** Some countries, like the Czech Republic, Lithuania, Russia and the Slovak Republic have opted for a "direct" system of distributing vouchers to citizens, who can invest them either in companies or through investment funds. In all of these countries voucher sales can be combined at the individual enterprise level with other methods of privatisation -- in Russia, they are predominantly combined with insider sales, i.e. to managers and employees. This approach has proved to be very efficient for the rapid privatisation of a large number of SOEs; however, it addresses to a very limited extent the problems of enterprise restructuring and corporate governance.

Other countries such as Poland, Romania and Slovenia have opted for state-created investment funds which own all or part of the companies to be privatised. Citizens become shareholders of the funds rather than the underlying companies. While this approach tends to address the issues of restructuring and corporate governance in a more effective way, the experience up to now indicates that these MPPs might be too complex from an institutional viewpoint; most of them have had to go through a lengthy process of political approval.

-- **Vouchers** are employed as a means of bidding for company shares in a large number of MPPs. Certain systems -- i.e. the Czech, Slovak and, to a lesser extent, Lithuanian -- have opted for non-tradeable vouchers which do not have a nominal value; these instruments can either be invested directly or through voucher investment funds but cannot be, in principle, sold. The advantage of this approach is that it "locks" the voucher holders, i.e. the population, in the process until they actually become shareholders, thus creating a lasting political engagement behind the MPP. It also simplifies decisions regarding the amount of vouchers to be issued. On the other hand, it seems that non-tradeable vouchers usually correspond to complicated allocation and bidding mechanisms that can only be implemented effectively in countries with a relatively small population and a limited number of SOEs.

Tradeable voucher systems are, in general much more sensitive to shifts in public confidence and require careful "supply side" management by the government; low credibility for the MPP might in this case result in a large-scale sell-off of vouchers for cash and a consequent loss of political support for the MPP. Such systems are also more vulnerable to corruption. On the other hand, they do not require the establishment of complicated bidding procedures for their implementation and might be beneficial in creating an *ex ante* concentration of ownership through the voucher market; thus, the transitional period between privatisation and the emergence of restructuring/effective corporate governance might prove to be shorter -- provided, of course, that no other obstacles are raised.

-- **Financial intermediaries** play a crucial role in the success of any MPP. The countries that have chosen compulsory intermediation in the context of the MPP are faced with the task of creating a real private sector governance structure and supervision for these state-created institutions. In the first place, this implies the "privatisation" of their management, as in the Polish MPP, and the establishment of an appropriate set of incentives for the private managers. Secondly, it requires a clear framework and timetable for the complete transfer of property rights from the state, their creator, to the citizens, their new shareholders; this is a prerequisite for subjecting the funds to capital market discipline.

Private intermediaries are playing a predominant role in countries with "direct" voucher systems. In the Czech Republic, more than 70 per cent of the shares sold in voucher auctions have been acquired by investment funds; the corresponding percentage for Russia is more than 50 per cent.

One of the more complicated issues regarding voucher funds is theirdual and to a great degree conflicting nature. They are, on one the hand, mutual investment institutions, in which thousands of small voucher holders have invested their (future) rights to property. An effective regulatory framework for the protection of these investors would require the maintenance by these funds of highly liquid asset structures. On the other hand, they are, under the circumstances, the only institutions capable of playing in the immediate future an important role in corporate governance of the newly privatised SOEs and, thus, of facilitating their rapid restructuring. Fulfilling such a holding function, however, requires extensive exposure to risk and much lower liquidity levels on the asset side of their balance sheets. Combination of the two functions might, at a preliminary stage, be unavoidable. However, regulation is needed for adequate protection of investor interests.

Another issue that is currently under scrutiny is the relationship between the banking sector and the funds. A captive relationship between the two might raise obstacles to a rapid restructuring of the corporate sector. A widespread combination of the lending and shareholding function in the banks might create conflicts of interests and incentives and delay the enforcement of market discipline, including bankruptcy procedures, on the newly privatised enterprises.

Some countries have involved newly created pension funds in the process of mass privatisation. Although limited participation of these institutions in the process seems reasonable, extensive exposure to the risks of mass privatisation, given the current level of uncertainty in the enterprise sector, might jeopardize social security policy in the future.

-- Most "direct" MPPs do not address the problems of corporate governance and enterprise restructuring as such. Privatisation is viewed more as a prerequisite of restructuring rather than the means to achieve it. In certain cases, restructuring concerns are reflected in the pre-privatisation process, mainly by combining voucher sales with a traditional method, such as a trade sale, for part of the equity capital of a firm. Moreover, the existence of investment funds and/or voucher markets might to a large extent mitigate the negative effects of widely dispersed share-ownership and the ensuing lack of effective corporate control mechanisms. In principle, however, it is expected that these mechanisms will emerge through active post-privatisation secondary markets.

-- **Stock exchanges** are playing an important role in the establishment of effective corporate control structures for newly privatised enterprises, and will do so increasingly in the future. In most central and eastern European countries (CEECs), their growth in value at the initial stage of their establishment as well as their volatility thereafter has been impressive. Exchanges were created as an immediate consequence of mass privatisation at least in three countries, i.e. the Czech Republic, Lithuania and the Slovak Republic; regional exchanges with little or no regulation are also becoming very active in Russia. In the Czech Republic, apart from the listed market of the Prague stock exchange

(PSE), which allows trading in a small number of enterprises, two competing over-the-counter (OTC) markets have emerged, the PSE OTC and the RM-S exchange. The latter represents an original approach to direct (i.e. without brokers), fully computerised trading. In comparison to its PSE counterpart, it is trading shares of a larger number of companies, which are however priced at lower levels.

The exchanges in the CEECs are still characterised by low liquidity levels. They have also been the object of an enormous influx of foreign investment fund capital. Although this is, in principle, a positive development which will contribute significantly in meeting the financial needs of enterprise restructuring it also contains an important risk, namely its highly volatile nature.

-- Although the development of exchanges is an important step in consolidating post-privatisation ownership structures, most block transfers of shares in privatised entities in the Czech Republic, Lithuania, Russia and the Slovak Republic have been taking place outside the exchanges -- sometimes outside the respective country. This **"unofficial" market** is likely to remain the predominant form of ownership consolidation in the near future, especially in countries in which stock exchanges are at their incipient phase. The existence of such markets is an indication that corporate control mechanisms for the newly privatised firms are starting to emerge. However, it might create serious problems for the further development of orderly equity markets. Important information asymmetries on share prices, supply and demand may result in unrealistic price formation in the exchanges and exacerbate liquidity problems. To avoid such problems, it would be useful to consider putting into place a framework for disclosure of price-sensitive information that would promote transparency in the marketplace.

-- Well functioning secondary markets in the post-privatisation phase will help to ensure effective corporate governance and impose restructuring on privatised enterprises. Obstacles that prevent the operation of secondary markets should be identified and removed. Enterprise insiders are often the source of obstacles through a variety of mechanisms, including "closed" employee ownership arrangements with share transfer and voting restrictions, extensive use of proxy mechanisms by incumbent management, companies buying back their own shares or other restrictions that limit shareholder freedom to dispose their shares. Company laws should be designed and enforced so that they effectively address these issues. Specific transitory rules for privatised enterprises, as is the case in Russia, might need to be developed and enforced by the governmental institution responsible for privatisation and/or state property management.

11

--   In many countries, an important role in the development of secondary markets will be played by **State Property Funds**, which retain considerable minority interests in a large number of privatised companies. In terms of corporate governance, these institutions, while being as neutral as possible in terms of company policy, should work to facilitate the involvement of outside shareholders in exercising management control. In any case, they will continue to remain a considerable source of equity supply for the markets; proceeds from these sales may be targeted, as in the Czech case, on meeting financial restructuring needs of SOEs that are still in the privatisation process.

Note

1.   This scheme has been discontinued by the new Hungarian government, after being implemented for less than a year.

Mass Privatisation in Central and Eastern Europe and the Former Soviet Union: A Comparative Analysis[1]

Ira W. Lieberman*

I. Background

The innovative method known as "Mass Privatisation" in Poland and "Large Scale Privatisation" in the Czech and Slovak Republics has been adopted by other Eastern European and CIS countries as diverse as Lithuania, Romania, Ukraine, Kazakhstan, and elsewhere[2]. Mongolia has also adopted and largely implemented such a programme. Russia has just completed its Mass Privatisation Programme (MPP) modelled, in large part, on the Czech and Slovak programme, but unique in its scope and complexity due to the need to extend privatisation to some 110 regions (oblasts), autonomous republics and major municipalities.

Mass privatisation schemes hold out the promise of rapid privatisation with widespread and equitable involvement of the populace. On the other hand, these schemes are exceedingly complex, hold many pitfalls, and if not developed carefully could both delay and undermine public support for privatisation. It is, therefore, of importance that countries beginning their privatisation programmes examine the various options open to them, and take account of the experience to date.

This report examines the experience of mass privatisation programmes in central and eastern European countries (CEECs) and the New Independent States (NIS) of the former Soviet Union. It draws on the lessons learned to see how these affect subsequent stages of implementation in these countries, as well as other countries currently developing or implementing MPPs.

Mass privatisation is seen as a critical component of the reforms to overcome the problems of the former centrally planned economies and their legacy. There were, for example, 25 000 state-owned enterprises (SOEs) in Russia, 8 500 in Poland, 7 000 large and medium SOEs in the Czech and Slovak Republics, most of which were and remain uncompetitive and unable to compete in a market-driven environment unless they are privatised and thereafter restructured. As part of a more comprehensive reform process (political, legal, economic, and social), countries in the region have to accelerate the formation of the private sector, and privatisation is a key part of that process. As Mr. Klaus, the Czech Prime Minister, has observed:

"We believe that the success of privatisation and, therefore, of the whole transformation crucially depends on a clear understanding of its nature, goals and strategies. It is not realized in a vacuum; in our case it is part of a very complicated transformation process from communism to free markets, to a free society"[3].

The demise of central planning and the halting transition to a liberal macro-economic environment made speedy transformation of property rights essential. In the case of Poland, Russia and Ukraine, there was a need to eliminate the vacuum that had formed in the governance of its SOEs, leading in many cases to "spontaneous privatisation" by the managers of these firms. "Thousands of these firms are now drifting in the limbo between a command economy without commands and a market economy still lacking the spur of private ownership. This makes rapid privatisation more, not less, urgent"[4].

This paper, therefore, seeks to accomplish the following:

--   define the conceptual approach towards mass privatisation in a number of CEECs and NIS, relying primarily on the Czech Republic, Poland, Russia and the Slovak Republic;

--   analyze the components of such a approach;

--   weigh the advantages and disadvantages, the potential risks and rewards of different approaches to MPPs in the political, social and economic climate that exists in these countries; and

--   examine the lessons learned to date.

II.   Mass privatisation defined

Mass privatisation involves the bundling or grouping of firms to be privatised utilising standard systems and procedures for their privatisation, as opposed to the more traditional case-by-case approach taken in the UK and other OECD countries, which has been widely emulated in many developing countries in Latin America and Asia, and Hungary in Eastern Europe.

The starting point for all MPPs is to decide on the universe of firms to be included in the programme. Mass privatisation requires a critical mass or core of firms to be privatised to create the supply side for the programme. The Russian MPP, for example, initially included all large firms (above 1 000 workers to a limit of 10 000 employees) and, on a voluntary basis, medium-sized firms (200 to 1 000 employees) in the tradeables sector. The universe of firms has subsequently expanded. The Polish MPP, on the other hand, includes a list of 400 to 600 primarily large enterprises.

The second key feature which distinguishes mass privatisation from classical privatisation is speed. MPPs create the basis for a market economy by privatising SOEs as quickly as possible. This requires mass corporatisation schemes to rapidly create the supply side -- a pipeline of firms ready for privatisation. There is no alternative if ambitious objectives are to be met. For example, in many countries, the specific objective is to privatise 50 per cent of the industrial sector over a three to five year period, but this is clearly not achievable on a case-by-case basis using classical methods of corporatisation, valuation and privatisation.

On the demand side, mass privatisation usually includes the wide distribution of shares (or vouchers to obtain shares) in SOEs to the public, either free or for a minimal charge, generally through a voucher allocation scheme. The vouchers are certificates or scrip that are distributed to the population entitling them to convert this paper either into shares in state owned enterprises (SOEs) through an auction process or into investment funds that have been formed to intermediate the vouchers as in the Czech and Slovak Republics and Russia. Poland differs as vouchers (called Master Share Certificates) can only be converted into shares in financial holding or investment funds, which in turn will own an interest in and manage a portfolio of SOEs. Kazakhstan is following a similar approach.

All of the MPPs discussed have included the development of financial intermediaries/voucher investment funds -- to accumulate and invest vouchers, to allow the public to diversify its risk, to strengthen governance over the newly privatised firms and to establish the basis for a capital market, a secondary trading market for the newly created shareholders.

In each of the MPPs, governments have faced the dilemma of what to do about "unsold" residual shares or portfolio holdings. The establishment of a state treasury or state property fund or committee in connection with the MPP is inevitable. However, these institutions will invariably end up being the largest single shareholders in the country, generally holding a diversified portfolio of shares, for example, 25 per cent of each of the National Investment Funds in Poland, up to 20 per cent of the large federal properties in Russia and up to 39 per cent in the newly privatised enterprises in Kazakhstan.

Finally, it has become apparent, as the initial MPPs have evolved, the critical point of closure for such a system is the formation of a capital (share) market. Capital markets allow the newly created shareholders to buy and sell shares, offering the potential for a real return on their vouchers. Capital markets reward companies and management which restructure and perform well. By contrast, they provide some degree of discipline over those managers and firms which perform poorly. Capital markets will allow ownership structures to change over time and provide the basis for the entry of foreign capital.

Each of these critical areas (portfolio selection, mass corporatisation, vouchers, investment funds, state property agencies and capital market developments) are discussed below. Other important but secondary issues, such as political will, property rights, corporate governance and restructuring, environmental liabilities, anti-monopoly programmes, institutional capacity, privatisation in the context of other economic reforms, and public information are discussed more briefly as complementary areas which affect the MPP.

III. Objectives of mass privatisation

Given the initial conditions in all ex-socialist countries such as little private capital formation; a lack of interest or confidence of foreign investors; political limit to the sale of SOEs to foreigners; and a desire to involve citizens in the process of economic transformation through widely distributed ownership, policy makers in many of these countries decided to initiate MPPs. The overall objectives were:

a) political: attempting to involve and commit the population at large to the economic transformation process;

b) social: seeking some form of distributive equity through the distribution of shares to the general public; and

c) economic: quickly privatising a large number of firms to deepen market forces and competition within the economy.

IV. Critical components of a mass privatisation programme

A. *Portfolio analysis -- selection of firms to be privatised*

The issue of selection or segmentation pervades the entire privatisation process. Countries in the region have a vast portfolio of SOEs to be privatised along with some that will remain as public enterprises. The experience of the CEECs is that no one method or technique of privatisation is applicable to every enterprise. But unlike other methods of privatisation, mass privatisation requires a critical core of enterprises to be privatised. These form the "supply side" of the programme. The first step is, therefore, to choose which enterprises are to be included in the mass privatisation programme.

For example, the Polish privatisation programme, created a rich menu of privatisation alternatives such as: small-scale privatisation for retail shops and service establishments; privatisation through liquidation (a form of management and employee buy-out) for small and medium-sized manufacturing and distribution companies; capital privatisation (which included the flotation of Poland's first five large privatisations on the Warsaw stock exchange); sectoral privatisation; privatisation through contracting out; and finally mass

16

privatisation. The MPP has repeatedly been delayed, however, because it has never been clear which firms would be slotted into one privatisation alternative versus another. The Polish Ministry of Privatisation eventually settled on a group of 400 to 600 large-sized firms for its MPP through a programme of voluntary participation. These firms are to be allocated between roughly 15 to 20 National Investment Funds, a form of diversified mutual fund, which are intended to provide corporate governance and restructuring assistance to the newly privatised firms. While the Polish MPP has been considerably delayed, it is expected to be launched during the course of 1995.

The Czech programme initially included all of its large SOEs in the large privatisation or voucher programme. In other words, corporatisation of large firms was compulsory. However, the firms had the right to establish their own privatisation plans, and competing plans from any interested party were allowed to keep the process "honest. "As a result of this, different privatisation alternatives emerged such as direct sales, auctions and tenders, and voucher sales. In this respect, the Polish and Czech programmes both employ a range of privatisation methods to privatise medium and large SOEs. But while the Czech programme has been able to secure popular and enterprise commitment to its programme through a bottom-up, market-driven approach, in Poland the programme has been blocked over the last three years by a fragmented *Sejm* (lower house of the Polish Parliament.)

The Russian MPP followed the Czech approach of compulsory corporatisation and privatisation, but it consistently maintained voucher auctions as the exclusive route to the privatisation of large enterprises. Almost every enterprise subject to privatisation (other than small-scale enterprises), therefore, has flowed through this single process. The Russian MPP offers three different incentive options for managers and workers to acquire shares via a closed subscription process as part of the MPP. In addition, certain industries deemed strategic by the government, such as the oil industry, employ variants of the MPP. The Russian MPP has generally emphasised speed and consistency of approach versus a menu of approaches. This is an important ingredient in its success given the size of the country, the extent of opposition to reform, and the emphasis on a decentralised implementation of the programme.

In all cases countries developing an MPP will need to decide how many firms form the universe of the MPP. There has to be a substantial supply of privatised firms to match the demand generated from the distribution of vouchers to the population and the creation of investment funds as intermediaries.

Deadlines and speed are extremely important. The Czechs chose to privatise all firms in two large waves over a two year period. The leaders of the Russian MPP, due to the decentralised nature of the programme, have kept the pressure on to maintain a high rate of regional voucher auctions -- reaching an average of 900 enterprises a month across some 81 oblasts and large municipalities. The programme was completed in June 1994, some two years from its inception and about 18 months from the initial pilot voucher auctions.

B.   Corporatisation

Mass privatisation requires mass corporatisation. This means that a pipeline or critical mass of firms has to be supplied to the MPP through a corporatisation process that is preferably simple and automatic. The Russian corporatisation process was compulsory. Firms were given, in principle, 60 days to comply, thereafter extended for another 30 days. In fact many firms took much longer to corporatise, but the compulsory nature of the process created the critical mass necessary to launch the auction programme. The process was administrative and not judicial. All SOEs eligible for were mailed a standard set of corporatisation documents, procedures and regulations. This set was also published in the large circulation daily newspapers so that firms had no excuses to evade the exercise. The standard documents included a charter, a method to value the firm, using book value as of 31 December 1992, as a valuation basis, and a procedure for choosing amongst three "closed subscription" options for distributing shares to managers and workers. Tying the closed subscription to corporatisation induced firms to corporatise rapidly.

C.   Vouchers

1.   Vouchers in practice

Vouchers are certificates or scrip that are distributed to the population that they can to convert into shares in SOEs through some form of auction process. Although mass privatisation schemes and vouchers are not inevitably linked, they are generally associated with each other. In at least ten CEECs and the NIS, vouchers are being used to speed up the privatisation process and to assure a more fair and equitable distribution of the wealth previously held by the state. By wide-scale distribution to the population, vouchers are intended to generate both popular support for the MPP and demand for shares in SOEs being privatised.

Czech and Slovak citizens had the choice of directly converting their vouchers into shares via auctions or placing them with investment funds, who in turn would bid for enterprise shares. For the first wave of the Czech and Slovak programme roughly 8.5 million citizens paid a nominal subscription fee to obtain vouchers. In Lithuania, subscription was virtually universal as vouchers were also used to purchase apartments. In Mongolia, vouchers were used primarily in a rapid and successful process of small-scale privatisation. Russia introduced a nation-wide voucher scheme on 1 October 1992, and vouchers were distributed to all Russian citizens for exclusive use in the MPP. In the cases of Poland and

Kazakhstan, on the other hand, holders of vouchers will use their vouchers to obtain shares in investment management funds, which in turn will own an interest in a portfolio of privatised SOEs.

2. Voucher economics

At first glance, it would seem that the use of vouchers would reduce the total cash proceeds to the state from the sale of SOEs, to the extent that vouchers displace cash in the auction process. However, a case can be made that the proceeds to the state will be reduced by much less than the amount of vouchers issued or not at all. Vouchers may stimulate the privatisation process as much as advertising and sales coupons stimulate purchase of consumer goods in the West. Information dissemination and educational materials related to vouchers and privatisation are likely to promote overall interest and willingness to participate in the process. Moreover, citizens of these countries only have a limited amount of cash or other financial resources to bid for shares in SOEs. In the absence of vouchers, the prices received for these shares may be lower than that justified by demand, reflecting the lack of cash. Issuing vouchers could increase the financial resources available for purchasing these shares, thus increasing the sale price -- and the overall proceeds to the state in the form of vouchers and cash. In the Czech Republic, spontaneously created investment privatisation funds (IPFs) started a bidding "war" for the population's vouchers through extensive advertising campaigns. They promised substantial returns to voucher holders who would place their vouchers with them. The Harvard Fund, for example, became famous for launching the first such mass media campaign and for cornering a large number of vouchers outstanding.

The use of vouchers may be inflationary. Vouchers are essentially an increase in the wealth of citizens and in most cases, a highly liquid form of wealth that can easily be sold for cash to finance consumption. While the Czech and Slovak programmes officially restricted trading, some citizens nonetheless traded their vouchers for cash. Moreover, the supply of shares (firms) available for privatisation and voucher conversion are likely to lag behind the demand created by the widespread distribution of vouchers, since it takes some time to organize a mechanism through which vouchers can be converted via auctions or bids for shares. This may increase the propensity to trade vouchers for cash (as is reportedly the case in Romania) and thereby increase current consumption and therefore inflation.

The monetisation of vouchers and the velocity of their turnover are, therefore, likely to have some impact on inflation; the magnitude of which must be estimated when the system is designed. The Czech and Slovak voucher system sought to mitigate the inflationary effects of vouchers by making them nominative, limiting their use to conversion for shares in funds or into shares in privatised companies, and denominating the vouchers in points, not in currency.

The Polish voucher is a bearer document and will become immediately tradeable off-line. Russia assigned a monetary equivalent of 10 000 rubles to its vouchers from the start. It also made vouchers immediately tradeable, thereby seeking to maximise popular support for its mass privatisation programme in order to counter strong political opposition in the Parliament and elsewhere. It created a large trading market throughout the country for vouchers, making them the dominant financial instrument in the country.

3.   The complexities of voucher schemes

The design of a voucher system and the associated system for auctioning enterprises to voucher holders is complex, requiring a series of decisions all of which affect the cost and complexity of the system. The key considerations are noted below:

-- Who is eligible to receive vouchers? -- all citizens, resident as of a specific date, all citizens above a given age, etc.;

-- How are vouchers issued? -- one or a series of vouchers, tied to the auctioning of firms in a series of tranches;

-- Should vouchers be assigned a monetary value? -- this affects issues such inflationary effects of vouchers, their tradeability, controls and security printing;

-- Who issues the vouchers? i.e. which institution(s) should control the physical issuance or distribution of vouchers, for example, the voter registration system, the savings banks, the social security, or pension system, etc.;

-- Are vouchers immediately tradeable? What other rules should govern trading of vouchers;

-- What are the roles of financial intermediaries? How will they be registered, regulated, and supervised? -- their linkage to the development of capital markets and prudential standards for financial institutions;

-- How are vouchers converted into shares? -- via an auction system, and inter-related features of the system for voucher cancellation, share registration and trading;

-- Can vouchers be used for anything other than SOE shares? -- buy land, apartments, etc;

-- How are vouchers and distribution of preference shares to employees linked?

-- Will the computer and accounting control systems for the vouchers be developed for alternative usage such as share registration and trading?

D. Investment funds

The Czech, Slovak, Polish or Russian privatisation approaches envisage an important role for financial intermediaries or voucher investment funds. The Czech and Slovak model is very market-driven and *laissez faire*. Initially it was thought that all the intermediaries would be domestically formed groups. Such groups were encouraged. Initially, little regulation or prudential supervision of these intermediaries was foreseen. Soon, however, major foreign fund groups -- for example, subsidiaries of Credit Anstalt of Austria and a subsidiary of Credit Commercial of France -- began to take a role in the process. The major domestic financial institutions -- the Czech and Slovak banks and insurance companies -- formed the largest voucher funds, the major exception being the Harvard Fund, which chose to invest a portion of its portfolio in local banks. Despite the large number of funds that initially formed to collect vouchers (in excess of 400 in both republics), ten funds only have accumulated 40 per cent of the Czech vouchers, and have eschewed a passive role, making these funds major players in terms of corporate governance and restructuring of the newly privatised SOEs. On the other hand, the concentration of asset holdings in a few financial institutions, concerns policy makers with respect to the independence of fund managers from the credit-worthiness decisions of the banks as owners. There is also a general concern that so large a proportion of total assets, and hence economic power, is concentrated in relatively few institutions.

Financial intermediaries are at the centre of the Polish mass privatisation process. An international investment bank and a consortium of foreign and Polish lawyers worked with the MOP to define the nature of these funds, their statutes, and governing regulations and a draft contract for the prospective fund managers. The investment bank solicited interest in these funds in capital markets throughout the world, testing initial market reactions. The government has received formal solicitations or bids and is in the process of negotiating final management contracts with these funds. The goal is to establish approximately 20 financial intermediaries in Poland as part of the MPP, primarily managed by "brand name" or world class firms, all actively traded on the Polish stock exchange. The key is to use these entities as "turn around" funds in their initial stage, and thereafter to float their holdings on the stock exchange, or otherwise divest fund assets. Each fund will take a lead share-holding of 33 per cent in some 30 firms, as well as smaller, highly diversified holdings, in a large number of the other SOEs to be privatised. Kazakhstan is following a similar approach. Its MPP will allocate enterprises directly to funds and shareholders will convert their vouchers to shares in funds.

The Russian MPP, like the Czech process, has allowed intermediaries to form spontaneously. The Russians learned from the Czech experience and put in place regulations to try to prevent fund abuse. About 640 regional and national funds have been licensed in Russia as of February 1994. They will not be as important as the Czech or Polish funds in the post-privatisation process due to the limits on share ownership, initially set at 10 per cent (modified to 25 per cent) of any one enterprise's capital. Moreover the Russian programme offers powerful incentives to managers and workers, resulting in large insider shareholdings. At present, managers are the dominant players governing most enterprises. Nevertheless, a few large funds in Moscow and Saint Petersburg appear to have collected well over a million vouchers and have contested management at the annual shareholders meetings. Russian funds are also very active in promoting privatisation and their strength has increased as the process continues. As of March 1994, Russian voucher funds held approximately 41 million vouchers (out of 150 million distributed to the population) and had invested approximately 63 per cent of their holdings though voucher auctions[5].

Intermediaries have become an integral part of all mass privatisation programmes. Their role is clearly established in the intermediation and accumulation of vouchers. As such, they diversify the voucher holders' risk by acting as mutual funds. They are also viewed as important sources of corporate power, providing transitional governance of the newly privatised firms are expected to deepen incipient capital markets. Some funds were developed to be turnaround or restructuring funds; and the role of these funds in corporate governance is particularly critical.

E. State property agencies

MPPs invariably leave the state with residual shareholdings. This arises from a number of circumstances: first, a decision may be made by the government at the time it develops the MPP not to sell all of its shares in the enterprises to be privatised or not to sell all of its shares in a specific class of enterprise; second, shares can simply be "unsold", that is left in state hands as a residual of the auction process; and third, timing -- not all of the enterprises can be sold in one round, so that the state most often has a large inventory or portfolio of assets until the MPP is completed.

For example, the Polish MPP proposes to leave 25 per cent of all enterprises in state hands initially. The Czech programme operated on the principle of two waves of auctions. Therefore, shares in a large number of enterprises, are being held by the Property Fund until the second wave. Also, for certain classes of enterprises a decision was made not to sell all the shares in one pass. The Czech Government decided to retain in the Property Fund, 40 per cent of the shares of the former state owned banks, (presumably out of a concern for financial stability) until it was able to assess the impact of the MPP. Finally, as a result of the first wave of voucher auctions the state was left with some percentage of the shares from the MPP, estimated as 8-11 per cent of all available shares, but skewed heavily toward relatively few companies in which the public and the funds apparently had little interest. Under the Russian MPP, the Federal Property Fund, a body which reports to the Parliament and acts as the final seller, exercised its right under the MPP to retain up to 20 per cent of the shares in many large, federally-owned enterprises. The Government of Kazakhstan has established branch holding companies for a number of sectors which will retain up to 39 per cent of all privatised enterprises held by the investment funds.

Continued state shareholdings presents all of the stakeholders with a dilemma. The state has to determine how to manage its large residual portfolio and what strategy it should apply to disposal -- rapid divestiture, revenue maximisation, finding core investors domestic or foreign, or deepening of incipient capital markets. In all cases, there are some who would argue that the state should hold a significant minority of shares into the indefinite future as the "shareholder of last resort" against systemic failure of the MPP.

Second, it has to determine how it will exercise governance rights over its portfolio -- possibly passively as in the Polish MPP or possibly actively as with branch holdings in Kazakhstan. The concern is that active governance gives the appearance of the state "clawing back" control over the same firms it has just divested. For the inventory of firms awaiting privatisation, interim governance has proved very difficult and is a major factor favouring speed in the process.

A third example is the Czech approach, where some of the portfolio holdings in the federal portfolio have been utilised to resolve specific problems in the transition from state to privatised enterprises. Some holdings have been transferred to municipalities as part of the MPP where the revenue from share sales will be utilised to cover the potential indemnities for environmental liabilities faced by these municipalities. Alternatively, the National Property Fund will utilise revenue from share sales to assist firms in cleaning up inter-enterprise liabilities, prior to the implementation of the country's bankruptcy laws.

In the case of newly developed, presumably thin capital markets, the state will often remain as the largest potential seller of shares with considerable influence over market results. Therefore, the state will need to act prudently in its divestiture of residual shareholdings to allow capital markets to develop and deepen. It is unclear, however, whether states will be able to resist social pressures and use these resources for political rather than economic ends.

F. Capital market development

A major and important benefit of mass privatisation is the development of secondary capital markets. Well-regulated, liquid, and efficient capital markets will play a critical role in providing corporate governance to the newly privatised SOEs. MPP creates a core of privatised firms rapidly. The Czech process has privatised approximately 1 500 such firms in the first wave and another 800 will go in the second wave. The Russian process privatised some 14 000 medium and large SOEs by July 1994 and the Polish programme plans to privatise between 400 to 600 SOEs by the end of 1995. Many of these firms will have widespread share ownership through financial intermediaries or via direct shareholdings. The development of secondary markets is therefore a natural outgrowth of the MPP. The Czech MPP has supported the development of an over-the-counter market in which many of the enterprises privatised through vouchers are now being traded. A second, more classical equity market has also developed, the Prague Stock Exchange, which currently lists the major banks, a few larger industrial enterprises and utilities and the major investment funds. The Prague Exchange also allows over the counter or off-market trading of some of the smaller issues resulting from the MPP. The Russian programme is developing supporting intermediaries (transfer agents, registrars, custodians and a Russian Securities Exchange Commission) and, in the course of 1995, expects to develop a series of regional exchanges. Already, shares of a number of the recently privatised firms are trading actively on the commodity and share exchanges in Moscow, Saint Petersburg and other major municipalities in Russia. In the Polish MPP, it is anticipated that shares will be floated in the financial intermediaries, National Investment Funds (NIFs), on the Warsaw Stock Exchange. It is expected that many of the enterprises held by the NIFs, once restructured, will be floated publicly. Indeed, this is the principal exit strategy for the Investment Funds.

Mass privatisation should be recognized for what it is: an initial transfer of ownership out of state hands by depoliticising ownership and by severing the link between industrial production and the state[6]. With capital market development there will be gradual changes in capital and ownership structures in firms. Workers and managers will "cash in" and sell to core investors. The markets will start to reward companies that restructure and perform successfully. Enterprises should be able to raise new equity capital for modernisation and expansion. Ancillary institutions will begin developing as new private firms in the service sector to support capital market operations. Information and research services should also develop to analyse these new privatised companies and to inform investors. Capital market development is, therefore, one of the most important by products of the MPP. It "closes the loop", that is brings closure to the voucher process by creating a liquid market for the newly created shareholders and intermediaries.

V. The supporting environment for mass privatisation

A. *Mass privatisation -- an intensely political process*

Experience reveals that mass privatisation requires strong commitment at the highest political level. Failure can rarely be attributed to technical reasons. The Czech Republic, for example, has been able to maintain the momentum of its privatisation process due to top-down political leadership from former Finance Minister and currently Prime Minister Klaus. The Russian programme has had the continuous support of President Yeltsin, who has enabled the programme to move forward against determined parliamentary leadership. It has also had the skilful and determined and continuous leadership of Anatoly Chubais, a Deputy Prime Minister and Chairman of the GKI (State Property Committee) since the start-up of the MPP. In Poland, the mass privatisation programme has stalled due to the political fragmentation which, until recently, halted Parliamentary approval of the programme. There have been several changes in privatisation ministers and constant in-fighting within the Government against the programme. Yet MPPs are also designed to bring bottom-up political support from the population for privatisation, and it is hoped other economic reforms. The widespread distribution of vouchers and subsequently shares in newly privatised enterprises or investment funds to the population, supported by public information campaigns designed to educate the population about privatisation and free markets, is intended to produce popular support for the transition to a market economy.

As such, a MPP is a highly political process, which under favourable circumstances, such as in the Czech Republic, has served its intended purpose. It has created several 8.5 million voucher holders, most of whom have become new shareholders. It has developed solid political support for the reform Government led by Prime Minister Klaus and it has served as the focal point in the transition to a market economy. Under unfavourable circumstances, as in Poland, the MPP has become a bone of contention in the highly fragmented *Sejm* (lower house of the Polish parliament) which has blocked the programme during the last three years. In Russia, where the politics of reform have been bitterly debated, the MPP has resulted in the Parliament creating its own privatisation institution, the Federal Property Fund, designed to oversee or control the activities of the more reformist government institution, the GKI. It has seen the MPP become somewhat distorted through parliamentary insistence that a privatisation option be created allocating 51 per cent of ownership to workers and management. On the other hand, it has resulted in widespread distribution of vouchers to the public and their ownership of shares in thousands of newly privatised firms. Moreover, the reform process has been decentralised through the active participation of some 81 oblasts and major municipalities in the MPP, working through the regional property committees (MKIs) and the regional state property funds, representing the regional soviets (both of which have generally operated under the influence of the regional governors.)

The MPP can, therefore, become either a focal point for market reforms, or the centre of the debate between reformists and anti-reformists due to its role in rapidly creating irreversible conditions for a market economy in the CEECs and the NIS. The primary issue is the political will of newly formed governments and parliaments. However, a poorly conceptualised or weakly-led MPP can also delay privatisation and setback the pace of reform.

B. Property rights

Mass privatisation is not viable in the absence of the unequivocal creation of property rights. The principles must be established by law and supported by institutions to safeguard and enforce them. New private owners need to know that through their shares they have proportionate ownership of all of the underlying assets that they have acquired in the newly privatised enterprise. They must have the right to buy, sell, and otherwise dispose of assets, and these rights must be upheld by the legal system. In addition, new owners need to understand property responsibilities, i.e. that they can benefit from the success of, and will be economically hurt by the failure of their investment, in short, that there are winners and losers in the process.

C. Preparation for privatisation: governance and restructuring

It has been assumed in the economic reform literature on Eastern Europe that with corporatisation and the imposition of the hard budget constraint, corporate governance would improve and the SOEs would automatically begin to operate autonomously and independently from government intervention. Above all, it has been assumed that these firms would respond to the economic reforms and emerging market signals, start to restructure themselves and become more efficient. It has also been assumed that they would embrace privatisation.

For many reasons, this has not generally been the case. Due to diverse factors such as lack of competition, rigidity of labour markets, restrictions on foreign investment, the importance of social services provided by SOEs -- including housing, child care, health care, vacations, sports facilities and even meals -- there has been an unwillingness to change the existing management, and a refusal to allow non-viable firms to exit the market. This structural rigidity has prevented resources from flowing into more productive areas of the economy. Faced with such circumstances, few governments have proven capable of imposing a hard budget constraint and enforcing and implementing bankruptcy legislation. Corporate governance is, therefore, an important issue from the time firms are corporatised until final privatisation. Also, governments in the CEECs and NIS have demonstrated an incapacity to restructure more than a handful of SOEs at a time[7]. The emphasis, therefore, must be on speed of privatisation, on decentralising the process, by placing governance and restructuring responsibility in the hands of new private owners.

One such approach is mass privatisation with its emphasis on speed, and a bottom-up approach which made firms responsible for preparing their own corporate strategies and privatisation plans, securing whatever outside assistance they deem advisable. In theory, to the extent the firm does this well and is committed to privatisation, it should become more attractive to the buying public during the voucher conversion and auction process. It has meant that these firms take responsibility for their own governance pursuant to or preparing for privatisation. Following the privatisation waves in the Czech Republic, the responsibility for governance and restructuring rests with the new owners, amongst whom, investment funds are seen as important players.

Given the initial strong commitment to privatisation in each of the countries in the region and the view that the process could be implemented quickly, interim governance has been given relatively scant attention at least by reformers. In fact, it is not clear that these governments have ever had the resources to impose interim governance during the transition process. A lesson from the experience to date is that firms that are part of an MPP need to be brought into the process at the earliest stage and their commitment to privatisation obtained. They should preferably prepare their own long-term strategies and plans for privatisation. Bottom-up commitment from the firms is essential. Moreover, given the fact that governance is difficult to establish, speed in privatisation is essential. Restructuring, with the exception of limited **passive restructuring**, for example to clear excessive indebtedness, should be handled by new private owners[8].

D. *Pro-competition policy*

Central planning left a legacy of heavily concentrated industrial sectors, marked by an absence of competition at all levels of production and distribution. This creates problems for the MPP with respect to sequencing and the interaction of privatisation and anti-monopoly or pro-competition policies. The Czech and Slovak MPP partially dealt with this issue by prior review and approval of all submitted privatisation projects. But it did not make anti-trust review a prior condition for privatisation. The Polish programme, on the other hand, anticipates a review of all enterprises entering the MPP and has a number of post-privatisation checks on the activities of the investment funds and their acquisition of shares in private enterprises. There are trigger points at which the Anti-Monopoly Agency needs to be notified of potential share purchases or acquisition of a firm by one of the NIFs. The Russian MPP seeks to prevent any cartels, associations or concerns from being privatised intact. It also requires that the lowest legal entity of an enterprise be corporatised and allows for plants or units of an enterprise to break away from a large multi-plant enterprise and privatise themselves. By July 1993, 1 237 sub-divisions of larger enterprises had been privatised[9]. Nevertheless, with the Russian Anti-Monopoly Agency basically focused on price controls and given the reformers desire for speed, the Russian MPP has clearly not made anti-trust considerations a first priority.

As with issues such as governance and restructuring, there has been considerable debate about privatising without first engaging in intensive anti-trust efforts. Part of the problem is the complexity of such programmes, the different approaches to pro-competition policies taken in the West and the capacity of any agency required to undertake such a programme. In general, the view has emerged that it is better to have imperfect competition than imperfect intervention and regulation of such monopolies. It is perhaps easier to address such issues with privatised firms, supposedly uncoupled from political protection, than when large monopolistic firms are protected by their branch ministries. At the same time, economic reform should also lower trade barriers, forcing enterprises to compete, thereby reducing domestic monopolies. However, this issue remains a real problem for countries seeking to privatise very quickly through a MPP.

E.   Environment

An important issue in privatisation in Eastern Europe and the CIS is the problematic environmental legacy of central planning. The Czech programme has dealt with this issue in two ways. First, by the Government agreeing to assume historic environmental liabilities. Some portion of the residual shares remaining in the National Property Fund will be used to pay for these contingent liabilities. Second, some enterprises were allocated to municipalities; their privatisation is to cover the cost of environmental cleanup in their area. The Polish MPP has largely sought to skirt the issue of environmental liability. The Government has generally taken the position that it will not accept liability for or give representations on the environment. The Russian MPP has also generally ignored environmental concerns.

While mass privatisation is basically a matter for the national governments (the republics in the case of the former Czechoslovakia), environmental issues are basically dealt with on a local or regional basis. Therefore, environmental problems may loom as an open issue for the newly privatised firms, as local authorities seek to enforce environmental standards in the future.

F.   Institutional support for the MPP

Mass privatisation programmes cannot be implemented successfully without institutional support, which must be unwavering once the process gets under way. In Poland, the Ministry of Privatisation established the Foundation for Mass Privatisation to allow it to attract talented local as well as external advisors. External consultants were hired to advise the Ministry on the organization of the Foundation, to prepare job descriptions and to analyze additional support requirements. The programme has been supported by external professional advisers -- investment bankers, lawyers, accountants, and consultants. Russia has established the Russian Privatisation Centre, as a way of recruiting advisers for the programme -- paying market wages to retain them. The Russian MPP has also been supported by substantial advisory assistance to make up for the relatively small staff and thin budgetary resources of the GKI.

Any MPP is a complex policy and logistical undertaking. Virtually all privatisation ministries, as new ministries, have been ill-equipped to design and implement such programmes. They require top level policy staff and advisors familiar with the operation of a market economy to assist with laws and regulations and implementation of programme modules for vouchers systems, corporatisation, investment funds, auction centres, equipment, training and public information campaigns. The amounts required are often trivial relative to the importance of the programme and the value of the assets being privatised; however, the sums appear large to government officials, and both governments and donors have often been slow to provide the necessary human and financial resources required to implement the MPP.

G. The financial sector

All of the CEE countries have learned that privatisation must proceed in tandem with the reform of the financial sector. The central credit allocation mechanisms and the weak banking system of the former socialist system are unsuited to a market economy. Moreover, in transition, countries such as Poland and the Czech and Slovak Republics have had to deal with a build-up of inter-enterprise arrears, potentially leading to systemic crises in both the enterprise and banking sectors. The Czech (and Slovak) government established a fund to clean up the commercial banks' portfolios in the course of privatisation. The major commercial banks have now been privatised, with the Government holding an initial 40 per cent stake in each of the five largest banks. Poland is currently recapitalising its banks and restructuring their portfolios. Direct linkage to privatisation has not been established; however, SOEs seeking debt forgiveness as part of the process will have to commercialise in preparation for privatisation. It is intended to privatise the commercial banks, once their portfolios have been restructured. Russia is presently beginning a programme to restructure and strengthen its commercial banking system and to twin a selected number of these banks with western banks so that they can reach international standards of operation.

In the short term, the commercial banks are important as a source of capital that will prevent the newly privatised firms from seeking government subsidies and soft, directed credits. The commercial banks are also a potentially important source of long-term restructuring funds to the newly privatised enterprises. They are clearly important for the provision of working capital for day-to-day operations. If the newly privatised enterprises cannot obtain such support from the banking system, there is a danger they will revert to government support. Moreover, over time the commercial banks should become an important source of financial discipline over enterprises through their evaluation of the credit-worthiness of firms. For the most part, they are not ready at present to assume such a role.

An area of direct linkage to the MPPs, is the role of the banks in assuming equity positions in newly privatised enterprises. Banks modelled after the universal banking system, as practised for example in Germany, could potentially become equity holders of the newly privatised enterprises and correspondingly play a major role in the newly emerging capital markets. This is clearly the case with the bank-owned investment funds in the Czech Republic. It should be noted, however, that this could result in concentration of equity and increase the fragility of the banking sector (e.g. first round of privatisations in Chile) and is a factor that should be taken into account when designing a MPP.

The Russian MPP has tried to keep the banks, particularly state-owned banks, at a distance from equity holdings in investment funds or the newly privatised enterprises. Actually the opposite is occurring with so called "pocket" banks -- banks owned by SOEs being privatised as their owners are privatised. A new phenomenon is emerging as increasingly new and private banks in Russia are owned by a number of enterprises in an industry or by a diversified group of enterprises in a region. The formation of these bank-industrial holding companies, modelled after the Korean "chaebol", is being actively discussed in Russia as an alternative form of industrial policy to supplant or augment present reform efforts. To the extent these holdings are anti-competitive, they represent a significant problem for pro-market reforms.

H. Public information and mass privatisation

Public information (public relations and mass communications) is vital to educate the public about privatisation in general and specific issues such as vouchers and investment funds. There is also a need to link privatisation in the public's perception to the overall reform programme and the transition to a market economy. The CEE countries have invariably understood this need belatedly and have rarely found the funding to carry out such a programme. Russia from the

beginning built a public information campaign in support of its MPP. In the Czech Republic, voucher funds essentially boosted the public's interest in the MPP and sparked demand for vouchers.

I. Privatisation and structural reform

Structural change and adjustment in the CEE countries will be a long drawn-out process and both political and public support are limited in terms of time. Privatisation is an essential but not a sufficient element of structural reform. Even where mass privatisation occurs and the process is accelerated, as in the Czech Republic, there is clear recognition that this is only the first phase of structural reform. Where privatisation occurs with little else in the way of structural reform, as in Russia, this leaves privatisation open to charges that it has failed. Extensive restructuring will need to occur and assuredly ownership structures will change substantially after the initial tranches of privatisation have occurred. The last lesson to be drawn is that privatisation needs to be viewed as a part of comprehensive reform programmes.

Notes

*   Based on a presentation made by the author (Ira Lieberman, World Bank, Washington, D.C.) at the fifth meeting of the Advisory Group on Privatisation, Paris, 2-4 March 1994.

The views presented in this paper are those of the author and do not necessarily represent the views of the World Bank.

1.   This paper is largely derived from a more extensive paper dealing with Mass Privatization in The Czech Republic and Slovakia, Lithuania, Poland, and the Russian Federation under preparation by Ira W. Lieberman, Andrew Ewing, Michal Mejstrik, Joyita Mukherjee, and Suhail Rahuja to be published by the World Bank.

2.   For convenience both processes are called mass privatisation in this paper.

3.   Prime Minister Vaclav Klaus, "Privatization Experience: The Czech Case," (1993), p. 1.

4.   The Economist, "Business in Eastern Europe," 21 September 1991, p. 5.

5.   Maxim Boycko, Andrei Shleifer and Robert W. Vishny, "Mass Privatisation in Russia", infra p. 163.

6.   See Boycko, Schleifer, and Vishny, *Opus Cited* for a detailed description of this issue.

7.   Ira Lieberman, Industrial Restructuring in Eastern and Central Europe and the CIS: an Overview, 1993, CEEPN (forthcoming).

8.   A debate within the countries and supporting donor institutions has persisted over before and after restructuring. At the extreme, the Czech Republic, with very few exceptions, has taken the view that every enterprise has a price and should be sold without prior restructuring. This is also the position of the Russian MPP. The Hungarian privatisation programme, until recently, has rejected a MPP, and has spent a great deal of effort on pre-privatisation restructuring in order to maximize revenue from restructuring and to avoid market failures of important SOEs post-privatisation. To date its approach has not been very successful. In donor institutions, on the other hand, the debate has focused on supporting the restructuring of large SOEs that will

not be privatised in the foreseeable future. It presents the danger of diverting donor resources away from the important agenda of privatisation and post-privatisation support and potentially sends the wrong signal to governments in the region, at this point in their transition.

9.   GKI, Monthly Mass Privatization Statistics, September 1993.

References

The Czech and Slovak MPP

BOHM, Andreja and Vladimir KREACIC (eds.) (1991), *Privatization in Eastern Europe: Current Implementation Issues,* The International Centre for Public Enterprises in Developing Countries.

CONTE, Michael and Jan SVEJNAR (1990), "The Performance Effect of Employee Ownership Plans" in: Blinder, A. (ed.), *Paying for Productivity,* The Brookings Institution Washington, D.C.

DORNBUSCH, Rudiger and Sebastian EDWARDS, "The Economic Populism Paradigm", NBER Working Paper, May issue, 1990.

GATI, Charles, "After Communism, What? The Political Agenda in Central and Eastern Europe in the 1990's", Third U.S.-Czechoslovak Roundtable on Economic Relation, Washington, D.C., 1990.

GROSFELD, Irena, "Privatization of State Enterprises in Eastern Europe: The Search for Environment", *Delta,* Doc. No. 90-17, Paris, 1990.

HANKE, Steve H. (ed.) (1987), *Privatization and Development,* International Centre for Economic Growth, ICS PRESS, Institute for Contemporary Studies, San Francisco, California.

HINDS, Manuel (1990), *Issues in the Introduction of Market Forces in Eastern European Socialist Economies,* World Bank, Report No. IDP/0057, Washington, D.C.

KLAUS, Vaclav, "Privatisation Experience The Czech Case", Speech at the Fourth CEEPN Annual Conference on Privatization In Central and Eastern Europe, 4 December 1993.

KLVACOVA, Eva, "Privatizace v Mezicase", *Ekonom,* No. 8, 1992.

KORNAI, Janos (1990), *The Road to a Free Economy, Shifting from a Socialist System,* Norton and Company, New York.

"Majetek Spocitan", *Hospodarske Noviny,* 13 April 1992.

MC DERMOTT, Gerald and Michal MEJSTRIK, "Czechoslovak Competitiveness and the role of small firms", Paper for the conference at the WZB, Berlin, 1990.

MEJSTRIK, Michal (1990), "Where are We Headed: The Case of Czechoslovakia," in: Colleen Duncan (ed.), *German Reunification: Privatization of Czechoslovakia, Hungary, and Poland: Implications for Western Business*, New York University Press, New York.

MEJSTRIK, Michal, "Innovation and Technology Transfer", Proceedings of conference, Institute of Economics, Prague, 1990.

MEJSTRIK, Michal, "The Transformation of Czechoslovakia to a Market Economy: The Possibilities and Problems", Seminar on Privatisation, UNDP, Warsaw, 1990.

MEJSTRIK, Michal and James BURGER, "The Czechoslovak Large Privatization", Working Paper No. 10, CERGE, Charles University, July 1992.

MILANOVIC, Branko (1989), *Liberalization and Entrepreneurship Dynamics of Reform in Socialism and Capitalism*, Armonk, M. E. Sharpe, New York.

MIZSEI, Kalman, "Experiences with Privatization in Hungary", World Bank Conference, Washington, D.C., 1990.

MLCOCH, Lubos (1989), *Behavior of Czechoslovak Enterprises*, Research Paper No. 348, Institute of Economics, Prague.

NELLIS, John, "Privatization in Reforming Socialist Economies", Conference on Privatization in Eastern Europe, ICPE/EDI World Bank /UNDP, Ljubljana, 1991.

RAMANADHAM, V. V. (ed.) (1990), *Privatization in Developing Countries*, Routledge, Chapman and Hall, Inc., New York.

SACHS, Jeffrey and David LIPTON, "Creating a Market Economy in Eastern Europe, The Case of Poland", BPEA, No. 1, 1990.

SHAFIK, Nemat (1994), *Making a Market: Mass Privatization in the Czech and Slovak Republics*, World Bank Policy Research Working Paper Series, No. 1231.

SHLEIFER, Andre and Lawrence SUMMERS (1988), "Breach of Trust in Hostile Takeovers", In *Corporate Takeover: Causes and Consequences*, University of Chicago Press, Chicago.

SVEJNAR, Jan, "A Framework For the Economic Transformation of Czechoslovakia", Plan Economic Report, Vol. V, No. 52, 1989.

TRISKA, Dusan, "Investment Privatization Funds on Securities Markets in the Czech Republic", Fourth Annual CEEPN Conference on Privatization in Central and Eastern Europe, Ljubljana, Slovenia, 1993.

VUYLSTEKE, Charles (1988), *Techniques of Privatization of State-Owned Enterprises*. Vol. I, *Methods and Implementation*, World Bank Technical Paper No. 88, Washington, D.C.

YOUNG, S. David, "Business Valuation and the Privatization Process in Eastern Europe: Challenges", *Issues and Solutions,* INSEAD, Fontainebleau, 1990.

ZAMRAZILOVA, Eva,"International Comparisons of Economic Development Levels Between East and West European Countries", *Jahrbuch des Ost-Europa Wirtsschaft*, November issue, 1990.

"Maly Zajem Dluzniku?", *Hospodarske Noviny,* 20 May 1992.

"Sest Fondu ze Hry", *Hospodarske Noviny*, 18 May 1992.

"Jasna Pravidla Predem", *Hospodarske Noviny,* 18 May 1992.

"Jsou Zahranicni Investice Dostatecne?", *Hospodarske Noviny,* 22 May 1992.

"Na Postach Prazdno", *Hospodarske Noviny*, 25 May 1992.

"Investicni Fondy Maji 72 Procent", *Mlada Fronta Dnes,* 22 May 1992.

"Natlak je Straslivy", *Lidove Noviny,* 27 May 1992.

Privatization Newsletter, Issues 1-10, October 1991-December 1992.

The Polish MPP

BELL, Joseph C., "Social Privatization: Vouchers Vs. Funds", memo to L. Balcerowicz, Minister of Finance, Kryzystof Lis, Minister of Privatization and Stefan Kawalec, Ministry of Finance, Warsaw, 1 September 1990.

BERG, Andrew (1992), "The Logistics of Privatization in Poland", Chapter 4, Harvard University Doctoral Thesis, Cambridge, Massachusetts.

LEWANDOWSKI, J. and J. SZOMBURG, "The Strategy of Privatization", The Gdansk Institute for Market Economics, No. 7, 1990.

LIPTON, David and Jeffrey SACHS (1991), "Privatization in Eastern Europe: The Case of Poland," Brookings Papers on Economic Activity, Spring.

Ministry of Privatization, *Program for the Privatization of the Polish Economy,* mimeos, Warsaw, 1990-1992.

Ministry of Finance, "A Plan for Citizen Ownership in the Polish Privatization Process", mimeo, 29 July 1990, Warsaw.

Ministry of Privatization, *Mass Privatization Programme, Invitation to Tender to Manage a National Investment Fund Under the Polish Mass Privatisation Programme (1992),* Warsaw.

Ministry of Privatization, *The Polish Mass Privatisation Programme (1993),* Warsaw.

World Bank, "Republic of Poland: Privatization and Restructuring Project, Staff Appraisal Report, 1992.

The Russian MPP

BOYCKO, Maxim and Andrei SHLEIFER (1993), "The Voucher Program for Russia", in A. Aslund and R. Layard (eds.), *Changing the Economic System in Russia,* St. Martin's Press.

BOYCKO, Maxim, Andrei SHLEIFER, and Robert W. VISHNY, "Privatising Russia", Paper prepared for the Brookings Panel on Economic Activity, Washington, D.C., 1993.

BOYCKO, Maxim, Andrei SHLEIFER, and Robert W. VISHNY, "Mass Privatization: First Assessment of the Results", OECD, Paris, 2-4 March 1994.

CHARAP, Joshua and Leila WEBSTER (1993), *A Survey of Private Manufacturers in St. Petersburg,* World Bank Technical Paper No. 228, Washington, D.C.

CHUBAIS, Anatoly and Maria VISHEVSKAYA (1993), "Main Issues of Privatisation in Russia", in A. Aslund and R. Layard (eds.), *Changing the Economic System in Russia,* St. Martin's Press.

Commission of European Communities, European Bank for Reconstruction and Development, and The State Committee of the Russian Federation for the Management of State Property (GKI) (1993), *The Privatisation Manual,* Vols. 1 & 2.

Debevoise & Plimpton (1993), "Privatization in The Russian Republic", mimeo.

DJELIC, Bozidar and Natalia TSUKANOVA, "Voucher Auctions: A Crucial Step toward Privatization", Radio Free Europe/Radio Liberty Research Report, Vol. 2, No. 30, 1993.

The Economist, "Russian industry: the revolution begins", 3 July 1993.

EARLE, John, Roman FRYDMAN and Andrzej RAPACZYNSKI, et al. (1993), *The Privatisation Process in Russia, Ukraine and the Baltic States,* Ch. 1, Central European University Press.

European Bank for Reconstruction and Development (1993), "Privatisation in Russia", Discussion Paper for the Consultative Group in Paris, June, 1993.

European Bank for Reconstruction and Development, "Privatising The Bolshevik Biscuit Factory", mimeo, April, 1993.

LIEBERMAN, Ira (1993), Poland's Mass Privatisation Program, mimeo, World Bank, Washington, D.C.

LIEBERMAN, Ira W., Andrew EWING, Michal MEJSTRIK, Joyita MUKHERJEE, and Suhail RAHUJA (1995), "Mass Privatization in the Czech Republic and Slovakia, Lithuania, Poland, and Russia: A Comparative Analysis", World Bank, forthcoming.

LIEBERMAN, Ira W. and John NELLIS, eds., "Russia, Creating Private Enterprises and Efficient Markets", World Bank, Private Sector Development Department, 1994.

MILANOVIC, Branko (1989), *Liberalisation and Entrepreneurship Dynamics of Reform in Socialism and Capitalism,* Armonk, M E Sharpe, New York.

NELLIS, John (1991), "Improving the Performance of Soviet Enterprises", Discussion Paper No. 118, World Bank, Washington, D.C.

NELLIS, John (1993), "Bolshevik Biscuit in Private Hands", *Transition,* Vol. 4, No. 2, World Bank, Washington, D.C.

Price Waterhouse (1993), "Funds Monitoring Report", mimeo.

Sawyer/Miller Group (1993), "Privatization and Popular Mandates: Using Communications to Ensure Sustainable Reform", mimeo, Washington, D.C.

ST. GILES, Mark and Sally BUXTON (1993), "The Role of Investment Funds in the Russian Privatisation Programme", mimeo, London.

The State Committee of the Russian Federation for the Management of State Property (1992) "The Russian Privatisation Program: A Guide for Foreign Investors", mimeo.

THOMAS, Scott and Heidi KROLL, "The Political Economy in Russia", *Communist Economies and Economic Transformation,* Vol. 5, No. 4, 1993.

The Polish Mass Privatisation Programme

Jerzy Thieme, Ph.D.*

I.   Introduction

The basis for implementation of the Mass Privatisation Programme (MPP)[1] is the Law on National Investment Funds and Their Privatisation of 30 April 1993. The Law came into force on 15 June 1993. Alternative concepts ("300 million" and others) never emerged in Poland in a shape which would allow for a serious analysis of their feasibility or for any serious steps towards their implementation.

MPP is the only programme of ownership transformation on a large scale which has been sanctioned by a Parliamentary act. This was a result of endeavours of consecutive governments which, even though they did not hold a majority in Parliament, used their best efforts to enact the necessary legislation.

II.   Towards mass privatisation

The state-owned sector of the Polish industry requires restructuring. Much of it is out-of-date and characterised by excessive employment, deficient organisational structure, low (often negative) profitability and lack of effective management.

Restructuring of almost one-half of the national economy (the rest was either private from the very beginning or has already been privatised) exceeds the financial and operational capacities of the country, as well as its capacities in terms of the number of required specialists. Therefore, fast and efficient privatisation is necessary. The process so far has been dominated by two privatisation methods.

A.   *Trade sales and flotations on Warsaw Stock Exchange*

During the last four years roughly 100 companies have been privatised by trade sales. These were primarily companies in good economic condition, for which a strategic investor could be found to purchase them and to pledge to make further investments. Some of them have been sold through a public offer. This method is limited, however, by its cost (up to 10 per cent of the value of privatised assets) which covers the valuation and the execution of the transaction, **implementation time** (on average, about one year) and **political controversies,** usually incited by the pricing and selection of a partner as well as the very decision "to sell out national assets". Another 30 firms were privatised through the flotation on the Warsaw Stock Exchange.

B. Employee buy-outs and leasing

This method consists of selling the state-owned enterprises' assets or leasing them to companies formed by the employees. It is a quick (it included over 1 000 firms) and not very expensive method. It can be applied, however, only to smaller companies that do not require a lot of money to be invested by employees.

The effectiveness of these two privatisation methods proved to be insufficient to meet the economy's restructuring needs and this is the main reason why the Mass Privatisation Programme was conceived.

The MPP envisages simultaneous privatisation of several hundred (circa 450) large state-owned enterprises, the ownership of which will be transferred to the National Investment Funds. Shares of the National Investment Funds will be distributed to all adult citizens.

Summing it up, the following economic rationale lies behind the MPP concepts:

-- companies need an active owner, capable of carrying out effective restructuring;

-- valuation should be avoided since it is costly, time-consuming and inaccurate.

In addition, there is a political rationale for the mass privatisation which is to give a chance to all people to participate in the privatisation process.

III. Implementation steps of the National Investment Funds Programme

A. Commercialisation

State-owned companies will be transformed into joint-stock companies. Initially, they will be held solely by the State Treasury. There are two conditions that the companies have to meet to qualify for the programme: an annual turnover above US$5 million and a non-negative profit before taxes.

B.   Establishment of National Investment Funds (NIFs)

NIFs will be joint-stock companies. Their assets include shares of privatised firms, contributed by the State Treasury. A Selection Committee, appointed by the Sejm, Senate, the government and the trade unions has selected members of the first supervisory boards of NIFs. The Committee was also responsible for carrying out a tender for fund managers.

C.   Contribution of joint-stock companies, held solely by the State Treasury

The State Treasury will contribute 33 per cent of shares in each joint-stock company held solely by the State Treasury into each "leading" NIF (the sequence of selection by NIFs of "leading" portfolios shall be decided by a drawing of lots), 27 per cent is distributed in equal parts among the remaining funds, employees obtain 15 per cent for free and 25 per cent remains with the State Treasury. The companies lose the status of state-owned companies held solely by the State Treasury.

D.   Distribution of Share Certificates

All adult citizens receive (upon payment of a small registration fee) bearer physical securities -- Share Certificates -- which give them the right to participate in the Programme. Those securities will be traded freely, both on and off the Stock Exchange.

E.   Introduction of NIF shares onto the Stock Exchange

After the Securities Commission admits shares in all NIFs to trade on the Stock Exchange, Share Certificates can be exchanged for a portfolio consisting of one share in each NIF.

IV. National Investment Funds -- the key to success

National Investment Funds will be joint-stock companies. Their assets will consist of shares in companies contributed by the State Treasury. Each NIF shall hold approximately 30-35 leading shares (33 per cent) and several hundred minority shares (2-3 per cent) in companies in the Programme. NIFs shall be privatised through offering to the general public Share Certificates (representing 85 per cent of shares in the NIFs) -- bearer securities in a physical form. In the later stages of the Programme, Share Certificates shall be exchangeable into shares in each of the NIFs.

Fund managers, selected through a tender operated by the Selection Committee, shall manage the assets of NIFs. Fund managers will be consortia formed by investment banks, fund management groups and consulting firms both Polish and foreign. In September 1993, 33 consortia submitted their proposals to manage NIFs. Their technical proposals constituted a basis for an initial evaluation of their offer. The second element of evaluation was their financial proposal.

Pursuant to the provisions of the Law on National Investment Funds and Their Privatisation, the fee for fund managers shall consist of three parts:

-- an annual flat cash fee for management services (it covers only the costs incurred by the fund manager);

-- an annual success fee for financial results (up to 1 per cent of the value of NIF shares for each year of management services);

-- a final success fee for financial results (up to 0.5 per cent of the value of NIF shares for each year of management services).

The success fee shall be payable by the State Treasury from the funds generated through sale on the Stock Exchange of NIF shares. The value of NIF shares shall depend on the condition of companies in which a given NIF is a shareholder. Therefore, it will be in the best interest of fund managers to manage their companies well in order to maximise their market value, since this will mean a higher success fee. However, it has been decided for political reasons that fund managers may not vote their NIF shares. They shall only make a decision on the time of selling on the open market their shares held for them on a special escrow account by the State Treasury.

In addition to the managing of the NIFs on a day-to-day basis, fund managers shall secure access to capital, new technologies and new markets for the companies in the Programme.

Transparent structure of ownership as well as professional management and stability resulting from legal sanctioning should be able to attract foreign capital to invest in the MPP companies and NIFs. It is expected that NIFs will effectively reach capital markets, e.g. through the flotation of corporate bonds or the placement of new share issues (of either companies or NIFs themselves) on the domestic and international equity markets.

The experience of foreign managers in managing and restructuring various industrial and financial corporations, combined with the knowledge of Polish domestic business and political conditions contributed by the Polish members of fund managing consortia, will make it possible to seek the best organisational and financial solutions for companies in the Programme. Access to new technologies, know-how and modern sales and marketing techniques will, among others, raise efficiency and hopefully reduce adverse environmental effects.

The well-developed network of international contacts of fund managers should also foster export expansion. In addition, NIFs solid capital base should help to re-establish trade relations with the East in the future.

V. Implications for the capital markets

The Mass Privatisation Programme (MPP) will significantly influence and accelerate the development of Poland's capital market over the next few years. Implementation of the programme will result in the issuance of three types of securities: share of the privatised companies, universal share certificates convertible in the future into shares of the National Investment Funds (NIFs) and, lastly, shares of the NIFs themselves. These three types of securities will differ not only with regard to their form (bearer versus registered, physical versus book entry) but also with regard to the mechanisms of their trading (public versus private, stock exchange versus OTC). These securities will be issued by various legal entities such as the companies in the MPP, the State Treasury and the National Investment Funds.

The various MPP issues will immediately increase the capitalisation of the Polish Capital Market by approximately US$3-4 billion. Further privatisation programmes will have impact on this market growth.

A. *Companies' Shares (CS)*

The first shares to be issued under the MPP will be the shares of the 444 companies participating in the Programme. Eligible employees of the MPP companies will obtain up to 15 per cent of the company shares free of charge. These shares will be issued as registered physical securities. More than likely, the companies concerned will deposit these shares with local banks and will issue depository receipts to the employees instead of physical shares. The company shares, before they are admitted to public trading on the Warsaw Stock Exchange or possible OTC market, will be traded privately on restricted company managed markets. These markets will initially take the form of notice boards maintained by the companies, continually matching buy and sell orders between eligible counterparties.

B. *Universal Share Certificates (USC)*

The universal share certificates[2] will be issued by the State Treasury and will be distributed among all eligible citizens of the country. Permanent residents over 18 years old will be eligible to obtain these certificates for a small nominal fee (probably about US$20) which is to cover the costs of their printing and distribution. The share certificates will be in the form of physical bearer securities, convertible to shares in each of the National Investment Funds. The share certificates are exempted from public trading regulations any may therefore be traded on a public unregulated market in their initially issued physical form. Resulting from this exemption, intermediaries such as banks, kantors, etc., will be able to trade the certificates in the same way as any currency they manage today. This form of trading will serve the needs of those holders wishing to sell or buy further USC's at minimal cost without the overhead of opening or running brokerage accounts. For those holders wishing to take advantage of the inherent security of the National Depository, the USC's will be eligible for deposit and dematerialisation via a brokerage house. In dematerialised form, the USC will be admitted to trading on the Warsaw Stock Exchange.

C. *Shares of National Investment Funds*

Following admittance to public trading, each National Investment Fund will issue shares. From the very beginning they will take book entry form in the same manner as other shares currently traded on the Warsaw Stock Exchange. Holders of universal share certificates will be able to convert each certificate into a defined number of shares of each National Investment Fund.

VI. Implications for the companies

The structure of a state-owned enterprise (SOE) is particularly impervious to attempts at reform. The director, formally reporting to the state and communist party administration, is, nowadays, in practice, a captive of the employees since his or her election depends primarily on the Workers' Council. As a result of the extremely powerful position of trade unions, any attempts at the transformation of state-owned enterprises by the management are only sporadically successful. Support for reforms is fostered by a difficult economic situation of companies, however, capital inflow from outside the company is usually necessary for their implementation. This requires a prior change of the legal structure of a company (commercialisation) and the dispossession of a majority of its shares by the State Treasury (privatisation). Only into such a transformed company would a potential investor "pump in" any new financial resources.

The Mass Privatisation Programme eliminates those inconveniences. SOEs become joint-stock companies as soon as their shares are contributed by the State Treasury to a NIF. Following that, there are various possibilities for capital investment in:

-- new issues of shares (after invalidating the pre-emptive rights of the existing shareholders);
-- joint-ventures;
-- credits or credit guarantees.

The ownership structure (33 per cent the leading NIF, 27 per cent dispersed among the remaining NIFs, 25 per cent the State Treasury, 15 per cent the employees) will be reflected in the composition of the Supervisory Board. The Management Board will be, in most cases, composed of the existing management, that supposedly knows best the peculiarities of the company and its business and social environment.

The leading NIF should not limit the autonomy of a company; its task is to stimulate restructuring and growth through efficient management of group's instruments capital. Fund manger guidance will help companies' management to develop effective business plans. International connections of fund managers and their position in negotiations with foreign partners will allow funds to seek investment capital effectively and to develop new markets for exports.

It may be reasonably expected that as a result of wage liberalisation, combined with participation in profits and in supervisory boards, employees will, to a greater extent, identify themselves with their companies. This is expected to help ease labour tensions.

VII. Implications for citizens

The Mass Privatisation Programme offers all citizens a possibility to participate in the emerging market economy in Poland. Share Certificates will be available for a small registration fee (not exceeding 10 per cent of an average monthly wage). For this price a participant can become a co-owner of several hundred reasonably good companies.

For investors who are beginners in the art of investing, the Programme provides a chance to become an owner of small equity capital (Share Certificates should more or less have the value of monthly wages). Share Certificates can be traded immediately after they are collected. After all NIFs have been admitted to public trading, shares of the Funds will be listed on the Warsaw Stock Exchange. For investors preferring the over-the-counter market, the Programme will create a chance to invest in several hundred MPP companies representing a full spectrum of technical parameters and risks.

For those small investors who will not be interested in trading on the Warsaw Stock Exchange, a Share Certificate provides either a safe investment or a source of additional one-time income. An information campaign developed and implemented by a professional advertising agency, contracted by the Ministry of Privatisation, will inform the general public of the advantages of holding a Share Certificate as a long-term investment. The objective of the campaign will be to convince those who may consider selling their Share Certificates immediately after purchasing them, to reconsider their decision, thus avoiding considerable lowering of the price of those share certificates.

VIII. Political advantages

The percentage of state-owned companies in the Polish economy remains high. More than one-half of the labour force still works in state-owned enterprises or in the public sector. This causes enormous political and logistical supervision problems beyond the capabilities of the public administration. In addition, it involves the state in conflicts with trade unions. Subsidies and growing social obligations covered by the state budget require a constant increase of budget revenues, which results in crowding out capital from the private sector. Social security reform is additionally hindered by a slow development of the capital market.

The NIF Programme should lead to a surge in capitalisation and turnover on the Warsaw Stock Exchange, generating a substantial increase by providing several hundred new securities to the Polish capital market. The creation of new financial instruments (Share Certificates, NIF shares, shares of companies in the Programme) should speed up the development of institutional investors, such as investment funds, pension plans and insurance companies.

The creation of a strong group of dynamic private companies, professionally managed, as well as new strong financial institutions (NIF) should help to reduce stress on the state as the main employer and a party in wage disputes. It should, at the same time, reinforce the state's role as an efficient regulator of economic processes.

Notes

*   Based on a presentation made by the author (Jerzy Thieme, Minister's Plenipotentiary for Mass Privatization, Warsaw) at the fifth meeting of the Advisory Group on Privatisation, Paris, 2-4 March 1994.

1.   According to the Law and amendments incorporated in its final form, the official name of the Programme is "The Programme of National Investment Funds and Their Privatization". MPP is a more common, "working" name, however, already well-established in the media.

2.   Share certificate is a legal term and media name used for an investment instrument having financial characteristics of an exchangeable participation certificate.

Polish Mass Privatisation Programme: The Unloved Child in a Suspect Family

Jan Winiecki*

I.   Introduction

The Polish Mass Privatisation Programme (MPP) stands out as a sort of curiosity among similar programmes in the post-Soviet world. The idea of citizens' privatisation (the term used in Poland in the early debates) has been around earlier than elsewhere in the area. Official considerations concerning such a scheme began probably earlier than elsewhere as well (except in the former Czechoslovakia). In early 1994, however, about four-and-a-half years since the beginning of Polish transformation, it has not yet been put into operation -- let alone implemented. Therefore, the role of the present writer consists not only of outlining and evaluating Polish MPP but also of explaining why it has been lagging so much behind other privatisation schemes implemented by a variety of methods.

This paper begins with a description of the programme's intellectual origins in pre-transformation times (Section II). The following two sections deal with its emergence in the political arena (Section III) and its basic features (Section IV). Stressed in these sections of the paper are, first of all, the reluctance with which successive governments treated this particular privatisation method and these governments' search for an almost riskless scheme, i.e. a scheme that would not supply political ammunition for those hostile to privatisation as such.

The foregoing, apart from other factors, must have had a strong impact upon both political economy and economics of a scheme that emerged in 1991 and has remained by and large the same ever since in terms of its fundamental features. Thus, in Section V the present writer evaluates lost opportunities that an early introduction of such a scheme would have offered in terms of creating a political coalition in favour of privatisation. Also, economic advantages and disadvantages of the scheme *vis-à-vis* some other schemes envisaging free distribution of shares to the population are discussed. The final section sketches the determinants of the future of the Polish MPP that are not regarded as particularly encouraging.

II. Intellectual origins of the Polish MPP

The idea of giving state assets back to the public, whose money was used to create them in the first place, was not completely new when it was launched by two young Polish liberal economists, Janusz Lewandowski and Jan Szomburg (1988; 1989a & b; Szomburg, 1989; and later both in an interview in the weekly *Solidarnosc,* 1990). It was first proposed in this fashion by Milton Friedman (1976) as a remedy for the ills of the public sector in Italy and the United Kingdom. It was reformulated a few years later by Samuel Brittan (1983 & 1984), as an alternative to the official privatisation programme of the Conservative government of Mrs. Thatcher.

Although hardly new as an idea, it was nonetheless formulated for the first time in Eastern Europe by the above-mentioned academics, strongly associated not only with the underground "Solidarity" but, within the broad anti-communist opposition grouping, also with the nascent liberal movement. The idea of citizens' privatisation stressed classical liberal, property rights-based arguments in favour of this method of privatisation. However, perceiving the Soviet system-specific aberrations, they added some other arguments in favour of the scheme.

They underlined the shortage of capital in Poland (in fact everywhere in the impoverished communist world) and its skewed distribution (largely in favour of *nomenklatura).* Furthermore, they expected the free distribution of state assets to have a **psychologically reinvigorating effect** of becoming owners of something, after decades of being little more than atomized objects of economic manipulations by the communist state. They called such distribution "propertisation" *(uwlaszczenie)* of Polish society.

In a later assessment, after the communist electoral debacle in 1989 and the formation of the first non-communist government, Szomburg (1989) stressed the **political** factor, namely an expected wide public support for the scheme. Understandably, political change made earlier intellectual considerations a raw material for political action and suggested privatisation alternatives had to incorporate political feasibility as an important component of a scheme.

In the original Lewandowski-Szomburg scheme all legally adult Poles (i.e. those 18 years old or older) would receive property coupons of a certain nominal value amounting to the estimated value of state assets to be privatised in that manner, divided by the number of persons entitled to receive the coupons in question. Coupons would be registered and would not be transferable. They could be used only to buy shares of privatised enterprises on the stock market.

It is worth noting that there is a striking similarity between the scheme debated in Poland in the 1987-1989 period and the one that later emerged as a dominant component of the privatisation programme in Czechoslovakia and its successor states. On the intellectual plane, similarity of thinking is clear; on the political plane, differences could not (unfortunately!) be greater.

Sticking to intellectual origins a while longer, I would like to mention the following developments with respect to free the distribution scheme outlined here. The first is that the scheme met initially with heavy criticism but intellectual support for it grew rather fast. An evidence of the latter fact is that the debate over the feasibility of a free distribution scheme spawned a number of similar schemes both within Poland and without. Various modifications were proposed that had an impact on the political debate about the shape of the programme -- and the shape of the programme itself (the term: "final shape" is consciously avoided here).

One kind of modification was formulated in response to criticism that the scheme was very costly in terms of transaction costs. With every citizen choosing individually from among the shares of many privatised enterprises, knowledge requirements for making reasonably sensible choices would be enormous. Modifications generally assumed that the entry of financial intermediaries would reduce these knowledge requirements. Those citizens who felt baffled by thousands of opportunities and/or did not find it worthwhile to invest their time to learn how to select the most interesting from among them, would turn to such intermediaries. The argumentation stressed also that such a pattern would be in conformity with the normal distribution of risk taking in the society, where only a fraction is ready to hold high risk financial assets such as shares.

One more strand of intellectual criticism with both economic and political implications is worth stressing in this section. It is an argument that free distribution of shares, or citizens' privatisation as it is better called, creates an extremely wide dispersion of ownership. Its consequence would be the dominant position of managers *vis-à-vis* shareholders, with all the consequences for efficiency known from the relevant literature.

The criticism was overstated, for the economic logic would suggest that reconcentration of ownership would proceed rather fast. Nonetheless, in the short to medium term the argument is valid. Here, the authors of the original scheme stressed initially (see, i.a., Lewandowski and Szomburg, 1988) the need for preferred shares to be distributed among employees, so that there were from the start a group of clearly identifiable shareholders. It is worth recalling that this concern was also shared by the authors of the so-called "Beksiak report", prepared in the autumn of 1989 for the parliamentary club of "Solidarity" (Beksiak, Jêdraszczyk, Gruszecki and Winiecki, 1989), although the vehicle used to achieve the same aim was somewhat different.

III. Emergence of the Mass Privatisation Programme: choice of bureaucratic over political approach to privatisation

Although citizens' privatisation has been around for at least two years at the intellectual level, the fall of communism and the formation of the first non-communist government did not turn the idea into an action plan. The government programme presented in mid-October 1989 stressed the aim to achieve the structure of ownership similar to those in western economies, but the means leading in that direction were left unspecified.

However, not only the programme but also the reality was not very encouraging. On the one hand, within the government's economic team there has been a strong preference in favour of public sale of shares as a "classical" method that, first, is in concordance with the principles of capitalist market economy, second, has been tried and tested recently in many countries (most conspicuously -- and successfully -- in the United Kingdom), and last but not least, has been seen as a clean, transparent method eliminating or at least reducing the suspicion of shady dealings.

Leaving aside the realism of expectations that public sale of shares would be able to accomplish the task of transforming ownership structure in a desired manner in a reasonable timespan (on this point, see, i.a. Winiecki, 1989, 1990 and 1992, as well as Gruszecki and Winiecki, 1991), a politically competing alternative to the government idea has not been citizens' privatisation. One should be aware that the compromise with communists at the Round Table envisaged the transformation of the state enterprises into self-management-based ones. More importantly, the idea had been incorporated into the agreement on the insistence of the then victorious "Solidarity".

Dissatisfied self-management activists continued to exert pressure on the government to return to this theoretically untenable and historically discredited idea. The pressure came both through parliamentary action (alternative privatisation bill) and from whipping up the militancy of workers in state-owned enterprises (SOEs), especially the large ones. All arguments seemed to be good to discredit privatisation. Even at that early stage accusations were made by the believers in the "third way" hostile to privatisation, that the government was pursuing a policy of purposeful destruction of enterprises so that some people could buy them cheaply (*Gazeta Wyborcza,* 28 March 1990). Accusations of that sort have, unfortunately, haunted the Polish political scene ever since.

Thus, the main political battle for the shape of the Polish ownership transformation programme has been from the start between the believers in self-management and, somewhat later, employee share-ownership plans (ESOP) on the one hand, and the government stressing the need for classical methods of privatisation on the other. At that early stage, citizens' privatisation was not even in the running.

This situation worried some liberal economists and politicians, for they understood, probably more clearly than the others, that the political attraction of the sale of small packages of shares to those willing to buy them would not fire the imagination and make privatisation popular. In other words, the political economy of privatisation was neglected. They also realised that there is a need to counteract the influence of a well-defined and organized lobby of self-management activists from large SOEs.

Such a countervailing power, they thought, would come from the launching of a privatisation programme that would be readily accepted by the public. A group of economists then wrote a letter to the "Solidarity" trade union leadership pointing out to Mr. Walesa, in December 1989, that the government does not see the need for political support with respect to this key measure, i.e. privatisation (see Letter, 1989). This political support was expected to come from implementation of a programme based largely on the Lewandowski-Szomburg principles, with some sweeteners for employees in SOEs to deflate their resistance. (Let it be noted that such a programme had already been in existence since the presentation of the "Beksiak Report".)

Nonetheless, the narrow, tunnel-like vision of the government continued to prevail. One version of the privatisation law succeeded another but all were products of technicians honing the details of basically the same programme centered on the public sale of shares. The government resisted demands of the politically strong believers in the "third way" but, at the same time, was impervious to arguments based on political economy. In the end, it pushed the privatisation law through the Parliament (the Law of 13 July 1990) but it turned out to be a pyrrhic victory.

The law established the rule that a state enterprise may be privatised at the joint request of the manager and the self-management board (which must have already sought the opinion of the general meeting of employees) or at the request of the respective supervising minister filed after obtaining the approval of the manager and the self-management board (an opinion of the general meeting is also needed). Thus the passage of law did not pave the way for rapid privatisation; each case still depends on the prior approval of the privatisation decision by employees. And, given the strong position of "third way" believers at the enterprise (SOE) level, the foregoing left privatisation at the mercy of those who fundamentally opposed it at the beginning and later rarely accepted anything except employee share-ownership.

Only thanks to the efforts of some liberals in the Parliament, the law of 13 July 1990 included the provision that allowed the government to proceed with privatisation using other methods than public sale. Thus, at least the room for future emergence of a citizens' privatisation programme was created.

It was also in the summer of 1990 that a partial change of heart took place within the government's economic team. With effects of the preferred public sale approach being nil for the time being (the first five SOEs were privatised in that manner only toward the end of 1990), with continuing domestic criticism from liberals and with the increasing acceptance of the idea by the international community of experts, the studies began on the most acceptable form of free distribution of assets to the citizenry. However, no specific proposals were officially presented for quite some time. The situation did not change until the resignation of Mazowiecki's cabinet in November 1990. Citizens' privatisation continued to be an unloved child in the increasingly suspect privatisation family.

Presidential elections brought citizens' privatisation into the political agenda. Moreover, the appointment of Janusz Lewandowski to the post of the Minister Responsible for Privatisation in January 1991 gave to the elaboration of this method somewhat greater urgency. The proposal of the programme was finally presented in summer 1991. The first proposal contained all the basic features that have been characteristic of Polish citizens' privatisation ever since.

Thus, it was conceived as a programme relatively limited in size (initially concerning 400 enterprises), as a programme based on the participation of citizens only in financial intermediaries (no possibility of buying shares of privatised SOEs with received investment instruments), and as a programme providing for intensive state involvement (not only adopting the rules of the game for financial intermediaries, but also establishing these intermediaries, running the selection process of teams managing them, appointing representatives to their first supervisory boards, etc.). Although at different stages of the debate financial intermediaries were differently called, they all had the same feature, namely they envisaged the intervention of these intermediaries in the management of privatised enterprises (thus they were of the active investor type).

IV. Shaping Polish MPP: much political ping-pong, few substantive modifications

Basically the programme in question was envisaged as a relatively safe one, that is, as a programme where neither people's own choice nor financial failures of privatised SOEs or their "core investors" (financial intermediaries) would turn some investment instruments into worthless pieces of paper. This playing safe approach, undoubtedly influenced by the increasingly charged atmosphere around privatisation, pushed those designing the programme in the direction of uniformity of investment instruments, making every potential participant (originally every adult Pole domiciled in Poland) an owner of an equal number of shares in all intermediaries taking part in the programme.

In fact, the whole design was made even more complicated as the process had been envisaged to have two stages. In the first, adult Poles would receive saleable bearer's investment instruments and at the later stage they could, if they wished, exchange them into shares of one or more intermediaries participating in the MPP. If they did not, they would become, during the existence of the programme (envisaged to last ten years), owners of a very safe financial instrument, because its dividend has been only to a small extent dependent on the success or failure of this or that privatised company or even intermediary. In this manner, an investment instrument in a few dozen financial intermediaries (and a few hundred companies) becomes something closer to a long-term government bond than to a private sector commercial paper (be it a bond or stock) in terms of its risk level. However, it should be noted, low risk level is usually associated with low return (be it interest or dividend).

In its intention to ensure that the degree of risk was as low as possible, the design of the programme envisaged that financial intermediaries, although under the state control initially, would have professional management. The selection process has been centralised from the beginning and the choice of the first management teams for these intermediaries has been left in the hands of a government-appointed committee. Low risk, then, and a high level of state involvement have been the hallmarks of the MPP from its inception.

Intermediaries were initially to start with similar portfolios. Each intermediary would receive an equal fraction of the state-supplied shares in transformed SOEs, participating in the programme out of that fraction of state-owned shares. Also, each intermediary was to receive a larger (33 per cent) fraction of state-supplied shares of some companies where it would be a core investor. As already stressed, financial intermediaries were in the nature of active investors that would not only receive financial returns from their shareholding in companies, as well as from buying and selling their shares, but would also be actively involved in the selection of management teams in companies, in which they were "core investors", in the financial restructuring of these companies and in lending to them for the purpose of expansion and/or change of their activities. Finally, they were supposed to sell the shares and in this manner complete the privatisation process of enterprises in which they were shareholders.

Innumerable modifications since the summer 1991 did not change the fundamentals. Although financial intermediaries at a certain stage acquired a name -- that of National Investment Funds (NIFs) -- their nature did not change. The range of beneficiaries have changed; public sector employees (health, education and administration) and pensioners have been added for special reasons. Employees of participating state enterprises got an increased stake (15 per cent rather than 10 per cent of shares). The number of potential participants in the MPP has fluctuated. But the heavy presence of the state and the extreme concern with the risk level -- features that, quite obviously, are not unrelated to one another -- have been present at every stage.

V. The political economy and economics of the Polish MPP

It is an elementary principle of politics that in order to introduce any change, let alone a change of such fundamental nature as privatisation of some 80-90 per cent of state assets, the support of at least a part of the electorate is a must. Otherwise, once reform fatigue sets in (Bruno, 1992), and resistance to change increases, the process of change may easily get stalled. However, as it was stressed in Section III, the Polish economic team managing the transformation process since late 1989 seemingly did not appreciate this principle.

Polish privatisation strategy is open to criticism on other grounds as well (see, i.a., Gruszecki & Winiecki, 1991; Winiecki, 1992), but disregard of politics has certainly had the gravest consequences. A comparison with former Czechoslovakia and its successor states (especially the Czech Republic) is instructive here. A few weeks after the velvet revolution, the then federal finance minister, Vaclav Klaus, announced, with much publicity, that the future mass privatisation programme would benefit all citizens, who for decades had been deprived of their ownership rights and, given their state of impoverishment, did not have many prospects of owning assets in the future. Mass privatisation, giving everybody an opportunity to own some privatised state assets, has been presented, and rightly so, not only as a shortcut method to the restoration of the ownership structure characteristic of a capitalist economy, but also as a morally justified effort to redress, to some extent, past wrongdoings.

As such, the programme fired the imagination of many and became a cornerstone upon which the popularity of privatisation has been built. The story has been different in Poland, though. There is a difference between giving to by and large everybody and selling to those who can afford it. There is no surprise, then, that the Polish preferred programme of the public sale of shares has not become as popular with the general public as the Czechoslovakian one.

This truth dawned rather belatedly upon Polish economic decision makers. However, once they became converted (at first, maybe, only half-converted!) to the idea of citizens' privatisation as a political support-building measure, it was unfortunately too late. The relentless anti-privatisation campaign pursued not only by the parties of communist *ancien regime,* but, even more importantly, by the utopian left wing of the victorious "Solidarity", made privatisation an increasingly suspect (and resisted) process. The Mass Privatisation Programme became just another child from this suspect family -- and the particularly unloved one at that.

As such, it has not been able to become a countervailing power to the ESOP-type privatisation based on utopian ideology and self-interest of workers in enterprises with positive asset value. Again, the contrast with the Czechs is very clear. When left-leaning former communist party intellectuals, who spearheaded the 1968 socialism with human face reforms, came up with the same alternative to privatisation, they were easily defeated. The popularity of citizens' privatisation played, in this author's view, a dominant role in the outcome in question, so different from that in Poland.

Thus, the political economy of citizens' privatisation has not been a strong point in Poland. The same thing cannot be said about the economics of MPP; however, the economic logic of the programme had much more to do with misconceived political economy than with free market principles. As underlined especially in Section IV, those designing the programme have been striving from the very beginning to reduce the risk of failure. They undoubtedly succeeded, but **at a cost.** The price has been the absence of choice -- again in contrast to the Czechoslovak scheme -- and the presence of the visible hand of government.

The present writer concurs with Roman Ceska's (1993) criticism that the Polish model does not put much faith in the people themselves. The state ensures low risk by giving each beneficiary the same thing -- each receives the same "state-created" portfolio ... in "state-established" investment funds. Ultimately, the Polish scheme protects citizens against effects of their potentially wrong decisions, while the Czechoslovak system rewards good investment decisions and punishes bad ones -- the same way markets function. Thus, the Polish MPP has been successful neither as a political support building measure nor as an educational device teaching people how markets behave.

It displays some more questionable economic features. This author dwells on two of them that concern the NIFs' role in the privatisation process. The first has already been stressed in the literature (see Hinds, 1990, and Gruszecki & Winiecki, 1991), namely that the creation of funds of the active investor type makes privatisation without the consent of a fund that is a core investor in a given SOE well nigh impossible. Thus, the role of capital markets in weeding out inefficient enterprises is attenuated. A potential investor cannot accomplish a takeover of a SOE whose assets it regards as undervalued against the will of a fund that holds a controlling stake in this enterprise. To be successful it would have to take over the fund itself. Given the limited financial resources of Polish private firms, such an approach is simply infeasible. In consequence, the role of capital markets is attenuated with respect to SOEs partaking in MPP.

A second criticism concerns the length of time NIFs are allowed to operate under unchanged rules of the game (ten years) and the relationship of that lengthy timespan to the need for rapid privatisation. A prescribed choice of new supervisory boards from among the shareholders of each NIF (see the preceding section) should not be equated with privatisation. After all, the core investor remains in each case a particular fund. Thus, at best it would become privatisation without owners' control, with all the "Berle-Means" type consequences.

The foregoing assessment reveals that free marketeers could not be very happy with the programme. Thus, it has had little support not only among privatisation opponents but also among its strongest proponents. Free marketeers criticised the MPP's defensiveness in political economy terms, i.e. its attempts to defuse potential accusations of recklessness. The unacceptable economic philosophy and the dubious economics of the programme did not make it more palatable, either. In the final analysis, they agreed that it would be better than no privatisation at all and that the programme should be implemented as rapidly as possible as the alternative (i.e. ESOP) was far worse; but this support was given without much enthusiasm and was based on the "lesser evil" principle.

VI. What the future holds

The Polish citizens' privatisation programme has been at least since autumn 1991 a hostage of the political fortunes of successive, systemic transformation-oriented governments. Since these fortunes have been getting increasingly worse, and the ability of governments in question to marshal a majority in the Parliament has been on the decline, getting the programme approved by the legislature, and off the ground, has continued to be beyond the reach of governments whose political will to pursue a privatisation path, including the MPP, was beyond a doubt.

Recent elections reversed the picture. A new government based on parties with their roots in the *ancien regime* (i.e. communist) commands a large majority in the Parliament. The problem this time is political will because the resistance to privatisation at the political level continues (in spite of *bona fide* declarations of the Minister for Privatisation on the need to continue a privatisation strategy). Furthermore, the political victory of parties that have opposed most privatisation initiatives since 1989 strengthened that resistance at the SOE level.

As usual, the MPP has been an early victim of that change. Although the new government declared its will to go on with the programme, it immediately began tinkering with its procedure.   The appointment of a new selection committee, whose task is to choose from among the teams competing for contracts to manage national investment funds (NIFs), slowed down the implementation process. Moreover, there has been no decision so far about the range of beneficiaries of the programme: adult Poles only or adult Poles plus pensioners and public sector employees (that is, groups slated to receive compensatory financial instruments -- see Section IV). This is a political decision that has to be made by the Parliament. Without it the programme will remain in limbo.

Again, decisions at the political level are influenced by other developments, at both the macro level and the micro level. As stressed already, election results strengthened the resistance to privatisation. Changes in the taxation of SOEs also added to that resistance, for they sharply reduced short-term incentives to avoid certain kinds of labour and capital taxation. Without these incentives and with strong anti-privatisation sentiments, some enterprises would consider opting out of the MPP (it should be remembered that participation in the programme is voluntary, thanks *inter alia* to parliamentary efforts of parties belonging to the present ruling coalition). And it should be kept in mind that there are too few SOEs to create the critical mass for the programme in the first place. Thus, the programme might not only remain in limbo. It may even be suspended or cancelled altogether due to the lack of interest in the programme by managers and workers, given the strongly attenuated property rights of the owner, i.e. the state.

It seems worth considering one more issue. As privatisation by other methods continues after all (although not without gathering clouds), a question may be asked: why MPP? Why precisely citizens' privatisation? Why does this particular child of the increasingly suspect family of privatisation methods remain so unloved that it never became fully recognised, let alone allowed to perform?

This writer sees two complementary answers. All other methods of privatisation have been tried many times. Nationalized assets have been re-privatised, or state assets have been sold through public sale of shares (and listed on the stock market), or some state-owned business units have been auctioned. In other words, even if privatisation has been increasingly opposed both at the macro (political) and at the micro (state enterprise) levels, the arguments against it did not put in doubt respective methods -- tried and tested around the world.

Undermining the efforts of privatisers took the form of a more or less unspecified general critique ("threat to economic sovereignty", selling family silver at rock-bottom prices, etc.) or case-oriented accusations of corruption. The former type of criticism required a successful majority vote in the Parliament against privatisation, *de facto* abolishing the programme. Politically motivated accusations of that sort could be levelled against privatisation **at any time.** Until the recent elections this was not politically feasible. The latter type was, of course, refutable in legal and economic terms, but political motivation did not deter levelling the same accusations again and again. However, given the propitious macro and micro conditions, these accusations could simply be shrugged off. (However, both types of unrelenting criticism have been increasingly successful in turning public opinion against privatisation.)

The novelty of citizens' privatisation allowed its enemies **to stall debates already at the conceptual stage** of this component of ownership transformation. Putting in doubt every aspect of the MPP always took place under the guise of the concern with the efficacy of this untried experiment. (The fact that this untried experiment became a major component of many privatisation strategies did not enter into the debates at any stage.)

This politically motivated procrastination strategy, much easier with respect to the MPP than any other privatisation method, has been coupled with the continuing incomprehension of SOEs with respect to the nature of MPP or even that of participating financial intermediaries. The kind of questions asked by representatives of state enterprises often reveal terrifying ignorance with respect to the workings of financial markets (see, e.g. *Zycie Gospodarcze,* 6 February 1994). Thus, political hostility has stalled the programme at the legislative and introductory stage, while ignorance has made it easier to turn SOEs against the MPP.

Note

* Based on a presentation made by the author (Jan Winiecki, Professor, Warsaw University) at the fifth meeting of the Advisory Group on Privatisation, Paris, 2-4 March 1994.

References

BEKSIAK, J., J. EYSYMONTT, T. GRUSZECKI, T. STANKIEWICZ, and J. WINIECKI, Letter: "Political Consequences of Certain Planned Measures in the Government Programme" (original Polish version: "Polityczne konsekwencje niektórych planowanych posuniec programu rzadowego"), mimeo, December, in Polish.

BEKSIAK, J., T. GRUSZECKI, A. JEDRASZCZYK, and J. WINIECKI, "Outline of a Programme for Stabilisation and Systemic Changes", 1989, In: The Polish Transformation: Programme and Progress, Centre for Research into Communist Economies, London, 1990. (Title of Polish original 1989 report: Zarys programu stabilizacyjnego i zmian systemowych).

BRITTAN, S., "Privatisation: A New Approach", *Financial Times,* 17 November 1983.

BRITTAN, S., "The Case for Capital Ownership for All", *Financial Times,* 20 September 1984.

BRUNO, M., "Stabilization and Reform in Eastern Europe: A Preliminary Evaluation", IMF Staff Papers, Vol. 39, No. 4, 1992.

CESKA, R., "Three Years of Privatization in the Czech and Slovak Republics", *Privatization Newsletter of the Czech Republic and Slovakia,* No. 17, June/July 1993.

FRIEDMAN, M., "How to Denationalize", *Newsweek,* 27 December 1976.

HINDS, M., "A Note on the Privatization of Socialized Enterprises in Poland", mimeo, World Bank, Washington, D. C., July 1990.

GRUSZECKI, T. and J. WINIECKI, "Privatisation in East-Central Europe: A Comparative Perspective", *Aussenwirtschaft,* Vol. 46, No. 1, 1991.

LEWANDOWSKI, J. and J. SZOMBURG, "Uwlaszczenie jako fundament reformy spoleczno-ekonomicznej" ("Propertisation as a Foundation of Socio-Economic Reform"). Paper for the Seminar on "Transformation Proposals for Polish Economy", mimeo, Warsaw, 17-18 November 1988, in Polish.

LEWANDOWSKI, J. and J. SZOMBURG, "Wlasnosc jako próg reformy gospodarczej, cz. 1" ("Ownership as a Threshold of Economic Reform, Part 1"), *Gazeta Bankowa,* No. 3, 1989a, in Polish.

LEWANDOWSKI, J. and J. SZOMBURG, "Wlasnosc jako próg reformy gospodarczej, cz. 2" ("Ownership as a Threshold of Economic Reform, Part 2"), *Gazeta Bankowa,* No. 4, 1989b, in Polish.

SZOMBURG, J., "Przeglad koncepcji" ["An Overview of (Privatization) Concepts"], *Zmiany,* No. 6, 1989.

WINIECKI, J., "Privatizacion en las economias de tipo Sovietico", *Quadernos Economicos,* No. 4, 1989.

WINIECKI, J., "Political and Economic Reform in Eastern Europe: A Case of Poland", paper prepared for The Mont Pelerin Society General Meeting on "Europe in an Open World Order", mimeo, Munich, 2-8 September 1990.

WINIECKI, J. (1992), Privatization in Poland: A Comparative Perspective, Kieler Studien 248. J. C. B. Mohr (Paul Siebeck), Tubingen.

Voucher Privatisation in the Czech Republic and Slovakia

Jan Mladek*

Introduction

The voucher privatisation in the Czech Republic has reached another stage of development. The programme has been executed, the shares have been distributed and the current key issues are the functioning of secondary markets and corporate governance. The issue of the initial distribution of shares and the functioning of the scheme is to a large extent an historical topic because the first wave of voucher privatisation was finished in June 1993, while the second wave is going on at the present time and is, to a certain extent, a routine matter[1].

Explained in the Section A is the scope of the Czechoslovak (Czech) voucher privatisation and its role as compared to other privatisation methods. In Section B there is a description as to how the vouchers were used. Section C highlights the enterprises involved in voucher privatisation. Section D addresses the creation of Investment Privatisation Funds (IPFs). The very limited possibilities for trading vouchers are explained in Section E. Section F is about privatised enterprises and the final chapter evaluates the importance of Investment Privatisation Funds. The key issue is whether they will be transformed into portfolio managers or into corporate governance funds. In the Annex is an additional description of voucher privatisation dynamics in former Czechoslovakia and in the Czech Republic, an issue which is not covered in standardised outlines.

A.   *The context and extent of voucher privatisation*

It is necessary to begin with a territorial specification of the subject. The first wave of voucher privatisation started in Czechoslovakia in 1991 as a federal programme and was finished in the two independent republics in the first half of 1993. The split caused certain problems for the execution of the program, but did not have fatal consequences. Also, it should be taken into account that in reference to the currency, a slight problem resulted. The Czechoslovak crown

(CSK) survived the federation for some five weeks. Afterwards, the Czech crown took over the tradition of the Czechoslovak crown and its stability was kept at a stable exchange rate with the DEM and the USD. In Slovakia a 10 per cent devaluation of Slovak currency later occurred. In this paper, the whole former Czechoslovakia will be covered in the first wave story, while the second wave will be only about the Czech Republic because Slovakia decided to postpone its second wave of voucher privatisation and play down the role of vouchers within the whole programme of large privatisation.

1.   Philosophy and theoretical background of voucher privatisation

The voucher privatisation programme in Czechoslovakia started to be developed in 1990. The main reason for the introduction of this programme was based on the following thoughts: In Czechoslovakia before 1989, 86 per cent of the GDP was produced in the state sector, 10 per cent in the cooperative sector and only 4 per cent was produced privately. It was understood by leading reformers that privatisation was needed. However, to privatise by standard methods of privatisation would either be too long because of limited savings of Czechoslovak citizens or would be equivalent to selling out the country to foreigners. Both outcomes were seen as undesirable. Politically, it was also argued that it should not be possible to allow old *nomenclatura* to sell out state companies to foreigners.

This provoked a discussion about the shape of the scheme. The discussion was initiated by Professor Jan Svejnar from Pittsburgh by publishing the first paper in December 1989. (Svejnar, J. 1989). This original project stressed the social justice aspect of voucher privatisation. These issues are central in both the approach that focuses on the establishment of state-created funds and the approach which emphasises the role of capital markets in enterprise restructuring. The leading figure in following discussions was Dusan Triska, an economist, mathematician and lawyer. Within the initial discussion, a scheme was developed which fully relied on the vouchers as an exclusive method of privatisation. The slogan was 97 + 3, which meant that every company should give 97 per cent of their shares to the voucher privatisation programme and 3 per cent to the Restitution Investment Fund (RIF) to cover potential restitution claims for properties which were indivisible, non-existent, etc. Later, however, this fundamentalist approach was changed and the use of other methods of privatisation, simultaneously with the voucher scheme, was allowed. The flexibility of the programme was its major feature. There were even greater changes during the implementation of the second wave of voucher privatisation compared to the first wave. A major change was recognisable in the attitude toward the exclusivity of voucher privatisation. The first wave started with the idea that vouchers were exclusive, but this idea gradually eroded. In fact, only 61.4 per cent of the shares of the companies which were involved in the first wave of voucher privatisation were privatised by vouchers, while the rest were kept in the hands of the Fund of National Property (FNP) or privatised by other means.

Table 1. **Methods used in the first wave of voucher privatisation (Czech Republic)**

Type of method	Value in billion CZK	Percentage of the whole value
Vouchers	203	61.4
Foreign investors	5	1.6
Domestic investors	5	1.4
Employees	3	0.9
Intermediaries	6	1.8
Municipalities	9	2.8
Temporarily in FNP[1]	33	10.0
Permanently in FNP	44	13.3
Restitution fund	10	3.0
Additional restitutions	7	2.1
Differentiation fund	6	1.7
Total	**331**	**100.0**

1. FNP = Fund of National Property.

Source: Mejstrik, M. (1993)

2. *Scope of voucher privatisation*

There is a certain confusion in the Czech terminology on large privatisation. For the first time, in 1991, it was believed that voucher privatisation and large privatisation were more or less equivalent. Nearly everything was supposed to be privatised with the help of vouchers. From this time period came the first privatisation plan of three governments: Czechoslovak, Czech and Slovak.

This plan is more or less followed. It is rather difficult to identify the exact number of state firms because some splits and spin-offs of companies have occurred. However, one point must be explained in order to understand the planning of the first wave of large privatisation. In the first wave of voucher privatisation, 2 285 firms were to be privatised. However, the result was that

1 491 firms were actually privatised, only 65 per cent of the original figure. Does this mean that the remaining 35 per cent were not privatised? No, this means rather that after public discussion within the preparation of voucher privatisation, it was decided, at least for smaller companies, to follow a bit of the German Treuhand model and sell directly to private entrepreneurs.

Table 2. **Privatisation plan of CSFR governments**

Government	1st wave	2nd wave	No privatisation	Liquidation	Total
CSFR	29	23	76	1	129
Czech	1 630	1 248	584	41	3 503
Slovak	626	573	611	40	1 850
Total	**2 285**	**1 844**	**1 271**	**82**	**5 482**

Source: Ekonom, No. 43, 1991.

3. *Standard methods and voucher privatisation in the Czech Republic*[2]

In the Czech Republic several methods of privatisation are used. In principle, there are five main paths of privatisation:

-- restitution;
-- municipalisation;
-- transformation of the cooperatives;
-- small privatisation;
-- large privatisation.

There exists a whole set of laws on restitution, which began with the law on restitution of church property and which will also probably finish with the issue of restitution of property to the churches. This is primarily because the first law was not comprehensive enough, at least in the opinion of Catholic Church leaders. Nevertheless, the main bulk of restituted properties consists of shops, restaurants, hotels, buildings, small factories and land. The amount of transferred properties is estimated to be at CZK 150-200 billion (US$5-6.7 billion)[3].

The Municipalities were rehabilitated at least partially by the transfer of properties which were owned by them before 1949, basically land and buildings, and also by the transfers of some assets originally owned by state companies (houses in particular). The estimate of the amount of those properties is CZK 350 billion (US$11.7 billion)[4].

The transformation of cooperatives represents a very special issue. A fierce political battle erupted around this transformation. Nevertheless, it was resolved with the transformation of some 500 productive, 200 consumer and other cooperatives, plus some 1 300 agricultural cooperatives. The amount of property transformed this way is estimated to be at least CZK 150 billion (US$5 billion).

Small privatisation has been, in fact, completed since the end of 1993. Some 22 000 shops, pubs, hotels, service establishment, stores, trucks and small factories were sold for more than CZK 30 billion (US$1 billion).

However, the largest share of privatisation is carried out through the large privatisation program. All four paths, which have been already mentioned, are responsible for the privatisation of some CZK 730 billion of properties. The large privatisation should privatise assets worth approximately CZK 1 200 billion (US$40 billion).

Within large privatisation, several methods have been employed:

a) public auctions;

b) public tenders;

c) direct sales to predetermined buyer;

d) privatisation of joint-stock companies (i.e. corporatised);

e) free transfers to municipalities, banks, pension funds, etc.

Voucher privatisation was the major method used for the privatisation of joint-stock companies. The original idea of the voucher privatisation architects was to privatise all companies by the voucher method. Later, however, they were forced to give up "voucher fundamentalism" and other methods were also employed. The structure of the large privatisation (both waves) according to the privatisation method used is shown in the following table.

In this table are summarised all privatisation projects which were approved by the Privatisation Ministry by the end of 1993. Some of those items have been already privatised, some others are waiting in the Fund of National Property for privatisation. Among those waiting in line are also companies scheduled for the second wave of voucher privatisation.

One should stress the role of Dr. Tomas Jezek, who contributed by his tremendous effort to the fulfilling of the supply side of voucher privatisation and also the role of Mr. Vaclav Klaus, who as Czechoslovak Finance Minister and later Czech Prime Minister delivered the political support for the voucher privatisation.

Table 3. **Large-scale privatisation in the Czech Republic: property
approved for privatisation and transferred from the Privatisation Ministry
to the Fund of National Property by 31 December 1993**

Form of privatisation	Number of units	Per cent of the total number of units	Property in billion CZK	Per cent of the total property
Public auctions	514	6.8	5.8	0.7
Public tenders	502	6.7	19.2	2.2
Direct sales	1 680	22.3	46.3	5.3
Joint-stock companies	1 777	23.6	754.3	86.5
Unpaid transfers	2 318	30.8	30.0	3.4
Restitutions	613	8.1	6.5	0.8
Restitutions with buy in	129	1.7	9.5	1.1
Total	**7 533**	**100.0**	**871.6**	**100.0**

Source: Privatisation Ministry, Prague.

4. *Operation of the voucher scheme*

The scheme began with the state selecting a group of 2 285 large companies for the second wave of voucher privatisation. This number gradually decreased to 1 491 large and medium-sized companies. The selection was rather arbitrary and based on very broad indicators pointing to the readiness of the companies for privatisation. The companies selected had an average employment of 915 people in 1991. These state-owned companies were first commercialised; meaning they were transformed into joint-stock companies with 100 per cent of their shares belonging to the newly founded National Property Funds (Federal, Czech, Slovak). All shares had a nominal value of CSK 1 000; thus, the larger the company, the greater the number of shares. A proportion of their shares was set aside for voucher privatisation. This proportion was usually proposed by the existing management in their "basic privatisation project". Shares allocated in this manner were available for exchange with vouchers through a bidding process.

While preparations for the voucher scheme were under way, the government invited privatisation projects for each of the 1 500 firms in the scheme: basic privatisation projects from the existing management (mentioned above), as well as competing privatisation projects[5] from other interested parties. The projects had to include a business plan and a proposal for the expected future ownership structure of the company. Given that the incumbent management had access to much more detailed information than outsiders, they were in an advantageous position *vis-à-vis* their rivals. This, however, did not stop the rivals from submitting alternative projects -- on the average, each firm was the subject of approximately four proposals.

Following such submissions, a cumbersome evaluation process of the projects in the branch ministries began. In every branch of the ministry, a privatisation committee was created which made detailed evaluations of the projects, discussed them with their authors, and finished their work with suggestions to the Privatisation Ministry which had the final word in project approval. (The branch ministry also passed on rejected projects to the Privatisation Ministry which was free to reopen them). The approval of the projects resulted in a first wave bottleneck and thus caused a few months delay in the start of the bidding. After project approval, however, the whole company, together with the approved project, was placed under the responsibility of the Fund of National Property, which served as a branch ministry until privatisation began. Nevertheless, it is worthwhile to stress that the Czech Fund of National Property serves like a waiting room for companies which were approved for privatisation and are waiting for its execution. This is not like in Germany where Treuhand first took over East German companies and then started to think about how to privatise them.

B. The vouchers

All Czechoslovak citizens over the age of 18 (at the start of registration) were, in the first wave of voucher privatisation, authorised to buy a book of vouchers entitling them to 1 000 voucher points for a total cost of CSK 1 035 (US$34.5), which was just about 25 per cent of the average monthly wage at the end of 1991. A registration stamp was CSK 1 000 (US$33.3) and a voucher book was CSK 35 (US$1.2). Vouchers were special tender documents which were issued only with a view to being exchanged for shares in a given privatisation wave following a specific bidding process. At the beginning, they were also considered for buying apartments, but later this idea was rejected. They could not be used in public tenders, auctions, direct sales or any other transaction involving the ownership of enterprises. In bidding for shares, the voucher holders could use as few as 100 voucher points for a company's share. Technically, every participant was sold 11 000 voucher points, in pieces of different value like 1 000 points, 500 points, 200 points, 100 points, which means that voucher holders could diversify their investment into as many as ten subjects (companies or Investment Privatisation Funds). The whole registration of voucher privatisation participants was computerised. The computer network covered the whole country with two central computers in Prague and Bratislava, which made it possible to check the registration of the voucher books. If more than one book was registered per citizen, the validity of the additional ones was cancelled. In the second wave of voucher privatisation all Czech citizens over the age of 18 (at the start of registration) were authorised to buy a book of vouchers entitling them to 1 000 voucher points for a total cost of CZK 1 050 (US$35), which was less than 18 per cent of the average monthly wage by the end of 1993. A registration stamp was CZK 1 000 (US$33.3) and a voucher book was CZK 50 (US$1.7). It was necessary for participants to prove their Czech citizenship before they could register themselves for privatisation in the second wave[6].

The trading of vouchers was not allowed, in principle. It was supposed that shares would be immediately tradable, but not the voucher points. Voucher holders were supposed to transfer their voucher points to the Investment Privatisation Fund through a computerised network during the so-called zero round of bidding or use them directly in the bidding for shares during the rounds of voucher privatisation. However, it was not always done this way. Voucher holders had a chance to pass the right to dispose of registered voucher points to another citizen or to the Investment Privatisation Fund. This was the only way to get around the forbidden trading of voucher points. Nevertheless, this does not mean that voucher points were traded freely.

Voucher points had no explicit monetary value. This fact was continually stressed by the architects of the voucher program. That was also probably the main reason why people were slow to register for voucher privatisation in the first months. Only later, when the privatisation fund Harvard Capital & Consulting made its notorious promise of ten-fold return within one year (CSK 10 350 or US$345) did people begin to register.

The participation of the citizens was very high in the first wave and in the second wave as well. The promotional campaign within the first wave was extremely successful, bringing home the message that voucher holders stood to gain from the process if they participated. In November 1991, public opinion polls indicated that some 25 per cent of the adult population was interested in participating in the scheme. As the advertising campaign and other marketing activities progressed, this proportion also increased, reaching 55 per cent by the end of January. The number of registered persons stood at just above half a million by the end of December 1991 but, with the massive advertisements all over the country from the beginning of 1992, this number rose to 2 million by mid-January and jumped to over 8 million by the end of the month, surpassing twice the most optimistic expectation and forcing the postponement of the registration deadline by another month. By the end of the scheme, 75 per cent of the adult population had participated in the voucher privatisation in former Czechoslovakia and an even greater 77 per cent in the Czech Republic.

C. The enterprises involved

The number of enterprises involved in large privatisation and in voucher privatisation is shown in Table 2. Large privatisation is supposed to be made up of a majority of the existing state companies and in large privatisation, the dominant part of the companies is to be privatised by vouchers. From the originally existing 3 500 state companies in the Czech Republic, 988 were privatised in the first wave of voucher privatisation. Another 676 companies will be privatised in the second wave. For those remaining companies standard methods will be used or they will stay in the state hands at least for some time. In Slovakia, the number of companies privatised by vouchers was 503, while the second wave has been postponed for the moment.

The structure of Czech companies privatised in the first wave of voucher privatisation is the following.

Table 4. **The Czech companies privatised in the first wave of voucher privatisation according to employment structure**

Employment category	Number	Total employment	All privatised property in CSK billion	Property privatised by vouchers in CSK billion
0-100	73	4 922	11.5	6.9
101-500	477	127 855	51.2	36.7
501-1 000	215	150 643	39.5	30.2
Over 1 000	223	620 534	232.3	138.7
Total	**988**	**903 984**	**334.5**	**212.5**

Source: Fund of National Property.

The average employment in companies privatised by vouchers was 915 employees, while the book value property was CSK 339 million (US$11.3 million), and by vouchers was on the average privatised CSK 215 million (US$7.2 million) per company. The decision about participation in the programme was undertaken by the three governments[7]. In some cases it happened that a company was taken out of the program, but generally they stayed there. The necessity to privatise was generally accepted by the public and there was no significant opposition against privatisation as such. What was, and still is, an issue is the way privatisation would take place. Will the company be privatised by voucher or by some standard method? If the latter is true, to whom will it be privatised? Those were the main issues for discussion. Managers usually wanted a management buy-out in the first wave and if they failed, then they were willing to accept voucher privatisation as a second best solution because they believed that its result would mean dispersed ownership, in other words, management control. However, after first wave, they have realised that such is not the case and they are less willing to accept the voucher method of privatisation.

For every company scheduled for large privatisation, it was necessary to prepare a basic privatisation project. The director of the company was responsible for this and was pushed to do the best possible by the very fact that everybody else was allowed to prepare competing privatisation projects. All of these projects were then submitted to the relevant branch ministry where a Privatisation Committee was established which was responsible for the evaluation of these projects. The committee spoke with all providers of the projects and suggested a solution. Sometimes they tried to merge the basic project with competing ones by changing the company into a joint-stock company and privatising by vouchers, for example. However, such assets as a recreation resort would be spun-off and sold by tender.

The criteria of selection which were used by branch ministries and by the Privatisation Ministry were never clearly defined. They were supposed to evaluate the quality of the business plan, promote de-monopolisation, keep employment, help restituents to buy additional property, support creation of small and medium-sized entrepreneurs, etc. What was the dominant criterium, if any, is not quite clear at the moment.

Finally, the recommended project, together with all other projects, was moved to the Privatisation Ministry, which made the final decision. After this decision, the final step of privatisation was executed by the Fund of National Property.

The whole scheme of the privatisation projects was very flexible. The only "hard" requirement was to give 3 per cent of the shares into the Restitution Investment Fund in the first wave of voucher privatisation and in the second wave was added the requirement to give 1 per cent of the shares into the Foundation Investment Fund. With the rest it was possible to combine different options like selling part of the company to a foreign investor, domestic investor, restituee, giving it free to the municipality, selling it to employees or keeping it permanently or temporarily in the hands of the state (FNP).

D.   Creation of Investment Privatisation Funds

By aiming to distribute enterprise shares to a very large number of people, voucher privatisation, like any other method of free or nearly free distribution of shares, is bound to create a highly diffused share ownership structure and an undisputed separation of ownership and control. The retreat of the state from the position of a dominant owner creates a massive vacuum which, it is hoped, would be filled by new private owners. But the highly diffused share ownership, and the separation of ownership and control, prevent the new owners from active participation in the affairs of enterprises or effective monitoring of their management. Thus, the problem of "corporate governance" becomes a major issue of concern to policy makers and analysts alike, and they create a serious obstacle to the development of an efficient and accountable management structure and a well-functioning market economy.

In an effort to increase the accountability of enterprise management and subject it to market pressures, the voucher privatisation scheme, and all other mass privatisation programs, are linked to, and rely on, the formation of intermediary financial institutions. These intermediaries, in pursuit of their own interests or acting on behalf of the new individual owners, can engage in the monitoring of enterprise management and the imposition of effective discipline on them.

There was no "central" or governmental establishment of the financial intermediaries. Triska's proposal relied on a Darwinian process of natural selection, whereby only those who were able to draw support from the citizens and combine their individual share holdings into large bundles succeeded in establishing themselves as investment funds with very profitable prospects. The individual citizens could participate in the scheme either directly or through one of these funds. The funds were, therefore, encouraged to compete for citizens' voucher points by offering them the right present or future reward. **This procedure was of tremendous importance for the Czechoslovak programme because it not only provided the individual citizen with a wide choice but also allowed the government to retreat from the scene without having to concern itself with the establishment and staffing of the funds or their mode of operation.**

From the aforementioned it becomes clear that the IPFs were created by private initiative of legal or natural persons. The entities which were at least commercialised were allowed to establish IPFs. The discussion was about the state enterprises' participation in the program. Finally, in the Czech Republic it became forbidden for state firms to participate in the program, while in Slovakia even the state enterprises were allowed to participate and some of them became important players, for example the Slovak Saving Bank.

For the first wave, the IPFs were created as joint-stock companies with a minimal requirement of capitalisation; only CSK 100 000 was needed for IPF and an additional CSK 1 million capitalisation was needed for the management company of the IPF. Later, because of a general change in legislation, CSK 1 million was needed for the creation of a joint-stock company.

The IPFs for the first wave were established in 1991 according to temporary regulation included in the Federal Government Decree No. 383/1991 Coll., of 5 September 1991[8]. This means that before the passing of the law No. 248/1992

Coll., on Investment Companies and Investment Funds, the IPFs were living in rather an uncertain environment. The IPFs were forced to accept the rule that they would change their regulation in accordance with the then non-existent law No. 248/1992 Coll.

It was necessary for the creation of the fund to fulfil three basic requirements:

1. to have minimum charter capital of the fund, which is now CZK 1 million (US$33 300) and which was earlier CSK 100 000;

2. to prove professional qualifications and civic integrity of the members of the proposed statutory bodies and members of the supervisory board;

3. to have the bank which shall act as the depository.

The biggest practical problem was with the proof of the professional qualifications of the fund managers and board directors. After initial attempts to have rather strict explanations of qualification requirements, rather bona fide explanations were accepted which allowed for the creation of hundreds of IPFs.

Citizens who are entrusting the vouchers to the IPFs are doing that against shares of those Investment Privatisation Funds. They are finishing the voucher privatisation, not with shares of the companies but with shares of IPFs[9]. Put options have been made available as an alternative, but are not required by law. Some funds promised something close to a put option, but they have done it because they believed that it would help them to attract more people who would give them their vouchers.

For protection of small investors the law stipulates that the IPF can invest only in securities which are traded on:

1. The primary list of the stock exchange.

2. The secondary list of the stock exchange.

3. Another market of securities where their prices are disclosed.

4. The primary or similar market of a foreign stock exchange provided that the choice of such stock exchange has been approved by the finance ministry. The IPF's silent partnerships and real estate ownership are also restricted.

The above-mentioned measures protect against using small investor voucher points or money for investment into suspicious securities or into other suspicious investments. To distribute properly risk is a goal of another regulations. Funds must diversify their assets at least into ten publicly tradable securities and they can not own more than 20 per cent of the nominal value of securities issued by the same issuer. The shares of funds themselves are also traded on the stock exchange and in the RM-S exchange. However, before this process, disclosure of the fund's assets is required.

A conflict which arose during the first wave had to do with cross ownership in the banking sector. Bank's established funds are not allowed to buy the shares of other banks. The majority of the banks went around this regulation by establishing a daughter company and this daughter company established the fund. The Savings Bank which directly established its fund was forced to sell the shares obtained in the first round of the first wave of voucher privatisation[10].

The major conflict which should be resolved in the short run is the conflict between the demand on the IPFs to be active as owners and the attempts to use US-like legislation, which restricts active involvement of the funds into company matters. Funds are supposed to be only portfolio managers. Some groups are pushing for the increase of a 20 per cent ownership limit in one company, because they believe that it would allow better execution of property rights by the owners than in the current situation. Some regulators, on the other hand, are pushing for strict adherence to the limits in order not to allow insider trading and misuse of inside information. The solution to this problem is not simple because experience in developed market economies is very different; even in the United States, "corporate governance funds" whose tendency is to be active in the boards have appeared.

E. The voucher market

A real secondary voucher market was never created in ex-Czechoslovakia. The vouchers were declared not to be tradable by the government, and because the voucher points were usable only for computerised bidding. The only possibility of trading vouchers was to sell them to somebody who would bid them in the original holder's name. Natural persons had a chance to make some concentration of vouchers before bidding, but it was an administratively cumbersome procedure for them. The funds were supposed to be given, the voucher points in the zero round through computerised system and citizens were encouraged by government to do just that. However, in some cases, the IPFs bought out the voucher books physically to be sure that the points would be given to them. The varieties of ways to do this were vast and ingenious. Some funds promised ten times more within one year, some others provided personal credits backed by voucher points. Other options were direct buy-out for different amounts of money from a few hundred CZKs to CZK 7 000. Other IPFs were supplying lotteries for trips to the Canary Islands, Fords or videos. Others were even developing schemes to help pensioners, students or families with children. PPF (one of the biggest IPFs) advertised the fact that they were involved in the Russian voucher privatisation.

One of the problems for those preliminary buy-outs of the voucher points was the multiple registration of the voucher books. That was not a problem for the system as such; rather it was a problem for the IPFs who bought out the voucher books too early. They may have found that they bought a voucher book whose validity was cancelled.

The revenues generated by the first wave were CSK 8.541 billion which was enough for covering the CSK 1.6 billion, costs for the technical execution of the program. Also, CZK 6.1 billion was obtained in the second wave which is supposed to be more than sufficient to cover all the costs of this wave.

F.   *The privatised enterprises*

In the first wave of voucher privatisation 988 companies were privatised in the Czech Republic, while 503 were privatised in Slovakia. This figure is smaller than the originally planned number because some companies were decided to be privatised by standard methods.

The best measure for evaluating the importance of privatised companies is employment. In the Czech Republic, after the first wave, nearly 1 million employees worked for privatised companies, which is roughly 20 per cent of the Czech labour force. The volume of property is less reliable, but roughly it can be said that out of CZK 1 200 billion, which is the value of large state companies, one-fourth was privatised in the first wave and another one-sixth was privatised in the second wave.

The special issue is what will happen with the state's stake in companies which were only partially privatised. In some cases, the state decided to keep 34 per cent, 51 per cent or 67 per cent in the companies. Those shares are supposed to be kept forever by the state, or to be sold later, directly by the state, on the capital market. However, it has not yet been decided when this will happen with those stakes and what the state will do with those shares in the meantime. Should the Fund of National Property be a passive owner or should it use its stake to push through government objectives? This issue is currently being discussed within the Czech government.

G.   *The role and importance of the Investment Privatisation Funds: corporate governance of portfolio management?*

The high cost of information gathering, together with the risk of ending up with obsolete assets and near-bankrupt enterprises, created the conditions for the appearance of outside agencies -- Investment Privatisation Funds specialising in information gathering and risk reduction. IPFs were able to collect the necessary information on individual companies, and served the needs of voucher-holders who were unable to make a rational decision by themselves. Also, by their sheer size, they were able to reduce the risk of ending up with worthless companies. In former Czechoslovakia they put their irrevocable stamp on the whole process within a short period of time. They were formed for the sole purpose of collecting voucher points and using them to bid for shares of enterprises in the scheme. The individuals who submitted part or all of their voucher points to a Fund became shareholders of that Fund and will benefit from its portfolio through dividends and capital gains.

During the first round of voucher privatisation, 429 Investment Privatisation Funds were established (in the former CSFR). These funds obtained 71.8 per cent of all available voucher points. As a proof of the high concentration of ownership held by funds it is often quoted that the 13 largest IPFs obtained more than 100 million voucher points each, which accounted for 40 per cent of all voucher points available in the first wave of voucher privatisation. However, this is rather misleading information. Much more important for understanding the level of concentration was the number of points controlled by one investment company. Any single investment company could establish several investment funds. In this way, for example, Harvard Capital and Consulting a.s. established eight funds. Investicni banka (IB) established a daughter company "Prvni investicni a.s. -- PIAS" and this company established 12 funds. Clearly, it is important for analyses of concentration of control to look at these investment companies. They will be called "Investment Companies" or "Groups".

The first 14 Investment groups controlled 4 744 364 700 voucher points, or 77.3 per cent of voucher points given to IPFs and 55.5 per cent of all points! These voucher points have been transformed into 119 149 916 shares, which was 67.7 per cent of the shares obtained by IPFs and 42.8 per cent of all distributed shares. Nine banks, two insurance companies, Slovenske investicie, Ltd., PPF and the Harvard group controlled voucher privatisation. Given the fact that the banks in the group are also major providers of credit to the economy and the fact that they can perform privatisation through other methods than vouchers, it becomes evident that banks have nearly absolute control over the Czech economy.

Out of these 14 investment groups, five were established as private legal persons: Creditanstalt, Agrobanka, Slovenske investicie, PPF and HCC. One group belongs to a 100 per cent state company -- the Slovenska sporitelna s.p. (Slovak Saving Bank). Another one -- VSZ Kosice -- is a steel maker, which was privatised by the voucher method. The other eight financial institutions were themselves privatised within the first wave of voucher privatisation, with the provision that the government keep an important packet of shares (compare tables above). In one case (Zivnostenska banka), the majority stake was sold to strategic investors (a German bank and the IFC).

A very peculiar fact in the Czechoslovak voucher privatisation scheme was the use of vouchers for privatisation of major financial institutions which were at the same time very active players in voucher privatisation.

From Table 6 it is evident that in eight out of nine financial institutions the state is the biggest shareholder. A triumvirate of three persons is responsible for

Table 5. Fourteen biggest investment groups in the first wave of voucher privatisation (groups which collected over 100 million voucher points)

No.	Name of investment group	Number of funds	Millions of points for the 1st wave	Number of shares obtained in the 1st wave
1.	Ceska sporitelna Praha	1	950 432 200	21 376 611
2.	Investicni banka group, Praha	12	724 123 600	13 594 068
3.	Harvard group	8	638 548 000	15 225 108
4.	Vseobecna uverova, Bratislava	1	500 587 700	11 985 444
5.	Komercni banka	1	465 530 300	11 931 808
6.	Ceska pojistovna	1	334 040 900	7 623 311
7.	Slovenske investicie s.r.o	1	187 917 000	4 432 770
8.	Slovenska sporitelna & VSZ Kosice	4	168 864 400	7 707 865
9.	Creditanstalt	2	166 256 000	3 610 773
10.	PPF	4	117 624 000	4 920 213
11.	Slovenska IB	12	145 128 400	4 432 770
12.	Zivnostenska banka	1	117 541 500	1 885 287
13.	Slovenska poistovna	6	116 682 500	4 362 299
14.	Agrobanka	17	111 087 900	3 941 916
	Total	**71**	**4 744 364 700**	**119 149 916**
	Total IPFs	**429**	**6 134 978 400**	**175 979 880**
	Total all		**8 541 000 000**	**277 800 000**

Source: Privatisation Ministry.

the state stake in commercial banks: the Minister of Finance, Chairperson of the FNP and the Governor of the Czech National Bank. At the moment they are very passive owners leaving corporate governance in the hands of bankers (bank managers).

Table 6. **Privatisation of major financial institutions in the former CSFR**

No.	Name of bank	Total property (in billion CZK)	For vouchers	Foreign ownership	FNP	Others
			Per cent			
1.	Sporitelna	5.6	37	0	40	23
2.	IB	1.0	52	0	45	3
3.	VUB	2.04	52	0	45	3
4.	KB	4.56	53	0	44	3
5.	Pojistovna	0.38	65	0	0	35
6.	Slovenska IB	0.5	52	0	45	3
7.	ZB	1.36	43.6	52	0	4.4
8.	Slovenska poistovna	0.94	48	0	37	15

Source: Kuponova privatizace, No. 5, 1992.

Despite heroic attempts of the architects of Czech voucher privatisation to create an American like capital market, we have finished with something much closer to the German system of "corporate bank ownership". The major commercial banks are, through their privatisation funds, the co-owners of many Czech companies. Further on, they do own each other. In some cases, the banks indirectly own their own shares. The champion in this game is Investicni banka (IB). The investment group of Czech IB owned 17 per cent of the shares of IB after initial distribution in June 1993.

H. *Conclusion*

Despite problems, the Czech voucher privatisation was a very successful privatisation program. As was shown above it helped to establish new owners in the economy who are active in company restructuring. There exists in the country a capital market with one thousand tradable securities. Several hundred companies have been traded. In the case of some of these firms, trade is already very significant. More and more companies are traded on the markets. However, what was not mentioned above was the tremendous political success of the whole program. It helped the government obtain political support for the overall economic transformation program.

However, caution should be taken in extending the scheme elsewhere in the region. It is quite possible that the success of the voucher programme was due to the credibility of the banking sector and the fact that Czechoslovakia was a developed country 50 years ago, not speaking about the Czech Republic's proximity to Germany, with whose economy the Czech economy gradually integrated. If those things are prerequisites for a successful voucher privatisation, then the chance to replicate the programme elsewhere is low.

Notes

* Based on a presentation made by the author (Jan Mladek, Central European University, Prague, Czech Republic, and Ministry of Industry and Trade, Czech Republic) at the fifth meeting of the Advisory Group on Privatisation, Paris, 2-4 March 1994.

1. This paper uses the term "voucher privatisation" instead of its alternative, "mass privatisation".

2. Unfortunately, a similar estimate is not available for Slovakia, but it is reasonable to believe that the situation there is not dramatically different.

3. CZK stands for Czech Koruna and CSK stands for Czechoslovak Koruna. Before 8 February 1993 -- the date of the split of the Czechoslovak currency -- CSK is used. After 8 February 1993, CZK is used. For the sums covering both periods the abbreviation CZK is used.

4. All estimates in this chapter are taken from Ceska, R. (1993).

5. Everybody had a chance to come up with a competitive action project, but usually those competing were groups of managers backed by domestic or foreign entrepreneurs.

6. Residents of the Czech Republic were not automatically given citizenship of the Czech Republic, rather they were forced to go through rather cumbersome administrative procedures. This resulted in long lines because it was necessary to prove the citizenship of 6 million people within a three-month period.

7. The attitude was as follows: a company was scheduled into privatisation by the government and, unless the government decided to remove it from the privatisation schedule, the company was privatised.

8. The rules as how to diversify portfolios were given by the amendments of the Decree No. 383: amendments No. 67/1992 Coll. and 69/1992 Coll.

9. Naturally, the combination was also possible. For example, the author of these lines gave 500 points to one IPF and the rest directly into the companies.

10. The regulation came into the force between first and second round of the first wave.

References

ANDERSON, R. E. (1994): Voucher Funds in The Transition Economies: The Czech and Slovak Examples, The World Bank, 21 January 1994.

BLAHA, J., O. KYN, M. MEJSTRIK and J. MLADEK, (1992): Tri uzly na kuponove privatizaci (Three Knots on the Voucher Privatization), Respekt 3, No. 5, February 1992, Prague.

CESKA, R. (1993): "Three Years of Privatization in the Czech and Slovak Republics"; *Privatization Newsletter of the Czech Republic and Slovakia 2*, No. 17, p. 1-5.

HASHI, I., and J. MLADEK, (1993): "Voucher Privatization, Investment Funds and Corporate Governance in Czechoslovakia", *British Review of Economic Issues 15*, No. 37, October 1993, p. 67-96.

KOTRBA, J. (1993): "Privatization in the Czech Republic: An Overview", CERGE Praha, Discussion Paper No. 18.

MEJSTRIK, M. (1993): "Second Wave of Czech Privatisation in Full Speed"; *Privatization Newsletter of the Czech Republic and Slovakia 2*, No. 18, p. 1-3.

MLADEK, J. (1992): "Transformation of Czechoslovak Agriculture", *Czechoslovak Privatization Newsletter No. 9*, October 1992, Prague, p. 1-3.

MLADEK, J. (1993): The Different Path of Privatization (Czechoslovakia 1990), in Earle J., Frydman, R., Rapaczynski, A. (eds.): Privatization in the Transition to a Market Economy: Preconditions and Policies in Eastern Europe; Pinter Publisher and St. Martin Press, London.

SVEJNAR, J. (1989): A Framework for the Economic Transformation of Czechoslovakia, PlanEcon Report, Vol. V, No. 52.

TRISKA, D. (1991): Voucher Scheme of Privatization, in Pöschl, J., Sohns, R. and Stadler, A. (eds.): Privatization in Eastern Europe, Proceedings of the Conference on Privatization: How to Use This Instrument for Economic Reform in Eastern Europe, Vienna, 17-18 November 1990, p. 101-115.

Annex

Short History of the Two Waves of Voucher Privatisation

A. The first wave of voucher privatisation

The first wave of voucher privatisation was finally finished in June 1993 by distribution of shares to individuals and investment funds. The whole process of the first wave lasted 21 months as can be seen from the Table 1.

Table 1. **The timetable of the first wave of voucher privatisation**

1.	1 October 1991	Voucher books for CSK 35 (US$1.2) were started to be sold.
2.	31 October 1991	Deadline for submitting basic privatisation projects.
3.	1 November 1991	Registration of individual investors for 1 000, - CSK (US$33.3) or 25 per cent of average monthly wage.
4.	20 January 1992	Deadline for submitting competing privatisation projects.
5.	29 February 1992	Deadline for investors registration deadline for founding and registering IPFs.
6.	1 March 1992	Zero round started (used for collection of voucher points to IPFs).
7.	26 April 1992	Deadline for submitting voucher points to IPFs.
8.	11 May 1992	Deadline for commercialisation and legal registration of companies privatised in the voucher privatisation scheme.
9.	18 May 1992	The start of the first round of auction bidding.
10.	22 December 1992	Publishing results of the fifth and final round.
11.	24 May - 30 June 1993	Transfer of shares to individuals and to the IPFs.

Source: Different issues of the newspaper Kuponova privatizace (Voucher privatisation).

Close to 300 billion CSK (US$10 billion) of property was privatised in the first wave of voucher privatisation. In the Czech Republic this figure was CSK 212.5 billion. The proportion designated for voucher privatisation ranged from between 7 per cent to 97 per cent of companies' basic capital. From every company it was necessary to reserve 3 per cent of vouchers for the satisfaction of future restitution claims. On average, Czech companies which participated in the first wave gave 61.4 per cent of their shares for voucher privatisation. Remaining shares were sold to foreigners, transferred to municipalities, or left temporarily or permanently in the Fund of National Property. In fact, only part of the shares went through voucher privatisation. The most important other holdings are those of the Fund of National Property. FNP holdings are, in fact, concentrated in a few large companies like the Czech Electric Company, steel works, etc.

One of the biggest fears before the start of voucher privatisation was the speed of convergence. It was quite clear that the scheme was convergent, but it was unclear how quickly. There was the risk that the wave would finish with many unsold shares and all voucher points used, or with all shares sold and a lot of unused voucher points remaining. These fears did not materialise, as can be seen from following two tables.

From these two tables it can be seen that after the fifth round of voucher privatisation only 22.4 billion CSK shares went unsold, i.e. 7.7 per cent of supplied shares and only 1.2 per cent of voucher points given to population were unused.

Table 2. **The results of the first wave of voucher privatisation**
Supply side

Round No.	Supply of shares (in CSK billion)	Shares sold in round (in CSK billion)	Percentage of supply (in a given round)	Shares sold cumulatively (in CSK billion)	Percentage of total supply
1.	299.39	89.44	29.9	89.44	29.9
2.	209.95	77.81	37.1	167.25	55.9
3.	132.13	32.30	24.4	199.55	66.7
4.	99.60	37.06	37.2	236.61	79.0
5.	62.50	40.94	65.5	277.55	92.7

Source: Kuponova privatizace (Voucher privatisation) 2, Nos. 6-11, Prague

Table 3. **The result of the first wave of voucher privatisation**
Demand side

Round No.	1	2	3	4	5
Number of points available in billion	8.54	5.50	2.10	1.05	0.54
Number of points used for D in billion	7.90	4.88	2.00	1.00	0.52
% of used points upon available ones	93.00	89.00	95.00	95.00	95.00
Satisfied D in billion points	3.04	3.40	1.05	0.51	0.44
% of satisfied D upon points used for D	38.50	69.70	52.50	51.00	88.10
Satisfied D cumulatively in billion points	3.04	6.44	7.49	8.00	8.44
% of cumulatively satisfied D upon total number of points	35.60	75.40	87.70	93.70	98.80

Source: Kuponova privatizace (Voucher privatisation) 2, Nos. 6-11, Prague.

The first wave technically finished in December 1992, although the distribution of shares was delayed until May and June 1993. New owners were finally given a chance to use their property rights obtained within the first wave.

B.   The second wave of voucher privatisation

There are several differences between the first and second waves of voucher privatisation. First, the second wave deals exclusively with enterprises belonging to the Czech Republic. After the split, the Slovak Republic government denounced voucher privatisation and indicated that it would rely on more traditional methods of privatisation.

Second, logistically everything is much easier. The computerised network for bidding, created during the first wave will be used for the second wave as well. This same system is used by the RM-S, an over-the-counter securities market. It seems that registration of the population will be much smoother than in the first wave.

Third, the attitudes of company managers are completely different than during the first wave. Now they are doing everything possible not to privatise by the voucher method. If this is not possible, then their goal will be to minimise the share of vouchers. In the first wave they were willing to accept the voucher method as the second best solution, because they believed that dispersed ownership would mean weak control. Now they realised that this is not the case and so they are trying to escape from voucher privatisation. This attitude has caused supply problems for the Privatisation Ministry. Initially, they promised CZK 200 billion of assets for the second wave, as they did in first wave. Then there was a time when they thought about offering CZK 100 billion. Finally, it was CZK 155 billion, but that is only because some minority stakes in large companies were allotted to the second wave of voucher privatisation (coal mines, petrochemical industry).

Table 4. **Funds in second wave of voucher privatisation in the Czech Republic**

Type of funds	Number of funds	Percentage of the total number of funds
IPF from 1st wave	133	37.6
New IPF for 2nd wave	63	17.8
Share funds closed	120	33.9
Share funds open	38	10.7
Total	**354**	**100.0**

Source: Kuponova privatizace No. 21, 2 December 1993.

The fourth difference is in the legal form of investment funds. In the first round, Investment Funds were only joint-stock companies which represented the voting rights of its individual shareholders. In the second round, because it was found that the joint-stock company arrangement was troublesome, the funds are very often standard mutual funds, which can be closed or open-ended. The major difference of these funds from the IPFs of the first wave will be the fact that individuals who give their voucher points to these funds will not have voting rights.

The fifth difference is in the transferring of shares to the new owners. In the first wave, instead of passing the shares after every round, it was done only at the end of the whole wave. In the second wave, shares will be transferred after every round at least to individuals, to the IPFs at the end, as in the first wave. The whole thing should be over by the autumn of 1994. The following table is a schedule for the second wave.

Table 5. **The timetable of the second wave of voucher privatisation**

1.	16 August 1992	Deadline for submitting basic privatisation projects.
2.	15 October 1992	Deadline for submitting competing privatisation projects.
3.	1 October 1993	Start of the registration of individual investors for CZK 1 000 (US$33.3) plus CZK 50 (US$1.7) for voucher book. Together CSK 1 050 represented 17.5 per cent of average wage by the end of 1993.
4.	15 November 1993	Deadline for IPFs registration.
5.	8 December 1993	Deadline for individual investors registration.
6.	15 December 1993	Start of the zero round for collection of voucher point to IPFs.
7.	4 March 1994	Final list of the companies was published.
8.	9 March 1994	End of zero round[1].
9.	11 March 1994	Start of the first round.
10.	25 March 1994	End of the first round.
11.	May 1994	The second round.
12.	Sept. - Nov. 1994	Possible end of the second wave (Transfer of share is supposed to be continued).

1.   Despite aggressive advertising, people gave to the Investment funds only 3.92 billion voucher points, which was 63.5 per cent of the whole. In the first wave IPF collected 72 per cent.

It is necessary to stress that the second wave has just started and a full comparison of the two waves will not be possible until results of the second wave are available. It will be particularly interesting to do so, as weak points of the original voucher privatisation scheme will be able to be identified.

Post-Privatisation Securities Markets in the Czech Republic

Dusan Triska*

I.   Introduction

Economically speaking, the major damage caused by the communist regime to the countries in the Central and Eastern Europe rests in the overwhelming destruction of an unquestionable and guaranteed system of property rights. In particular, the destruction of ownership structures towards the means of production created the basis for the ever-present inefficiency of the performance of economic agents.

Where they exist, the seemingly natural character of the ownership rights, their routine and everyday presence, can lead their beneficiaries to forget that it has taken centuries of evolutionary development for systems to emerge that supply goods and services to the country with some degree of efficiency.

Unlike many outside observers, the Czechoslovak (and, later on, the Czech) government has constantly stressed its awareness of the institutional core of the transformation problem and its political, legislative and economic aspects[1].

Bearing in mind the institutional concept, it must be stressed, in the first place, that it is the **economy as a whole,** not a particular state-owned enterprise or group of enterprises that calls for transformation. In other words, however disabled individual businesses may appear, it is not **they,** but the overall economy, which requires therapy.

The economy cannot be cured, transformed or restructured without comprehensive "property reform". There is no doubt that it is privatisation that distinguishes a genuine, systemic change from **perestroika,** or "reform". The Czech government never wanted to reform the unreformable. Its target has always been to establish an entirely new institutional set-up.

Capitalist countries have also embarked on privatisation, the best known of which is the Thatcherite privatisation of Great Britain in the late seventies and early eighties. The obvious focus of that process was ownership transfer within **an already existing** property rights structure.

Unfortunately, this western-style privatisation has almost nothing in common with the post-communist privatisation. As a matter of fact, the very terms and concepts of western privatisation may be misleading when used in the context of transformation in Central and Eastern Europe. No wonder that the very term has confused both analysts and many politicians. Unlike in the west, eastern privatisation amounts to the very **establishment of a heretofore non-existent property rights structure** (and associated institutions). Privatising in the West may be viewed as a "reform" process. In the East, however, privatisation must fulfil the most fundamental transformation objectives.

In order to distinguish the above defined two types of privatisation, we shall refer to them as W-privatisation and E-privatisation, according to whether they occur in the context of a market economy or constitute a fundamental part of post-communist transformation, respectively.

II. Tradability of "capital goods" in a post-communist country

For the sake of simplicity, we shall use the term "capital goods" to represent a concept complementary to the notion of consumer goods (and public goods, of course). By capital goods we understand items usable as production factors such as whole enterprises or their constituents: land, buildings, labour, etc.

Due to nationalisation and central planning, almost all of these items lost their status of tradability. In fact, under communism, those capital goods lost a great portion of their economic content as they ceased to be subjects of market transactions. While consumer goods markets existed even within the centrally planned economy, the capital goods markets must be established from scratch in all post-communist countries.

E-privatisation (in contrast to that in a market economy), therefore represents a process of re-creating capital good as a fundamental economic category. By ascribing an owner to, e.g. every piece of land, every building, the land and the building become tradable goods and the "capital market" emerges. In order to allow for changes in ownership, **the first owner** has to be established. Unlike the western experience, E-privatisation is **not** a process within which property changes hands. Rather, it is the process within which the "non-owner", the government, "packages" and transfers **newly created capital goods** to their first (initial) masters.

III. E-privatisation and securities markets

In organising the privatisation programme of a transforming economy it is always important to emphasise what are and what are not the objectives of the programme, or what are the major principles upon which the process can and should be based.

With this in mind, a number of different (often correlated) questions have to be clearly raised and answered. Given the topic of this paper we shall address only the following ones:

-- speed;

-- ownership structure and corporate governance;

-- efficiency of the newly-emerging capital goods markets.

A. *Speed*

Dozens of privatisation techniques of different speed characteristics have been elaborated, various criteria have been established for their evaluation, one of which is of the Czech origin. According to this original criterion, the techniques can be grouped as standard (some analysts state there are now 56 different such techniques) and non-standard [so far, just one such technique has been successfully implemented: the Czech (and, at that time, also Slovak) **voucher** privatisation scheme].

Czech agents of privatisation believe non-standard, voucher privatisation to be rapid and comparatively cheap[2].

Still better, in the Czech Republic the non-standard (voucher) privatisation is believed to facilitate application of standard privatisation techniques and, in a somewhat indirect manner, speeds up their implementation.

B. *Appropriateness of the ownership structure*

Unfortunately, the Czech concept "privatise first, restructure later" gave rise to the following voices: "should restructuring be postponed after privatisation, the government bears responsibility for organising privatisation in such a fashion as to select owners who would be responsible enough to fulfil the restructuring tasks".

At this stage of the debate the experts on so-called corporate governance take the opportunity to explain what patterns of ownership are and are not optimal. According to their views, privatisation should not begin until legislation allows for ownership optimisation and "fine tuning".

1. *Initial and final distribution of property rights*

The architects of the Czech privatisation programme always believed that the highly needed stable distribution of ownership has to be an evolutionary process of which as many people as possible should become a part. Whatever ownership structure emerges during the transformation process, it should be the outcome of free choice by the population and there is practically no reason why the government should interfere -- especially after privatisation -- with this **spontaneous** ownership restructuring[3].

It is, then, noteworthy that the **initial** ownership structure may say very little about the **final** distribution of property rights[4]. This latter may be constituted only as the result of thousands of operations in capital markets.

While the opposition towards the so-called spontaneous privatisation is extremely strong in the Czech Republic, the restructuring of the initial ownership structure is as deregulated as possible. The government has no ambitions to affect (not to mention "fine tune") changes in the initial ownership structure. At the same time, the government is very cautious that everybody be offered a fair chance to participate not only in the privatisation process but also in the follow-up ownership restructuring.

2.   *Corporate governance*

As already noted, there have never been any serious doubts in the Czech Republic that it is **the new owner not the government** who should find ideas, time and resources for the necessary restructuring. The Czech government has never listened to the advise that its agencies should attempt to increase the efficiency of a state-owned enterprise before it is subjected to privatisation.

In the early weeks and months of 1990, the approach of the Czech government always provoked harsh criticism from all imaginable sources. Today, even the most prominent international financial organisations have realised that:

-- a government of a transforming country is **the worst imaginable agent** to take care of restructuring tasks;

-- internationally renowned consultant firms (and/or their representatives appointed for particular assignments) are very expensive and not always fully aware of all the specifics of the post-communist environment.

It is, then, a wrong strategy for E-privatisation to design techniques and legislation with respect to the objective of creating responsible owners. An objective like this is far beyond the capacity of the post-communist government and, as already stated, the first (initial) owners may not be the final ones, anyway.

The worst of all possible worlds is, then, the practice, maybe applicable in W-privatisation, within which the government determines the "optimal owner" and at the same time prevents the owner from changing his/her products or even selling his/her business unit.

3. Investment privatisation funds

As an intermediary within the voucher privatisation scheme the investment privatisation fund (or IPF) is in the Czech Republic conceptualised as a joint-stock company established with the objective to attract voucher-holders, to accumulate their investment vouchers and, with the help of the vouchers to bid for shares of the privatised companies. After this, the IPF is obliged to issue its own shares and to distribute them among "its" voucher-holders thus turned shareholders[5].

The Czechoslovak voucher privatisation scheme was designed in such a fashion that, theoretically, two extreme outcomes could have resulted:

In the first (totally improbable) extreme case, only one IPF would be established and this IPF would concentrate in its hands all the investment vouchers. (This would represent a full-scale collapse of the scheme.)

The second (relatively more probable) extreme case is that even though the intermediary services of the IPFs were offered, no one would take the opportunity of using them.

The real-world outcome in the CSFR was such that the IPFs have played an exceptionally significant role in the first wave of voucher privatisation and their role in the second wave will be important, too. The degree of their role, however, was not pre-determined by the law or the government. It was an outcome of the free choice of voucher-holders.

As the requirements for establishing an IPF were relatively easy to meet, basically any citizen or institution was offered the opportunity to establish one. This liberal approach for allowing funds to participate in voucher privatisation led to the fact that in the Czech Republic alone no less than 264 IPFs took part in the first wave of voucher privatisation. Investment privatisation funds were set up by domestic banks, private consulting firms, as well as by some privatised enterprises.

The participating investment funds competed against each other, primarily through massive advertising campaigns. The success of IPFs in gaining the trust of individuals was not only the result of advertising campaigns or of any guarantees that were provided if an individual decided to entrust his/her investment points to a particular fund.

The actual result was that 72 per cent of all investment points were assembled in the hands of the investment funds. Of this amount, a significant portion was concentrated in the hands of the following ten largest funds:

-- seven IPFs were established by domestic banks; in the Czech Republic these were: Ceska Spooitelna, Komercni Banka, Investicni Banka, Zivnostenska Banka and Ceska Pojisovna; in the Slovak Republic: **Vseobecna uvirova banka, Investicni banka;**

--   one IPF was established by a subsidiary of a foreign bank (**Creditanstalt**);

--   two IPFs were established by companies created by private agents for this special purpose. (In addition to the notorious "Harvard", i.e. **HC\C,** there was another founder of the type called "The First Privatisation Fund", or **PPF**).

These ten largest IPFs collected approximately one-half of the total points entrusted to investment privatisation funds in the first wave of voucher privatisation.

As a direct consequence of voucher privatisation, trading with privatised shares started in May 1993.

C.   *Efficiency of the newly emerged capital goods markets*

Privatisation creates the first (initial) owners who, of course, immediately play the role of potential sellers. Where there are (potential) sellers there must also be (potential) buyers. Whether these two types of players actually meet, and the magnitude of their transaction costs depends on the efficiency of the market place.

Unlike in W-privatisation, an interestingly sharp asymmetry is produced during and especially after E-privatisation between the following two types of agents:

--   the new owners of huge value of privatised assets who suffer from an enormous shortage of disposable cash;

--   agents with large funds of cash and no assets.

This situation, of course, implies that there is a large potential for a massive "secondary" shift in the initial ownership. It is in the interest of the economy that these secondary transactions of capital goods (land, buildings, labour and securities) are carried out smoothly and rapidly. The great scale of the secondary transformation in the Czech Republic is given by the scope of the overall privatisation programme which is implemented not only within the voucher scheme but also on the basis of: (1) transfer of state property to municipalities, (2) restitution to original owners, (3) transformation of "soviet-type" co-operatives, (4) small-scale privatisation through public auctions, and (5) privatisation of medium and large-scale enterprises through direct sale and joint ventures.

Being constrained by the topic of the paper, we shall confine ourselves only to this sector of the capital goods market which is associated with securities. However, most of what applies to securities trading is true for other markets as well.

D. Two types of securities markets

Voucher privatisation turned more than 75 per cent of Czech adults into shareholders. Each of them now owns shares in either the 1 500 privatised companies or the investment privatisation funds. Given such great market potential, two types of securities exchanges were established (spontaneously, without any government initiation and with only limited regulation): the traditional stock exchange (established mainly by banks) and the non-traditional electronic RM-System.

Trading on both exchanges started in May 1993, right after completion of the first privatisation wave. As already mentioned, access to both markets, in particular in the case of the RM-System, is extremely liberal.

Developments in these exchanges are observed with great interest by both analysts and investors, not to mention the government. The reason is that the emerging securities industry will supplement the, so far, only slowly recovering Czech banking sector. The crucial function of these markets derives from the eminent need for the most rapid reallocations of existing resources and the most efficient injections of highly needed fresh capital. The more efficient the securities industry becomes, the better the chance for the optimal restructuring of the economy.

This is also the reason why the current fierce **competition** between the two securities exchanges established in the Czech Republic is highly welcome not only by the government but also by all participating investors.

The fundamental differences between the two exchanges established in the Czech Republic are as follows:

Prague Stock Exchange

It was founded on the basis of membership which means that the members of the Stock Exchange (its shareholders) are, in comparison to other persons, in a privileged position. The most important privilege is that Stock Exchange members can decide who may and may not directly enter the market.

If another person wants to enter the market, he or she has two possibilities:

-- either he or she will gain approval from the Stock Exchange to enter that market;

-- or he or she enters this market indirectly through one of the members of the Stock Exchange or some agent that has already acquired the above-mentioned authority from its members.

In addition to this, the Stock Exchange has the right to select which securities are "good enough" for its market. If the Stock Exchange members believe that the quality of a given security (its issuer) does not comply with its investor protection policy, they may decide not to accept this security on the market.

RM-System

The market organised by RM-S can be directly accessed by anyone regardless of whether they are legal or physical persons, providing they fulfil the very simple conditions of the RM-S Trading Rules. Participants may be professionals in the field (securities traders) or persons who are engaged in another business area, or are not businessmen at all.

In principle, therefore, the RM-S organs are not entitled to refuse to provide their services to anybody, with the minor exception of people who breach the law or the RM-S Trading Rules. As a consequence, RM-S has no right to refuse the introduction of any security on its market.

Compared to the Stock Exchange, the role of the so-called intermediaries (brokers) is also somewhat modified on the RM-S market. The peculiarity of RM-S, therefore, is that it gives its customers the option of whether they want to make their sales and purchases directly by themselves, or whether they want to use the professional brokerage services of securities traders.

IV. RM-S Securities exchange

A. *Organisation*

RM-S consists of a central workplace and a network of entry workplaces.

The most important task of the **central RM-S work place** is to process all orders delivered to it from the entry work places. On the basis of the so-called central algorithm, the central work place will define which of these orders can be satisfied, to what extent and at what price.

The entry places of RM-S are divided into groups that correspond to the types of customers who will be entering the RM-S market through them:

-- retail (ordinary) customers, that is primarily individual citizens, will be mainly visiting the trading places where they will submit their orders in the so-called order forms;

-- medium and large (special) customers, that is primarily investment companies and dealers/brokers, can select from the following two methods of entering the market:

  a) at specialised entry work places they can submit their orders on computer diskette;

b) on their own premises they can submit orders through a work station, that RM-S will build upon request in one of the two basic modifications:

- modem, through which it is possible to submit to the market orders prepared in batches, similar to the disk but with higher user-comfort than on disk;
- on-line station, enabling deals to be concluded in real time.

As to the delivery, the RM-S has a direct access to the Centre for Securities. As to the payment side of the executed trades, the RM-S organises it through the so-called jumbo account established in the **Investicni banka.**

B.   Self-regulation

By law RM-S is obliged to publish the conditions on the basis of which it is providing services to its customers. RM-S must submit its **Trading Rules** for approval to the Ministry of Finance, which also approves all the future changes and additions to these Trading Rules.

The existence of these Trading Rules, their correctness and availability at each commercial place are therefore the most important protection of RM-S customers. The Trading Rules contain, in particular, a detailed description of orders that can be submitted to RM-S, and the basic methods of satisfying them. The Trading Rules further define the principles by which the prices (rates) of securities being bought and sold are defined and published on the RM-S market.

C.   Customers and services

The **ordinary customer** submits his/her orders on a certificate, or an order form. The use of the certificate replaces the necessity to sign a contract between the customer and RM-S. The relations between the special customer and RM-S are regulated by the above Trading Rules.

Unlike this, a special contract must be signed between RM-S and anybody who wants to become a **special** customer, that is a person who is able to submit his/her orders on a computer diskette, through a modem or through an "on-line" station.

Save for unimportant exceptions, RM-S provides its service on the basis of an **order** submitted to RM-S by its customer. At this stage of development, RM-S is offering to its customers one **basic** and hundreds of **special** services. The latter services are, in one way or another, an enhancement or improvement of the basic service.

The principal orders (services) are of the buy or sell type. These orders are satisfied by inclusion in auction rounds of either a **periodic** or **continuous** character.

D. *Trading places*

Any ordinary customer can submit his/her order form at any of some 400 outlets ("trading places") established and run by RM-S.

The trading place accepts the order form in the following manner:

-- it will print the day, month, hour and minute of the order form being submitted;

-- it will enter the signature of an employee of the trading place and the imprint of its rubber stamp;

-- it will hand over a copy of the order form to the customer and send the original to the central processing.

Both buy or sell-orders can but need not bear a concrete price specification. By not explicitly expressing his/her opinion on the price, the customer relies on the fact that RM-S will, through its internal rules, set this price according to "what the market gives".

E. *Pre-trade validation*

By definition, newly emerged markets cannot be built upon a mutual trust among business partners. All entrepreneurial agents, be they the "old" (transformed or even privatised) ones or the "green field" ones, are only learning the standard manners of trading and business behaviour. This general truth holds firm also for securities markets and, in particular, those of them which allow for a direct access, as is the case of RM-S. In a transforming economy, many cases occur when the buyer does not have enough cash for the payment and/or when the seller is incapable of delivering what he/she offers for sale.

Therefore RM-S regards as one of its most significant services to its customers the fact that it is capable of controlling and securing their mutual "solvency". This service RM-S offers in the form of pre-trade validation.

For this purpose, RM-S has set up a special cash account or "jumbo account". Every customer who wants to **buy** is then required to deposit beforehand a sufficient amount of cash on this account. This amount must be sufficient as to cover fully the payment of:

-- the price that will have to be paid to the **seller** if the submitted buy is fully satisfied;

--   the price that RM-S charges the buyer for its services.

If the amount of cash on the "jumbo account" is not sufficient, RM-S is entitled to "scale-down" the respective buy-order of such customer.

It is somewhat simpler to validate sell-orders dealing with book-entry securities. In this case RM-S acquires the right to dispose of the securities and their owners are registered in the Centre of Securities.

In all cases when the P-order passes through pre-trade validation, the appropriate number of customer's securities are "frozen" or "blocked" or, more accurately, suspended as to the right of their owner to dispose of with them.

F.   Fees

RM-S offers a wide range a diverse services. Some of these are provided free-of-charge, others for a fee.

For using the basic service, the ordinary customer pays the price defined by the RM-S price list. This price is defined as a **percentage of the monetary value of the satisfied order.**

In reality, this tariff could be either lower or higher. RM-S can differentiate its tariffs, in particular based on the following two criteria:

--   the extent of the service being provided;

--   the position of the customer whose order is being satisfied.

The second of the above criteria basically does not apply in case of an ordinary customer. All ordinary customers will be equally important to RM-S and therefore will be charged the same price for the provision of the basic service.

However, differentiation can be exercised based on the first of the above mentioned criteria. In accordance with this, RM-S will apply the principle that the higher the monetary value of a satisfied order, the lower will be the price for the service provided.

RM-S has ordinary and extraordinary customers. Ordinary customers are divided into regular and special. A market maker is an extraordinary customer. It is possible to become **an extraordinary customer, that is a market maker,** by applying to RM-S for a special registration.

A person who wants to enter the RM-S market by means other than only the order form (e.g. on computer disk, through modem or an on-line station) must be a **special customer.** In order to become a special RM-S customer, that person must sign a special contract with RM-S.

For the sake of completeness let us mention that the **ordinary customer** is defined as a person who is registered on the RM-S market and who can submit his orders to the RM-S market only by a **single** method -- on the order form.

Not everybody can become a special customer. Those who want to become one must:

-- prove that they have sufficient technological, organisational and personnel prerequisites for this;

-- undertake, if need be, training organised for them by RM-S;

-- accept from RM-S the necessary software, hardware and other technological tools and use those in line with RM-S orders.

RM-S will also require that special customers set up, in accordance with instructions from RM-S, a special monetary account at a bank and, for the purposes of pre-trade validation, sign a contract with RM-S and this bank.

V.   Prague Stock Exchange (PSE)

A.   *Organisation*

The "Law about stock-exchange" defines what exact type of the securities market organisation can be referred to as a "stock exchange". Organisers of other market types are then not allowed to use the term in their business names.

The "Law about stock-exchange" does not say that there may be only one such exchange, however only PSE has been licensed to operate in this field. The law states in detail under what conditions an applicant may by granted a licence for providing the exchange. It is not likely that in the near future another stock exchange will be established in the Czech Republic.

PSE has been initiated by the largest Czech Banks who are now its most influential members. It is organised traditionally, i.e. it established its floor where -- so far twice a week -- its members meet to execute their orders. So far some 60 members are entitled to enter the PE floor.

As to the delivery, attached to PSE is its own Register through which PSE organises the settlement in the Centre for Securities. As to the payment side of the transactions, PSE organises it through the Clearing Centre of the Central Bank.

B.   *Self-regulation*

Regulation of PSE is derived from the law and in detail based upon its own "Stock-exchange rules" which are subject to the approval of the Ministry of

Finance. The major rules of the regulation are derived from the membership principle upon which PSE is established.

C. Customers and services

For the right to enter PSE's floor each broker/dealer has to apply for membership first and, if accepted, pay the annual membership fee.

D. Trading places

The stock exchange floor is so far the only place where the trades can be executed.

E. Pre-trade validation

PSE runs a special fund to guarantee payments attached to the executed trades. Every member is obliged to contribute to the fund.

F. Fees

PSE offers two major types of services. One on a so-called central market, the other consisting of direct purchases and sales. The latter service is free of charge. The fees for the former service are defined as a **percentage of the monetary value of the satisfied order.**

VI. Direct purchases and sales

Apart from the two "official" exchanges there also exists a third -- "unofficial" -- market consisting of direct trades executed without any restriction by anybody who is interested. As all the privatised shares are dematerialised and registered in the Centre for Securities, all such trades have to be reported to the Centre. The transaction becomes valid only after it has been registered. At the same time, the Centre for Securities has no right to refuse the registration.

So far the estimates are that some 80 per cent of the monetary value of the overall transactions is executed on this "unofficial" (third) market. The Ministry of Finance as the government regulatory body (See section VII) closely watches its development and is ready to react to any development that would be regarded as inadequate.

VII. Regulation

A. *General principles*

The approach of the Government to the securities markets developments is strongly affected by its inherent liberalism. However, as a direct outcome of implementing the voucher privatisation scheme two major problems arose:

-- in what form would the "voucherised shares" be issued?;

-- what types of market organisation would be the most appropriate for the post-privatisation trading with the shares (and, of course, other securities)?

The first question was answered with respect to the enormous number of share-holders and under the provision that there is literally nobody in the country who could provide sensible depository services. These were the reasons why all the privatised shares were immediately dematerialised by law and now exist "only" in a book-entry form in the central government-sponsored registry -- so-called **Centre for Securities.** It should be stressed that the securities dematerialisation is a difficult process which requires solving many complicated conceptual, organisational and legislative problems.

The second question was mainly addressed by the "Law about Securities", the most important provisions of which are the following two[6]:

Firstly, the law established the Ministry of Finance as the regulatory body over the "securities industry"[7]. Secondly, the law introduced into the legal frame such entities as securities owner, dealer/broker (trader) and securities exchange organiser. The law defined the rights of the owner and the licensing procedures for the latter agents.

B. *Listing requirements*

In the Czech Republic the notion of listing lost most of its traditional meaning due to the adopted concept of so-called public tradability.

According to the "Law about Securities" only publicly tradable securities may be admitted to **public exchanges** such as RM-S and PSE.

The status of public tradability of a security is ascribed by the Ministry of Finance whose decision in this matter is based upon proper evaluations of the issuer. All the relevant information is included in the respective **prospectus** of the security produced by the issuer. Without the prospectus being approved by the Ministry the security must not be publicly traded.

C.   Investor protection

The corresponding section in the "Law about Securities" is very short and relatively vague. The Ministry of Finance has established a special commission for reviewing the markets with the objective of specifying such amendments to the law that would, if necessary, make the relevant provisions of the law more elaborate.

So far the overall approach is that no special measures must be taken in the short-run.

D.   Capitalisation

Traditional stock exchanges need enough capital mainly in order to guarantee the executed trades. On the contrary, capitalisation requirement imposed upon RM-S are, thanks to its policy of the pre-trade validation, almost negligible.

VIII. Current developments

As the securities trading started only in May 1993 it is, generally speaking, too early to derive reliable trends for the existing time series.

A.   Market versus nominal values

The nominal values of the privatised shares were derived from the book-value of the privatised companies. The initial market value of the shares reached some 35 per cent of the nominal value (around June-July 1993) and, by March 1994, increased to some 78 per cent. The price development is illustrated in Annex I.

It should be noted that the higher price level on PSE (compared to that on RM-S) is due to the fact that only about one-third of the "issues" traded on RM-S is also traded on PSE and that the "issues" traded in PSE belong to the relatively more expensive ones.

At the same time, it is also true that the prices of the shares traded on both markets are different and that the prices on PSE are higher as a rule. This situation provides scope for arbitrazh, within which some investors buy on RM-S and sell on PSE.

B.   Main players in the market

As to the profiles of market participants, the major questions are the following:

What is the situation between domestic and foreign buyers/sellers? What role do "professionals" play *vis-à-vis* the "amateurs"? In what proportions do the foreigners and/or amateurs participate directly and/or indirectly? What differences are there in the above respects, in the two official markets (RM-S and PSE)?

Already in this area the situation changes literally every day. However, both the organisers of the exchanges and the government do not find anything in the development to raise concerns. Generally speaking, again, the development is regarded as highly positive and encouraging.

IX. The IPFs on the exchanges

IPFs have two roles: a dealer/broker and an issuer. IPFs are thus becoming both the subject and the object of the market.

A. *IPFs as buyers/sellers*

1. *Forced purchases/sales*

The information about buyers and sellers is regarded as confidential in the Czech Republic. Official data are, therefore, not available.

It is generally believed that the relatively high volumes of direct (i.e. outside the exchanges) purchases and sales are to a large degree realised by the IPFs. These activities, however, are not regarded as forced by the shortage of IPF liquidity. Rather, the IPFs are assumed to restructure their portfolios.

On the other hand there may be observed some "forced purchases" when the IPFs participating in the second wave submit to the market buy-order for their own shares as to support their price. (See section IX.*B*)

2. *Active and passive IPFs; collaboration between IPFs*

Paradoxically, the "Law about Investment Companies and Funds" includes provisions which could prevent IPFs from becoming active agents in the restructuring of enterprises[8]. In order to avoid this unwise regulation, the IPFs establish subsidiaries and/or enter into various types of collaboration. The government regards this as a healthy process.

B. *Trading on IPFs' shares*

The exchanges opened for the shares of the privatised enterprises in May 1993. In October 1993, the IPFs started issuing their own shares. Just like in the case of the enterprises, the IPFs' shares were dematerialised by law. Unlike in the case of the enterprises, the IPFs had to apply at the Ministry of Finance to receive public tradability status for their shares. The great majority of the IPFs fulfilled the tasks by the end of 1993.

X.   Conclusions

The concern of governments in post-communist countries must be focused not on transforming individual enterprises but on their economies as a whole. Therefore, the governments' privatisation strategies have to keep in mind, unlike those in western countries, the importance of the follow-up processes, namely the emergence of the entirely new capital goods and securities markets.

The experience of the Czech Republic fully demonstrates that its voucher privatisation scheme and its extremely liberal approach to the institutional formations stimulated by the scheme has been an appropriate tool towards such objectives.

However, the logistics and mechanics of mass privatisation implementation has to take into consideration not only the short-term objectives of privatisation in the narrow sense, but also the institutional short and long-term objectives of the post-privatisation era. In particular, the role of various institutions on the emerging capital markets has to be reviewed and the entry of these institutions has to be made as liberal and costless as possible.

In the Czech Republic (and similarly in Slovakia), the proceeds from voucher privatisation were used largely to directly and indirectly ease the otherwise enormous incumbent costs of the financial institutions such as investment companies and funds, securities firms and exchanges.

The architects of the Czech (and Slovak) privatisation scheme are still careful in declaring the voucher project a success. Whether the design and its implementation brings about a successful transformation will be judged, apart from other things, on the basis of how fast and smooth the capital goods market will emerge and, consequently, how efficient will become the most needed reallocation of capital.

Notes

*   Based on a presentation made by the author (Dusan Triska, Project Director of the RM-S Securities Systems in the Czech Republic and Slovak Republic) at the fifth meeting of the Advisory Group on Privatisation, Paris, 2-4 March 1994.

In this paper weighted average price = aggregate monetary value of trades/number of pieces traded.

1.   For more comprehensive analysis see Vaclav Klaus: Privatisation Experience: The Czech Case. (Speech at the International Chamber of Commerce Meeting, Cancun, Mexico, 21 October 1993.)

2.   The major characteristics of the voucher scheme are summarised in, e.g. Dusan Triska: *Political, Organizational, and Legislative Aspects of Mass Privatization -- Czechoslovakia.* (Marko Simoneti and Andreja Bohm: Privatization in Central and Eastern Europe 1991, Proceeding of the Second Annual Conference of the CEEPN.)

3.   The evolutionary process on secondary markets must not be confused with another phenomenon entirely unheard of in W-privatisation, i.e. the so-called spontaneous (wild) privatisation. As to this, it is rarely mentioned that the Czech government has been by far the toughest amongst other governments in the Central and Eastern Europe. The assets of the state-owned enterprises were frozen by law so that managers and former nomenclature officials in particular could not turn large-scale privatisation into "whole-sale looting". It is also little known that this aggressive approach was possible only due to the promptness with which the well-defined privatisation programme was presented and approved. It is, therefore, largely overlooked that the infamous wild privatisation is mainly the direct outcome of the governments incapability in preparing a trustworthy large-scale privatisation strategy.

4.   The initial ownership structure created by voucher privatisation in the Czech Republic is illustrated in, e.g. Dusan Triska: *Voucher Privatization in Czechoslovakia -- 1992.* (Andreja Bohm and Marko Simoneti: Privatization

in Central and Eastern Europe 1992, Proceeding of the Third Annual Conference of the CEEPN.)

5. More detailed description can be found in Jan Pauly and Dusan Triska: *Investment funds in the Czech Republic.* (The CEEPN Workshop on Investment Funds as Intermediaries of Privatisation 29-30 October 1993, Prague, Czech Republic.)

6. In addition to the "Law about Securities", the "Law about Stock-exchange" and the "Commercial Code", the most important parts of the relevant legislation are the "Law about Investment Companies and Funds" and the "Law about Bonds".

7. Alternative solutions were the Central Bank and a special Parliamentary Commission. (The Central Bank is the regulatory body of the commercial banks.)

8. IPF cannot have in its portfolio more than 20 per cent of the shares of one company. This regulation was included as an attempt to harmonise the law with the "standard legislation". In fact, any such provision only demonstrated the total lack of understanding of the nature of what we refer to here as E-privatisation.

Privatisation in Lithuania

Albertas Simenas*

I. The privatisation process

A. *The system of privatisation*

The main objective of the privatisation of state-owned property was to rapidly develop the private sector (in particular, its middle layer including small and medium-sized entrepreneurs and farmers), to abolish the non-effective monopoly of state property and, at the same time, to create the conditions indispensable for the development of a market economy.

The peculiarities of the privatisation policy were caused by the following conditions:

-- a rapidly increasing economic crisis accompanied by the recession of the standard of living and reduced possibilities to privatise state-owned property due to the low incomes of the population;

-- the non-existence of controlled economic borders with the USSR resulting in a threat of the possible interference into the Lithuanian privatisation of the USSR economic structures possessing huge sums of rapidly devaluating currency (roubles);

-- the tradition of the centralised management of the economy and the negative attitude of officials to the development of the private sector and their interest to have privileges in the privatisation of state-owned property;

-- weak economic relations with the western countries and an insufficiently stable political situation.

On the basis of these conditions, the system of privatisation was formed according to the following regulations:

1. Privatisation shall be carried out rapidly and, within two to three years, two-thirds of the state-owned property shall be privatised;

2. Mass privatisation shall be emphasised at the initial stage. Therefore, public subscription for shares shall be applied and property shall be sold at auctions. Conditions for the majority of the population to participate in the privatisation shall be created and the high tempo of privatisation and reduction of social pressure dangerous to economic reforms ensured. In order to carry out mass privatisation, the **investment vouchers** (IVs) shall be allocated to the citizens. In order to eliminate roubles as the main means to acquire the privatisation property, the selling possibilities of IVs shall be secured. The restrictions shall be abolished only after the introduction of national monetary units. The methods of privatisation shall be expanded and additional conditions for the concentration of capital created.

3. An autonomous structure of privatisation bodies shall be created in such a way that the officials of other public institutions shall not be able to influence their activities. In order to minimise the abuse, the transparency of the privatisation process and the effective system of accounting and control shall be ensured.

4. Three groups of privatisation objects, the property of state enterprises, public housing funds, and the property of agricultural enterprises (farms), shall be distinguished. Mass privatisation shall be applied to all object groups. Nevertheless, individual laws regulating privatisation shall be worked out facing the specificities of each of them.

5. In order to ensure the approval of the employees of the privatisation of an enterprise, in the course of privatisation of the state property, 10 per cent of the shares of the enterprise shall be sold to them on favourable terms. No other privileges shall be given.

6. In all the stages of privatisation, it shall be sought to attract foreign investors and sell assets and/or blocks of shares for convertible currency.

7. The overall privatisation program shall be worked out in such a manner that after its realisation the private sector shall predominate in the branches of industry, construction, trade, consumer services and agriculture while the branches of energy, communications and, to a great extent, transportation (railways, sea, air transportation), shall remain in the public sector.

These regulations of mass privatisation were successfully used albeit slightly amended. Significant amendments were introduced after the elections to the Parliament when the opposition won the elections.

B. Objects and subjects of privatisation

Mass privatisation objects are considered to be shares of state enterprises, blocks of shares (sold only for convertible currency), small entities (the value of which does not exceed Lt 30 000), separate means of production (assets), the property of agricultural enterprises (farms), public apartments and land. Only nationals of the Republic of Lithuania and investment companies founded under the established manner (ICs) are entitled to acquire state property. Individuals having the right to citizenship of the Republic of Lithuania may acquire public apartments, and natural and legal persons of Lithuania and other states may acquire property sold for convertible currency.

C. Means of payment in privatisation

IVs and money circulating in Lithuania (at the initial stage it was roubles, later coupons and at present, national currency -- Litas) or convertible currency is used for the acquisition of objects of privatisation.

At the beginning of 1991, IVs were allocated to all the citizens of the Republic of Lithuania according to their age (from Rb 1 000 to 5 000). Special accounts of investment vouchers with a bank were opened. In all, more than 2.5 million investment accounts were opened (family members as a rule use the same investment account). It was permitted to deposit roubles on the investment accounts though the deposited sum could not exceed the amount of IVs allocated for one person.

During the inflation period of 1991-1992, IVs and money deposited in investment accounts were indexed and their value increased eight times. After the indexation, the total value of investment accounts was Lt 1.3 billion.

At the beginning, the sale and transfer of the IVs was limited, but after the introduction of the national currency the restrictions were abolished. At present, they are sold at market price for Litas. They can be acquired and utilised for the privatisation of the state property by all subjects of the Lithuanian economy except for state organisations. The main turnover of IVs is generated by stock investment companies (ICs).

In the manner provided for by law, the state-owned property may be acquired for means deposited on investment accounts (IVs and cash). No less than 1.25 per cent (it was 5 per cent at the initial stage) of the acquired property price shall be paid in cash and, in the case of the purchase of apartments, no less than 20 per cent.

With the sale of IVs it is possible to purchase apartments and state-owned property, the sale of which is informed by a decision of the Central Privatisation Commission (CPC). Monetary quotas are not applied in these cases nor for enterprises sold through tender offers.

According to the law, the government has a right to fix the terms for the utilisation of IVs to be used for acquisition of state property. It is provided to convert the IVs which have not been utilised in state treasury bills. At present, the terms provided by the government for the circulation of IVs will last until 1 August 1994.

An important role in privatisation is also played by another means of payment, i.e. the currency circulating in Lithuania. The importance of money especially increased when IVs became tradable. Lithuanian economic subjects may acquire the basic means of payment, IVs, for Litas and participate in the mass privatisation.

Only those objects and blocks of shares which have been approved by the government may be acquired for convertible currency. Under the manner established by the Government they are sold by way of tender.

D. Bodies of privatisation

According to the law, the privatisation of state-owned property is implemented by the Central Privatisation Committee (CPC) and by privatisation commissions of towns and districts subordinate to it. In the process of privatisation, certain functions are also performed by the administrative bodies of an enterprise, its founder (the municipal council or ministry), and the department of privatisation functioning within the framework of the Ministry of Economics.

The chairman of the CPC, upon the motion of the Prime Minister, is appointed by the President (the first chairman of the CPC was the Deputy Prime Minister, later the Ministers of Economics). The CPC is composed of the representatives of public institutions, banks, industrialists and entrepreneurs competent in the issues of privatisation. The composition of the CPC is approved by the Prime Minister. Privatisation commissions of towns and districts are, upon the motion of municipal councils, appointed by the Government.

The main executive body in the privatisation process is the department of privatisation which, according to the instructions of the CPC, prepares the drafts of normative acts, provides information on the course of privatisation, prepares the projects of privatisation programmes, the documents on approval (or non-approval) of the privatisation objects, etc. It maintains direct communications with the town and district privatisation institutions. The information system of privatisation is also under its jurisdiction.

Thus, the CPC is a decision making body and the department of privatisation an executive body. At the level of municipalities, the similar functions are distributed between privatisation commission and agencies.

For the privatisation of the state-owned property, the following decision making procedure is followed:

The CPS presents privatisation targets for ministries and municipalities, according to the value of the objects under their supervision. The municipalities privatise the objects under their jurisdiction themselves, the CPC interfering only in cases of disputes. Ministries choose enterprises for privatisation and the latter prepare all the information necessary for privatisation which is submitted to the Department of Privatisation by the ministry. On the basis of the received information, the department prepares the draft privatisation programme for the following month which is presented to the CPC for examination. The initial prices and degree of privatisation is thoroughly controlled by the CPC. The privatisation programme which is approved by the CPC is obligatorily under the established terms published in special public privatisation bulletins. The said bulletins contain the list of the objects to be privatised, their basic data, methods applied for privatisation, procedure and time limits thereof. These bulletins also contain resolutions of the CPC, normative acts and their amendments.

The direct privatisation procedure is performed by the privatisation agencies which organize and hold auctions and the subscription for shares. After the expiration of the term fixed for the privatisation of an object, they furnish implementation information to the privatisation commissions of towns and districts according to the established manner. Where the object of privatisation is under the jurisdiction of a ministry, the closing decision on the privatisation of an object is made by the CPC, while where the object is under the jurisdiction of municipalities, it is made by privatisation agencies of towns and districts. The functions of privatisation institutions and the decision-making procedure in the privatisation of apartments, agricultural enterprises, land and also objects to be sold for convertible currency are governed by individual normative acts and have their own peculiarities.

The CPC regularly informs the government of the course of privatisation.

E.   Methods of privatisation

At the initial stage it was provided that state property may be sold at auctions, by announcement of public subscription for shares, or tenders held for the purchase of the privatisation objects for convertible currency. Later, other methods were introduced: closed auctions, closed subscription for shares, tender for the best business plan.

The price of objects to be sold at auctions can not exceed Lt 30 000. Only natural persons, groups of persons (no more than 20) and closed stock companies may participate in auctions (ICs have no right to participate).

The auctions are organised by privatisation agencies. Information on the auction shall, at least 20 days prior to its beginning, be published in privatisation bulletins. An auction may be held if at least three days before the day of the auction no less than two participants have been registered which have paid the registration fee and transferred into the indicated account 10 per cent of the initial price of the object they wish to acquire. If the initial price at the auction is not increased by at least 5 per cent, the auction transaction is considered invalid. Due to abuses, the procedure of auctions has been changed. At present, they are organised by way of "mail". Persons wishing to participate in the auction present in advance the price they offer in closed envelopes and send them to the privatisation agency. The envelopes are not closed till the beginning of the auction. Therefore, both the participants and the prices they offer remain unknown. The auction is won by the participant who has offered the highest price.

State joint-stock companies are privatised by public subscription for shares of the public, provided that their value is not less than Lt 10 000. Natural and legal persons as well as ICs may participate in subscription for shares.

The degree of privatisation (i.e. part of the capital to be privatised) of an enterprise is recommended by the administrative body of the enterprise. The suggested degree is revised by the ministry-founder and the final decision is made by the CPC. Should an enterprise be under the jurisdiction of a municipality, the final decision is made by the privatisation committee of the municipality. The degree of privatisation should be such that after the privatisation of an enterprise the state would be a holder of at least 11 per cent to 50 per cent of the shares of the enterprise, i.e. more than 50 per cent though not more than 89 per cent of the shares should belong to the private sector after the privatisation of the enterprise. At the initial stage, employees were given at favourable conditions 10 per cent of the shares. At present, they may acquire 50 per cent of the shares. As a rule, the latter are sold for their nominal value.

The price of issued shares is suggested by a ministry-founder and the decision is made by the CPC. The price of issued shares of the enterprises which are under the jurisdiction of a municipality are set respectively by the municipality and the privatisation committee.

Subscription for shares is announced in the privatisation bulletins not later than 15 days before the beginning of the subscription. The subscription for shares lasts for 45 days.

Subscription of shares may be performed in several stages. If more than 80 per cent, but not more than 110 per cent, of shares planned to be issued have been subscribed for their initial price and the minimum rules on company capital have not been violated, the subscription of shares is considered as made. If more than 110 per cent or less than 80 per cent of shares have been subscribed, the CPC reduces or increases their nominal value and a new subscription for shares is announced.

The procedure of tenders for the selling of objects for convertible currency has been worked out after the consultations with the western experts and it is similar to the practice valid in western countries. The tenders are organised by the CPC.

The closed auctions and closed subscription for shares apply for the privatisation of special objects (for instance, institutions of medical service, pharmacies, veterinary, media). Smaller objects are sold at auctions, bigger through subscription for shares. The main feature of these privatisation methods are that only the persons with the respective degree of education in this sphere are entitled to participation.

The tender for the best business plan is held in case an object has failed to be privatised by the public subscription for shares in three stages. Private natural and legal persons, Lithuanian or foreign, may participate in a tender. This method of privatisation has not yet been applied in practice.

F.   The critical evaluation of the development of the privatisation process

During the period of preparation for and in the course of mass privatisation, the mass media paid more attention to criticisms than commentaries on the progress and characteristics of privatisation. Even during the privatisation of apartments, when the absolute majority of the citizens acquired them under the most favourable conditions, dissatisfaction spread because of the varied quality of the apartments. "Unfairness" is especially felt when state-owned property is to be privatised, though all the citizens are given an opportunity to acquire an equal part of state-owned property sold for IVs at the initial stage of privatisation. This mood of the public was cultivated mostly in order to change the initial system of privatisation and to legalise privileges.

The aim that all citizens who were given IVs understand the peculiarities of participation in privatisation has failed. The market price for IVs is considerably low due to the fact that part of the citizens do not know how to acquire the shares of enterprises or to participate in auctions. They sell their IVs for any offered price. Thus, participation of a certain part of the citizenry in the process of privatisation is rather passive.

Privatisation and the developing private sector has given rise to new possibilities for the activities of criminal structures. The law enforcement system, at the initial stage in particular, was not prepared for the prevention of the new kinds of crimes. The criminal structures are an obstacle to the formation of a middle class (small and medium-sized entrepreneurs and farmers).

The development and activities of the private sector were weakened by the delayed reform of the financial and credit systems as well as the lack of a securities market. The privatisation system has been significantly deformed and, in our opinion, weakened by the modifications introduced by the new Seimas Government since 1993. The right of employees to acquire up to 50 per cent of the shares of an enterprise which is under privatisation, the introduction of closed auctions and subscriptions for shares and limitations of the possibility to acquire a controlling block of shares by ICs has enabled the formation of a system of privileges favourable to officials. In some cases, the prices of freely sold shares (their amount should not, according to new regulations, exceed 39 per cent of the enterprise capital) are 100 times higher than their nominal value, while employees acquire shares for their nominal value. Such a difference in the prices of shares is especially favourable to the administrative bodies of enterprises and creates preconditions for different abuses.

The government has also adopted a number of resolutions which, in our opinion, have a negative effect upon the privatisation process.

Shareholders and employees have a right, upon the approval of the governing body of an enterprise and the CPC, to purchase state shares (except 11 per cent which should belong to the state) either for IVs or money and as a rule for their nominal value. The employees are allowed to use the profit funds (reserves) of the enterprise for the purchase. The shareholders and employees of non-privatised closed stock companies are entitled to acquire the state shares for the profit, IVs or money. Under the decision of the administrative bodies of the enterprise "depreciated" means of production may be sold, provided that their book value does not exceed Lt 10. (When the value is higher the permission to sell has to be given by the founder). The lack of an indexation system for asset values creates favourable conditions for the plunder of the means of production.

Changes of staff in the privatisation institutions had a negative influence on mass privatisation. This significantly increased the influence of the administrative bodies of enterprises and ministries and weakened the role of the CPC and other privatisation agencies in the decision making process with respect to overall privatisation policy and individual privatisation objects.

Due to the provision of the law providing for the possibility to increase the capital of the state enterprises by profit reserves belonging to the employees, the indirect method of privatisation has become widespread. It is a very "convenient" method because the value of property of enterprises has not been indexed since 1992 while the total level of prices has grown more than 30 times within that period.

Changes in the privatisation system have significantly weakened the former system of privatisation. The enactment of privileges in the privatising of state-owned property and the increase in the influence of officials limits competition and creates the conditions for the accumulation of capital for persons whose privileges are guaranteed by their positions and places of work. It has reduced the possibilities for the formation of the middle layer (small and medium-sized entrepreneurs and farmers) and for a harmonious economic structure. On the other hand, the state loses the income which could be acquired by selling state-owned property for market prices and gains the means to support economic reform, employment creation and a social safety net. Under the conditions of economic crisis these problems are extremely serious.

II. The basic results of privatisation

A. *The indices of overall privatisation*

Mass privatisation in Lithuania started in September 1991. At that time there were Lt 1 313 million IVs and cash in the investment accounts (after the indexation of Litas deposited on these accounts).

Until 31 December 1993, Lt 781 million were used for mass privatisation. The remaining Lt 532 million amount to 40 per cent of the initial sum of investment capital available. Investments capital was used to acquire state-owned property (enterprises, means of production and premises) as well as public housing, property of agricultural enterprises (farms).

Total data on the course of the state-owned property privatisation (privatisation of apartments, property of agricultural enterprises and land not included) are indicated in Table 1. The planned programme of privatisation according to the number of objects has been implemented by 66 per cent and according to the amount of capital -- by 40 per cent. The highest degree of privatisation according to the capital has been reached in the branches of the economy where smaller objects predominate -- 73 per cent in consumer services, 83 per cent in "other economical" branches and 74 per cent in the construction industry.

Approximately 50 per cent of the state-owned objects has been privatised which represents 27 per cent of the total capital (value). More than one-half of state capital has been passed to private sector in certain **areas,** including 69 per cent in consumer services, 66 per cent in the construction industry and 56 per cent in "other sectors". According to the number of privatised firms the private sector is now dominant (55 per cent). Nearly one-half of industrial enterprises are controlled by the private sector. Privatisation is slower in the utility sector. Low profitability of this branch causes low demand.

Only 26 per cent of capital has been privatised in heavy industry. The great problem is privatisation of large enterprises which had a great importance in the economic context of the USSR. Due to the deep economic crisis in Russia and other states of the CIS, and other factors of an economic and political character, the demand for their production has significantly reduced. They should be either reorganised or liquidated. In any case, the privatisation of these enterprises is causing many problems at present. The private sector is developing not only due to the privatisation of state-owned capital but also due to new capital investments, the creation of new enterprises or the capital increase in enterprises in which the state still retains a share.

Table 1. Cumulative data on state-owned property privatisation (1 September 1991 - 31 December 1993)

Sector	Total no. of objects	Objects subject to privatisation		Privatised objects		
		No.	%	No. of privatised objects	As a percentage of objects subject to privatisation	As a percentage of total objects
Industry						
Number of enterprises	1 132	863	76	525	61	46
State capital*	968	645	67	251	39	26
Transportation						
Number of enterprises	293	165	56	113	68	39
State capital*	198	99	50	17	17	9
Construction						
Number of enterprises	782	646	83	462	72	59
State capital*	89	80	90	59	74	66
Commerce						
Number of enterprises	2 583	2 065	80	1 412	68	55
State capital*	119	107	90	40	37	34
Utilities						
Number of enterprises	620	352	57	165	47	27
State capital*	133	67	50	5	7	4
Services						
Number of enterprises	1 168	1 102	94	903	82	77
State capital*	13	12	92	9	75	69
Other branches of economy						
Number of enterprises	1 906	1 257	66	653	52	34
State capital*	88	59	67	49	83	56
Total						
Number of enterprises	**8 484**	**6 450**	**76**	**4 233**	**66**	**50**
State capital*	**1 608**	**1 069**	**66**	**430**	**40**	**27**

*   In Lt million.

The agricultural capital privatised amounts to Lt 155.4 million or 83 per cent of property which was subject to privatisation. Six thousand new agricultural enterprises have been established since privatisation started. The employees have been given additional investment subsidies to acquire shares of their enterprise's property. These subsidies have amounted to more than Lt 120 million.

Until 1 December 1993, 497 300 public apartments in multi-flat houses and 30 300 single-flat houses were sold to the inhabitants. This equals approximately 94 per cent of all apartments which were planned to be privatised or 75 per cent of all public housing funds. (Approximately 25 per cent of former public apartments and dwelling houses are, under the law, provided for restitution to former owners).

Two hundred and fifty-five million Litas of IVs and Lt 72 million in cash have been used by the citizens to acquire the apartments.

Privatisation of agricultural land for IVs has not yet been started. Up to now, only lots for building of dwelling houses and economic objects were being sold. Until the beginning of 1994, only Lt 40 million from the investment accounts had been used for this purpose.

Since August of 1992, the privatisation of the state-owned property for convertible currency has been started. Thirty-six objects have been sold for US$21.8 million.

At the beginning of 1994, there were 379 registered investment companies (ICs) in Lithuania which played an important role in privatisation. ICs own Lt 290 million of capital. They have participated in the privatisation of 783 objects (18 per cent of all objects) and acquired property for Lt 169 million or 39 per cent of privatised state-owned property.

Amendments and new restrictions mentioned above have greatly influenced the speed of privatisation. In 1991 and 1992 an average of 193 enterprises per month were privatised while in 1993 only 102. Therefore, the decision of the government to finish mass privatisation by July 1994 is not realistic. A significant amount of the IVs would not have been used and part of the state-owned property planned to be privatised would not have been.

The system of mass privatisation in Lithuania as the means for transfer of state-owned property to the private sector has justified itself. Within two years, and without great social tension, more than one-half of the former state subjects have become private, though in terms of the amount of capital the state sector still predominates.

The economic state of private firms is better than of that of the state-owned. The best results were achieved by private companies where the capital is controlled by a few owners, while in large companies with a lot of shareholders the situation has only slightly changed since privatisation.

The subjects of the Lithuanian economy have to adapt to the new market conditions and their requirements, the necessity to reorganise enterprises and ensure the quality of production. At this point, even after the privatisation of an enterprise and the means of production and technology, qualifications of the staff and methods of work remain the same.

B.   Tasks, problems and perspectives

First of all, the provisions which enable individual persons or groups of persons to enjoy special privileges in the acquisition of state-owned property should be abolished. Such distortions create conditions for the formation of a polarised structure of economy and eliminate the possibilities for the formation of the middle social layer of entrepreneurs and farmers. In such an economic structure, the competition in production and services decreases to a minimum and long-lasting social tension should be expected.

In order to normalise the process of privatisation, the right of employees of enterprises to be privatised to acquire for favourable conditions 50 per cent of shares should be abolished and a limit of no more than 10 per cent should be established. In the privatisation of the agro-food industry, provisions under which it is required to sell more than one-half of all shares to workers engaged in agriculture should be rejected. We should also reject the obligation providing for 11 per cent of shares to be left to the state. The policy of closed auctions and subscription for shares, which is gaining strength, should also be abolished as well as any other privileges granted for the acquisition of the state shares of enterprises to be privatised and closed joint-stock companies.

It is necessary to prevent an indirect manner of privatisation. In order to achieve this aim, the value of the state-owned property should be indexed in such a way that its price would be nearly equal to the market price, and it should be prohibited to increase the authorised capital of an enterprise from the profit reserve funds without the permission of its owner (state).

In order to ensure competition, the activities of ICs should be regulated more precisely and the restrictions for participation in privatisation should be abolished.

Activities of the law enforcement institutions should be strengthened so that the protection of private property and income is guaranteed. This is indispensable for solving problems inherent in the formation of the capital market. The activities of the Committee of Securities and the National Exchange of Securities are rather weak and do not satisfy the requirements imposed upon them.

For the successful end of mass privatisation, the activities of privatisation organs should be strengthened so that opposition of the structures of bureaucracy was eliminated and an adequate number of enterprises may be introduced into the privatisation process so that all the unused IVs can be used for privatisation. It is wise to refuse the conversion of unused IVs into the state treasury bills because they are means of distribution of the state property and not means of the circulation of capital. The unused IVs should be bought up by the state and the necessary means for this purpose may be accumulated by selling objects of privatisation for cash.

When mass privatisation is accomplished and the stability of the private sector is ensured, the goals in the second stage of the privatisation will be of a commercial character. For that reason, property should be sold only for money and IVs should no longer be used as a means of property acquisition.

Until the beginning of the second stage of privatisation, the new management scheme of state property has to be prepared and the establishment of the fund of state property (state holding company) has to be provided for. Shares of state property and, at the same time, the rights of shareholders have to be transferred to the fund of state property. Thus, the supervision functions of ministries would be taken over.

A privatisation agency should be established for the privatisation of state property and legal preconditions for the establishment of property valuation institutions should be created. New methods of privatisation of the state property should be enacted. Requirements for participation in property privatisation and conditions for commercial activities should be the same for both local and foreign investors.

In order to ensure the effective functioning of both the private and the state-owned sector, special attention should be paid to the amendments of the laws regulating commercial activities. They must correspond to the requirements of the European Union.

Note

* Based on a presentation made by the author (Albertas Simenas, Deputy Director, Economics and Privatisation Institute, Vilnius) at the fifth meeting of the Advisory Group on Privatisation, Paris, 2-4 March 1994.

Post-Privatisation Secondary Markets in Lithuania

Algirdas Semeta*

I. The primary ownership structure of privatised enterprises

Lithuania is one of the first among central and eastern European countries which has implemented a mass privatisation scheme into the privatisation process. Started on September 1991, the mass privatisation program is to be finished by August 1994. There have been a lot of changes in the program in two-and-a-half years. Therefore, it is rather difficult to describe the primary ownership structure of privatised enterprises. It depends on when a company was privatised. The privatisation process may be divided into three stages for the purpose of analysis of ownership structure in the privatised enterprises. The companies privatised from September 1991 to early 1992 usually have the following ownership structure:

-- 10-20 per cent of equity is owned by employees and managers;

-- 40-50 per cent is owned by small investors; and

-- 30-50 per cent is owned by the government.

At the beginning of 1992 investment companies were allowed to participate in the mass privatisation process. The employees were given a privilege to acquire 30 per cent of their company shares for their nominal value at the same time. Therefore ownership structure of enterprises privatised at that time differs substantially from those mentioned above. As usual, 30 per cent of the shares in these enterprises belong to the employees and managers, 30-50 per cent to investment companies, and 10-20 per cent are owned by small investors and the government.

The third group of companies consists of enterprises privatised after February 1993. The amendments to the Privatisation Law approved at that time granted additional privileges to the employees. Therefore the employees and managers own 50-60 per cent of the shares in these enterprises, investment companies have

30 per cent, 5-10 per cent are owned by small investors and the rest belongs to the government.

There have not been many companies in Lithuania privatised by standard methods. In cases when these methods have been used the privatised companies are majority owned by the so-called "strategic investors". The stake of the employees varies from 10 to 30 percent and 5-10 per cent remains with the government.

The next chapters outline how such an ownership structure influences the development of the secondary markets in Lithuania.

II. The structure and functioning of secondary markets

A. *The concept of securities market*

A rapid securitisation of the former state-owned enterprises subject to the mass privatisation program called for the creation of an environment for securities trading. Lithuania has taken a top-down approach in this area. According to the law on initial privatisation approved by the Parliament in March 1991, shares of privatised enterprises would not be tradable until 1 July 1992. The regulatory authority of the securities market -- the Lithuanian Securities Commission -- was established by government decree on 26 June 1992. According to the regulations approved by the government in September 1992, the Securities Commission was empowered to perform the following basic functions:

-- to design the legal framework for primary and secondary markets;

-- to control an implementation of Lithuanian laws in the securities market;

-- to supervise the observance of rules of fair trading and competition within the public trading in securities;

-- to provide official explanations and recommendations to the public on any issue connected with the securities market;

-- to give licenses for broker-dealer and stock exchange activity;

-- to authorise and register public offerings of securities.

The Lithuanian Securities Commission consists of seven members. They are appointed by the Prime Minister for five years. The Commission has its own administration and it is funded from the state budget.

The legal framework for the securities market was approved by the Government of Lithuania in October 1992. The "Temporary Regulations on Issuance, Public Trading in Securities and Stock Exchange in the Republic of Lithuania" sets out the requirements for:

-- public offering of securities;

-- content, format and dissemination of prospectus information;

-- organisation and performance of primary and secondary markets of securities;

-- performance of securities intermediation by securities brokerage firms and their brokers;

-- establishment and operations of stock exchanges and member firms admitted thereto;

-- continuous disclosure requirements;

-- accounting of securities.

Public offering of securities requires a prior authorisation on the part of the Commission. This authorisation shall not be issued without adequate prior disclosure through prospectus of all material information concerning the issuer and the securities to be publicly offered and only implies that, at the date of approval, the issuer has complied with all disclosure requirements.

The securities intermediation is subject to license. Both brokerage companies and individual brokers shall be licensed by the Commission. Brokerage companies must be specialised in securities activity with one exception -- they can also trade real estate. They also shall comply with minimum capital requirements set forth by the Securities Commission.

Banks are allowed to engage in the trading of securities. However, they are required to establish separate branches for this activity and can act solely as agents for their clients.

The requirements for foreign brokerage companies are the same as for domestic ones.

The stock exchange may be established only with the prior approval of the government. This restriction is temporary and is valid for two years until 1995. The entity running the stock exchange shall be established in the form of a not-for-profit organisation and shall engage only in this activity. Both the Statute and the Internal Regulations of the stock exchange requires the prior approval of the Commission. The Internal Regulations shall include the procedures regarding membership, listing requirements, trading, clearing, settlement and arbitration.

The issue of securities may be organised either by the issuer himself or through financial intermediaries. For the time being there are no specific rules for underwriting. The issue shall be accomplished during the six months after registration of appropriate amendments in Articles of Incorporation.

The rules for secondary trading in securities depends on the legal status of persons intending to engage in this activity as well as on the size of the issuer. If the equity of the issuer is more than Lt 250 000 (a bit more than US$60 000) the secondary trading in securities may occur only on the stock exchange, unless both the transferor and transferee are physical persons. In the latter case, the transfer of ownership may be conducted either in an organised over-the-counter market or through direct transaction. There are no restrictions for secondary trading in securities of the issuers with equity capital less than Lt 250 000.

B. The organised secondary markets

As one can see, the Government of Lithuania from the very beginning decided to promote the concept of a "National" Stock Exchange instead of allowing each city to establish a local one. Although the "Temporary Regulations" do not prohibit the establishment of several stock exchanges there is only one stock exchange in Lithuania. Moreover, there is no other organised market in the country.

The establishment of the National Stock Exchange of Lithuania (NSEL) began in September 1992. The rights of the NSEL founders and the right to organise the issue of shares were granted to the Ministry of Finance, the Investment Bank of Lithuania, the Lithuanian Commodity Exchange and the Baltic Commodity Exchange. The NSEL was registered by the Securities Commission in May 1993. The authorised capital of the NSEL is Lt 1.23 million. It is divided into 246 ordinary registered shares without dividends. The face value of one share is Lt 5 000, emission price Lt 5 500. One share of the stock exchange grants one seat on the trading floor. The owner of a share may use this seat either himself (in case the owner is a licensed brokerage company) or may lease his seat to another licensed brokerage company.

The State of Lithuania (through the Ministry of Finance) owns 110 shares, or 44.7 per cent, of the authorised capital. The remaining shares belong to other natural and legal persons, mainly to the private brokerage companies. Only three shares are owned by the banks.

C. The trading system of the NSEL

The trading system of the NSEL is based on the French model. It was prepared with significant advise of the Paris Bourse and French depository -- SICOVAM. The French model is based on the concept of a centralised order-driven market operating on a fixing basis. Seemingly, this approach is well-suited to both trading and post-trading needs and the constraints of an emerging market because it constitutes:

--   a pragmatic solution: frequency of quotation session is determined according to both the liquidity of the market and the back-office capacities of brokerage companies;

124

--   a cost-efficient solution: capital requirements on the brokers side are very limited since they are not obliged to act as principal for all orders as market-makers do;

--   a fair solution: the same price for everybody, the same access to the market for all brokers wherever they are located;

--   a flexible solution: without modifying the system, the latter provides for a possibility to implement further developments: multifixing and continuous market.

The concept of dematerialised securities used in the French model was another important reason why it was chosen. This concept is particularly useful for countries which implemented mass privatisation schemes because it allows them:

--   to avoid printing millions of costly share certificates;

--   to organise transfers on a pure and safe book-entry basis.

D.   *The procedure of quotation and clearing-settlement*

Any person, before being able to send an order, shall open two accounts (securities and cash) with a brokerage company operating on the NSEL. An order may be sent only through a licensed broker. Since the market is operating on a strictly cash basis, it is necessary to cover all orders with relevant cash/securities provision, without any netting. Orders may be stipulated with or without a price limit, and with or without a maximal delay for execution. When a limit price is specified, this limit is the maximum price the buyer is prepared to pay and the minimal price the seller required. When no price is specified, the order is said "at best" and it may be executed at any price.

Prices are determined on a fixing basis. This means that the price results from the simultaneous confrontation of all orders. This quoted price is determined in order to maximise the volume of transactions. Only one price exists per session, and all trades are done at this price. Prices cannot fluctuate more than 10 per cent between two weekly sessions if the volume of trading is more than 10 per cent of the whole issue of security. In case of lower volumes the fluctuations may be higher but in any case cannot exceed 60 per cent.

All orders are supposed to be centralised on the market in order to take part in the price setting mechanism. However, brokers are authorised to directly transact between themselves in case of a large deal which may have disturbed the market (providing that the transaction price is connected to the last market price).

Since only dematerialised securities may be traded on the stock exchange, clearing-settlement operations are processed on a pure book-entry basis. This means that no physical delivery of certificates takes place. The Central

Depository initiates operations between brokerage companies according to information received from the NSEL. A statement of account has to be sent by the Depository to brokerage companies after each session. Clearing-settlement operations are performed by the Central Depository according to international standards. In this respect, the main function of the Central Depository is to ensure that delivery will take place simultaneously with the cash transfer, in a fixed time limit of four days after quotation day.

In order to ensure the proper resolution of all operations done on the Central Market, the NSEL requires that all brokers contribute to a "Market Guarantee Fund" which handles the responsibilities of a defaulting broker in case of bankruptcy.

E. The principle listing requirements

The Rules and Regulations of the NSEL provide that securities may be traded either on the Official List or on the so-called "Current List". For the time being, the quotation process is the same for all securities, whether they are listed on the Official List or quoted on the Current List.

Securities may be admitted to the Official List of the NSEL if:

--   they are admitted by the Lithuanian Securities Commission for public trading;

--   transferability of the securities is not limited;

--   equity capital of the issuer is not less then Lt 750 000 and the nominal value of the issue applied for listing is not less than Lt 250 000;

--   at least 25 per cent of the issue was, or is, subject to public offering;

--   distribution of ownership will ensure adequate liquidity;

--   information about assets of the issuer, source of financing, financial situation and prospects of development, profits and losses and any rights attached to the securities has been disclosed to the investors;

--   securities were listed on the Current List within the last six months.

An issuer who wants his securities to be listed on the Official List of the Stock Exchange shall submit a written application to the Board. The application shall be accompanied by the prospectus and information about the most recent financial activity, which occurred after the publication of the prospectus and could influence the financial status of the issuer. An applicant, whose securities are traded on the Official List, is obliged to submit annual, semiannual and quarterly reports. Financial statements of the annual report shall be audited by an independent auditor and compared with the relevant data from reports of the previous three years.

The Current List is created in order to let all the investors who own securities publicly issued but not listed on the Official List know the market price of these securities and trade them using the infrastructure of the Stock Exchange. The Exchange gets all information concerning securities traded on the Current List from the Securities Commission. An important feature of the Current List is that securities may be traded on it without any agreement of the issuer. Any investor who wishes to buy or to sell the publicly issued security may apply for listing on the Current List through his brokerage company. The Board of the Exchange will include the security into Current List if it is registered with the Securities Commission and the global account for this security is opened in the Central Depository. The disclosure requirements for securities listed on the Current List are a bit less strict than those for officially listed securities. For instance, companies listed on the Current List are not required to prepare quarterly reports. Another difference between the two lists is that, in the case of current listing, the issuer is obliged to provide all necessary information only to the Securities Commission and his investors, but is not obliged to do so for the Stock Exchange.

The concept of the current listing is very important because it allows trading on the stock exchange of all securities issued through the mass privatisation program.

F.   The trading activity on the NSEL

The NSEL was officially opened on 14 September 1993. Twenty-two securities and 20 brokerage companies were admitted for the first trading session. The total market capitalisation was slightly more than Lt 30 million. During the five months after the opening session, the market capitalisation substantially increased. By March 1994, it exceeded Lt 160 million. Seventy-five securities are traded on the Current List of the Stock Exchange. Among them there are 36 securities of industrial companies, 11 securities of banks and 28 securities of investment companies. Trading activity on the Stock Exchange is still not very high. Average turnover per session is approximately Lt 350 000 (approximately US$90 000). Total turnover per 20 sessions exceeds Lt 7 million. More than 90 per cent of turnover comprises large block transactions. This means that the liquidity on the Central Market is very low. The financial analysts expect that market liquidity will be significantly increased after payment of dividends for the 1993 financial year. The other factor which may increase the liquidity is the recently announced government intention to sell through the NSEL some of the remaining shares of privatised enterprises listed on the Current List.

Fixed quotations have occurred for only nine securities from the 75 which are listed on the Current List. Therefore, it is difficult to speak about trends in prices of shares of privatised enterprises. Among the nine securities whose prices have been fixed on the market, the highest prices of four were higher than their book value. Taking into consideration the buy orders which have been sent to the market but not matched, the prices of shares of privatised enterprises have tended to increase.

Very clear trends are seen in price fluctuations of shares of listed investment companies. The buy order quotations for these shares are at present decreasing at each session. For the time being, these prices are very similar to the prices of vouchers traded on the unorganised OTC market.

As mentioned above, most transactions on the NSEL take place through block trading. Usually sellers in these transactions are investment companies. Buyers vary from transaction to transaction. Nevertheless, they may be divided into a few groups:

-- investment companies which already own some shares in the company concerned but are trying to take a control of that company;

-- so-called "strategic" domestic or foreign investors who have decided to purchase the business of the company concerned;

-- insiders of the company (mainly managers).

Buyers and sellers on the Central Market are mainly trade and small investors. Some brokers are relatively active in trading on their own account. However, most of them can not be very active in such type of trading due to a lack of cash in their accounts.

Foreign investors are still not using the infrastructure of the Central Market for their investment, though there are no restrictions for their participation. Such inactivity is due to the following reasons. Firstly, foreign investors usually belong to the category of strategic investors. If they are investing, they seek to acquire a substantial or even majority stakes of equity in privatised enterprises. Currently, this goal is easier to achieve by making direct investments on the primary market or using the system of the block transactions because the volumes on the Central Market are relatively low. Secondly, foreign investors are not well-informed about the Lithuanian securities market. Thirdly, some investors deem the Lithuanian securities market too small for their activities. The last two reasons are interlinked because usually investors who deem the Lithuanian market too small are not aware of the mass privatisation program.

G. *Secondary trading on unofficial markets*

In January 1994, the Lithuanian Securities Commission carried out a survey concerning the trading activities outside the organised stock exchange. All companies with securities registered with the Securities Commission were asked how many transactions they registered in their registers of shareholders in 1992 and 1993. Not all companies responded to this poll. However, 63 answers more or less reflect the situation in the market. The first conclusion made after analysis of the answers is that trading outside the organised market is not active either. Only 10 per cent of all issued shares of these companies were transferred outside the stock exchange over two years. Nevertheless, the comparison of data about transfers of shares on and outside the stock exchange showed that most of the transactions were made on the over-the-counter market. Less than 1 per cent of all transactions were executed on the stock exchange in 1993. The number of shares transferred through the stock exchange in 1993 amounts to 5 per cent of all shares transacted. Evidently, the results of the poll have to be adjusted taking into consideration that the stock exchange was opened only in September 1993.

The prices of transactions outside the stock exchange are more or less comparable to those on the stock exchange. It is difficult to make a more exact assessment of their fluctuations due to lack of information in this area.

Concerning the profiles of sellers/buyers in transactions on the over-the-counter market, information exists only on internal transactions between employees and managers of the privatised companies. According to the results of the above-mentioned poll, this type of transaction amounts to 7 per cent of all transactions outside the stock exchange. The transactions between employees have a clear tendency to increase. In 1992 this type of transactions amounted to only 1 per cent of all transactions, while in 1993 this figure increased to 17 per cent. The other major transactors on the over-the-counter markets are investment companies. Their behaviour on both markets is described below.

III. The behaviour of the intermediaries

A.   *Activities of investment companies on the secondary markets*

The establishment of a trading facility for both investment companies and their investors was one of the goals of the establishment of the stock exchange. Investment companies were prohibited to trade the securities of their portfolio outside the organised markets. Most experts expected that after the opening of the stock exchange the investment companies would become very active players. But such expectations were overestimated. The investment companies are involved in most transactions executed on the stock exchange. However, as was mentioned above, the trading activity on the stock exchange is rather low and the investment companies do not significantly improve it. Most of the transactions executed on the stock exchange with participation of investment companies were block trades. Counterparts of investment companies in these transactions were either so-called strategic investors or other investment companies. What are the reasons of such low activity of investment companies on the secondary market?

Firstly, most investment companies in Lithuania prefer to act as holding companies with active participation in the decision-making process. The strategy of the passive portfolio investor is unpopular with them.

Secondly, due to very liberal legislation regulating the activities of investment companies, they do not feel serious liquidity problems. The current expenditures of investment companies are usually covered by sponsors, i.e. by private entrepreneurs having some long-term interests in assets of sponsored companies. At the present time, all investment companies in Lithuania are of the closed-end type. Therefore, they do not need to keep cash for redemption of their shares.

Thirdly, most privatised enterprises wrote into their statutes a provision according to which shareholders could not sell their shares without permission of the Board of Directors. Therefore, very often the investment companies are not free to sell their securities even if they are willing to. Such a provision restricts not only activities of investment companies but also the development of the securities market in general. A new draft law on joint-stock companies has already been submitted to the Parliament for approval, stipulating that public companies are prohibited from writing such restrictions into the Articles of Incorporation.

Fourthly, in order to be tradable on the stock exchange, shares of privatised companies should be registered with the Securities Commission. The registration means a disclosure of all material information about the company. Many privatised enterprises still do not conform to this and, therefore, their shares can not be traded on the stock exchange. If an investment company owns shares of such enterprises they temporarily cannot sell them on the stock exchange.

Perhaps investment companies also have some other reasons for limited activity on the organised secondary markets. However, it seems that the four reasons mentioned above are the main ones.

Although there is no official information about trading activity of the investment companies outside the organised market, financial experts in Lithuania recognise that it is far more active than on the stock exchange. As was mentioned above, such transactions are illegal and prohibited. In order to avoid a direct violation of the law, the investment companies use a number of future contracts for their transactions. The exchange of portfolio shares between the investment companies is the most popular type of transaction outside the organised market.

B.   The secondary market for shares of investment companies

Among the 75 securities listed on the stock exchange, 28 belong to investment companies. Only four of them are quoted on the Central Market. The market prices for all quoted shares of investment companies are lower than their face value. The analysis of orders submitted to the market shows that there are more investors willing to sell than to buy. The other problem is that, in most cases, sellers are asking higher prices then buyers are ready to pay. Therefore, the liquidity on the secondary market of the shares issued by investment companies is still very low. However, the data of the last few trading sessions show decreasing supply quotes. Thus, there exists a probability that in the near future the trading volume in investment companies shares may increase.

There is no standard pattern of behaviour of investment companies towards the enterprises they have invested in. As was mentioned above, most investment companies have felt that in order to best pursue their investments, they must get into a position of control, through which they allegedly seek to assure that the industrial company they invest in is run properly. But even being in a position of control, the investment companies usually do not directly manage the industrial companies because they do not have, in fact, enough personnel. In most cases they limit their direct involvement to the election of members of the Supervisory Board -- by law, that Board cannot manage the company, but chooses the Board of Directors and supervises its activities. On the other hand, the investment companies can not provide fresh capital for privatised enterprises because their own assets comprise still illiquid securities and vouchers. Therefore, some of them concentrate their attention on the search for foreign and even domestic investors being able to provide fresh capital for restructuring of privatised enterprises. Sometimes they are even ready to relinquish their control in order to attract new investments.

It should be mentioned that relations between the investment companies and privatised enterprises are not always very good. There are a lot of conflicts between managers of privatised enterprises and investment companies. These conflicts are mainly caused by both sides trying to gain control of privatised companies. On the other hand, the investment companies usually require improvement of the management of privatised enterprises or even a change of the managers. Naturally, the managers do not like that.

C. *Future development of investment companies*

As one can see, investment companies in Lithuania are currently quite different from those in western countries. They are a type of hybrid between passive investment, active control and operation. In this context, the Lithuanian Securities Commission has decided to prepare a draft law on investment companies. The objectives of the Securities Commission are:

-- to ensure better protection of shareholders against the risk entailed by the lack of diversification, and;

-- to reinforce the monitoring of the management of investment companies.

An ancillary objective would be to favour the transformation of investment companies into institutional investors who would play an important role on the stock exchange and thus increase market liquidity.

However, in order to prevent investment companies which have successfully started acting as holding companies of industrial enterprises from being forced to dispose of their controlling interest, an option should be made available to investment companies. Under this option, they could either become holding companies or remain investment companies, in which case they would become subject to rules similar to those existing at an international level for undertakings in transferable securities.

IV. The behaviour of insiders

Insiders play a very important role in privatised enterprises. In particular, this role increased when the Parliament adopted, in February 1993, the amendments to the privatisation law allowing employees and managers to acquire 50 per cent of shares on a non-competitive basis (20 per cent are privileged non-voting shares). Taking into consideration that employees may acquire additional shares in public bids, most companies privatised after approval of the amendments are controlled by insiders.

There are no restrictions imposed by the law for insiders to sell their shares. However, insiders of most of the privatised enterprises face the same problem as investment companies, i.e. even if they wish to sell their shares they need to receive permission of the Board of Directors. This burden, as well as natural conservatism of employees, explain why insiders are not active on the organised market. In the direct transactions between the insiders, managers usually are buying shares from the employees. There are more and more companies where managers have already become the principal owners. Such a situation has two sides. On the one hand, the concentration of ownership in the hands of managers is a healthy thing because it simplifies the decision-making process. On the other hand, it allows freezing or postponement of reforms in management, because a lot of old managers are not ready to introduce new, modern management systems. Unfortunately, there is no comparable analysis of the performance of the companies privatised over the initial stage, i.e. when outsiders had an equal opportunity with insiders, and the enterprises privatised after privileges for employees were introduced. But few general conclusions may be drawn. Many companies privatised over the initial and middle stages replaced their managers. Companies privatised over the last stage are usually managed by the same managers. The shares of the companies privatised over the initial stage find an easier way to the stock exchange than the shares of companies privatised after the privileges for employees were introduced. A more detailed assessment of the situation of the companies with a different structure of private ownership will be possible to do later when clearer trends in the behaviour of the companies appear.

Note

*   Based on a presentation made by the author (Algirdas Semeta, Chairman, Lithuanian Securities Commission, Vilnius) at the fifth meeting of the Advisory Group on Privatisation, Paris, 2-4 March 1994.

Small Investor Share-ownership Programme (KRP)

Report by the KRP Project Management Group*

I. Background

Prior to 1993, the thrust of the Hungarian privatisation programme has been the sale of state property to foreign trade investors. Since 1993, foreign investors have kept their significant participation, but domestic entrepreneurs are taking an increasing part. The privatisation programme has also resulted, to a lesser degree, in transfer of ownership to managers and employees. However, ordinary citizens and financial institutions have not had many opportunities to participate in the privatisation process, even though such investors are essential to the longer term development of Hungary's capital markets.

As the average citizen has so far been largely excluded from the privatisation process, part of the domestic savings which could go some way to financing economic restructuring has remained untapped. The longer term prosperity of the Hungarian economy and corporate sector will require the development of the country's capital markets to enable businesses to raise finance from a wider range of sources. An efficient capital market will lead to a wider choice for raising equity or debt capital, whilst competition in providing capital will result in cheaper sources of finance for business development.

On 15 April 1993, the government approved the recommendations of the Small Investor Share-ownership Programme (KRP), the objectives of which are to:

-- accelerate privatisation of state assets; and

-- facilitate wider participation by citizens in the privatisation process.

In developing the recommendations of the Programme, particular attention was paid to the advanced state of Hungary's economic development and to the progress made to date in its privatisation programme.

Table 1. **The means of payment for privatisation**

Sale for	1982-1992	1993	1989-1992	1993
	Billion HUF		Per cent	Per cent
Foreign currency	66.1	25.5	65	34
Domestic currency (HUF)	22.5	15.3	21	20
Sale for privatisation credit	11.0	21.7	11	29
Compensation note	2.2	13.0	3	17
Total value of sold state property	101.8	75.5	100	100

On the demand side, the strategy for the Programme fully recognises:

-- that a "free" voucher scheme, adopted by some countries in the region for accelerating demand, is more suitable to economies that have less tradition in market economy than Hungary. Hence, the recommended Privatisation Investment facility for facilitating wider share-ownership amongst citizens, and its requirement for paying for shares acquired over five years in interest free instalments is, by comparison, more like the model of mass privatisation adopted in highly developed economies; and

-- the government's existing commitments to compensation coupon holders, by using certain features of the infrastructure which will be put in place in support of the KRP, to widen the existing opportunities for the exchange of compensation coupons.

On the supply side, the strategy for the Programme fully recognises the need for:

-- the early introduction of domestic and foreign strategic investors into those state-owned companies that would benefit from the financial, managerial and technological resources of such investors;

-- preparing companies for a public offering by allowing strategic investors or managers to strengthen or restructure the company, and in the case of utilities, by putting in place an appropriate legislative and regulatory framework, and thus increasing the value of the public offering; and

-- placing greater emphasis on individual public offerings as a means of creating investment opportunities for compensation coupon holders, small investors and financial institutions, and of developing the capital markets.

The key thrust of the Programme will be a five-year programme of public offerings, aimed at the listing on the Budapest Stock Exchange of shares with a value of over HUF 120 billion in over 70 high quality and well-known companies, drawn from both the State Property Agency (SPA) and the State Holding Company (AVRt) portfolios. Whilst the public utility companies from the AVRt portfolio would represent a large part of the public offering programme, in general these would take longer to prepare and part of them could not be expected to be ready for a listing on the Budapest Stock Exchange for at least two years. Therefore, in the short term, companies from the SPA portfolio are likely to form the basis of the public offering programme. The active involvement of the AVRt is essential if the required level of supply for the longer term is to be secured.

Over the five-year period, up to 500 000 original holders of compensation coupons and between 500 000 and 1 million small investors would be expected to benefit from the investment opportunities created through the Programme, though there may be some overlap between these numbers.

The benefits of the programme of public offerings envisaged in the context of the Programme can be summarised as:

Hungarian economy

-- The significant increase in the small and institutional investor base will be a major contributor to the development of the country's capital markets. It would triple the number of listed companies and more than quadruple the value of shares traded on the Budapest Stock Exchange.

-- The mobilisation of domestic savings in financing economic and corporate development.

-- A more systematic and disciplined approach to developing privatisation plans of state-owned companies, and to their preparation for a public offering, leading to an acceleration of the privatisation programme.

-- The continuing ability to attract foreign capital and technology. Evidence suggests that, given the choice, foreign investors would prefer to invest in, and would indeed place a higher value on, companies which will be partly owned by the public rather than by the state.

-- Halting the fall in value of state property and reversing the process through greater competition on the demand side.

-- Scope for potential savings in privatisation costs, for example,through the coordination of educational and information campaigns addressed to compensation coupon holders and other small investors in respect of investment opportunities in the context of public offerings.

Small investors (including original holders of compensation coupons)

--   the public education and promotion campaign in support of the programme of public offerings will greatly enhance citizens' understanding of the privatisation process and their awareness of the investment opportunities in which they can participate;

--   both original compensation coupon holders and small investors will receive a personal service by being sent through the post information about all investment opportunities in public offerings and how to take part; by bringing privatisation to the people's door steps, the process will be transformed from one which is carried out in a "black box" to one which is simple and transparent;

--   the 150 or so registration centres around the country will serve as points of contact for citizens and will deal with their questions on share-ownership and participation in the programme of public offerings;

--   some of the features of the scheme and the systems and logistics infrastructure required in support of the KRP can be applied to improve the capability of the existing scheme for compensation coupons, thereby increasing the rate of participation of original compensation coupon holders in the programme of public offerings.

Companies

The expansion of the capital markets and investor base will offer companies wider choice and significantly improved terms for financing their business development, for example, through a capital increase on the Budapest Stock Exchange.

As noted above, the original holders of compensation coupons can benefit by extending to them certain features of the infrastructure that will be required in support of the KRP. In addition, the scheme and the systems and logistics infrastructure required in support of the KRP could be adopted to facilitate the participation of other specific social groups in the privatisation programme, including in connection with:

--   the acquisition by employees of quoted and unquoted shares in their respective companies; and

--   the acquisition by citizens of unquoted shares in companies within their local community.

The concept could be adapted to further facilitate the sale of state-owned real estate and physical assets to entrepreneurs, managers and employees.

Work on the design and implementation of these additional schemes will, however, be dependent on the implementation of the main scheme for the KRP which is outlined in this report.

II.   Overview of the Accelerated Privatisation Programme

A.   *Programme of public offerings*

Subject to further evaluation, further supplies in excess of HUF 120 billion could be secured for public offerings, by:

-- The creation of holding companies, portfolio management companies and residual shareholding companies from within the portfolio of the SPA. This could include those companies formed with the assistance of PHARE and the EBRD under the proposed Special Restructuring Programme (SRP).

-- Reducing the long-term state ownership in certain of the companies within the AVRt portfolio; including certain of the assets of local municipalities in the event that they would be interested in participating in the Programme.

-- Including, if possible, any suitable assets owned by the treasury.

-- Significant restructuring and rationalisation of a number of industry sectors and companies. This would serve to increase both the quality and the amount of the medium to longer-term supply for public offerings.

-- Selective reductions in the significant levels of debt suffered by a number of companies in the state's portfolio, for example, through debt-equity conversion or debt write-off.

-- Extending (if possible) the scheme for the purchase of shares in companies by employees.

-- Extending the scheme to the purchase of unquoted shares. This is likely to be possible only on a regional basis in respect of companies with strong local recognition.

The Programme proposes that when a state-owned company is floated on the Budapest Stock Exchange, its shares will be offered to three main groups of investors:

Group 1:   small investors (comprising citizens registered under the instalment payment facility, or "IPF" scheme). These will be allowed to pay by instalments, or to pre-pay, for any shares acquired through the IPF scheme either in cash or in compensation coupons;

Group 2: compensation coupon holders, comprising:

     a)   the original holders registered under the compensation coupon scheme; and

     b)   secondary holders; and

Group 3: cash investors (for example, domestic and foreign institutions and wealthy individuals) to ensure a liquid secondary market.

Under these proposals:

--   Shares in any company which is allocated to compensation coupon holders by the respective decisions of the Boards of the SPA and the AVRt will be offered to them.

      If deemed desirable, the original holders of compensation coupons can be given priority over the secondary holders.

      If compensation coupon holders do not subscribe for the full allocation given to them, the surplus shares could then be available to instalment payment (IPF) or cash investors.

--   Equally shares in any company which is allocated to small investors will be offered to IPF investors.

      If IPF investors do not subscribe for the full allocation given to them, the surplus shares could then be available to compensation coupon holders or cash investors.

The practical effect of the above will be to:

--   provide a consistent and easy administrative mechanism for the withdrawal of compensation coupons from the market in exchange for quoted state-owned shares;

--   ensure that an appropriate balance is struck between raising proceeds for the state (through the cash and IPF segments) and withdrawal of compensation coupons (through the compensation coupon and IPF segments);

--   ensure a liquid secondary market in the shares;

--   withdraw compensation coupons from the market to a greater extent than at present, since IPF investors will be allowed to pay or pre-pay some or all of their instalments in compensation coupons;

--   generate major savings in privatisation costs, for example, through the coordination of educational and information campaigns for marketing each public offering to compensation coupon holders and other small investors; and

-- increase the market value of compensation coupons through creating greater demand on the secondary market and providing performing and marketable securities in the exchange.

III. Potential demand

A. The instalment payment facility (IPF) scheme

The results of the nationwide market research undertaken in June 1993 suggest that there is:

-- more support for, than opposition to, the policy of privatisation;

-- widespread mistrust of the implementation of the privatisation process to date, derived from a perception of its political motivation; and

-- a lack of understanding of, and a sense of exclusion from, the privatisation process.

The research also suggests that:

-- 10 per cent of the adult population has considered buying shares; and

-- 35 per cent of the adult population is interested in knowing more about the details of the IPF scheme, and of these:

    • most would be satisfied with an initial instalment payment facility of HUF 100 000;

    • the vast majority feel that a five-year payment period for the IPF is appropriate.

On the basis of the research carried out to date, we estimate the registration of approximately 500 000 people. With an effective communications programme this could increase substantially. Therefore, in planning the logistics and other systems in support of the IPF scheme the possibility of around 1 million people becoming involved in the scheme needs to be accommodated. In any event, the level of registrations is dependent upon the public being convinced that the government will ensure a continuing supply of quality companies throughout the Programme.

B. Compensation coupon scheme

By the end of the first quarter of 1994, up to HUF 220 billion (including accrued interest) of compensation coupons are expected to be issued to some 1 million citizens. To date, the take-up of opportunities for exchange of compensation coupons for state property has been very limited; this is reflected in the low valuation placed on compensation coupons in the secondary market. Whilst it is impossible to estimate the number of original compensation coupon holders that are likely to retain their coupons for exchange with shares listed on the Budapest Stock Exchange, it is likely that this number will be influenced by the ease with which they can participate in public offerings and by the quality of shares made available through the public offerings. For planning purposes, however, it needs to be assumed that up to 1 million original holders of compensation coupons may wish to participate in the programme of public offerings.

C.   *Communications programme*

The communications programme required to achieve a level of up to 1 million IPF registrations will take place in three stages:

-- pre-registration -- to educate the public about share ownership, the IPF scheme and how to take part;

-- during registration -- to encourage maximum public participation in the IPF scheme; and

-- in support of each public offering -- to maximise the number of IPF registrants investing through the IPF scheme.

The communications strategy will be based on three key elements:

-- a balance between public education and promotion to ensure that as many people as possible understand that the IPF scheme is aimed at them and recognise that it offers them the opportunity to participate in share ownership with minimal risk;

-- the co-ordinated use of the full range of communications techniques: research, advertising (television, radio, press and poster), PR, educational broadcast, information materials and roadshows -- at both a national and a regional level; and

-- the presentation the IPF scheme as a non-political, easy to understand and well-managed programme in which citizens can have confidence.

The above communication strategy for the IPF scheme can be easily adapted and extended to educate compensation coupon holders on share ownership and to encourage their participation in the investment opportunities presented by the programme of public offerings.

IV. Overview of the schemes

A. *The IPF scheme*

The IPF scheme can be divided into six distinct stages. The main features of each stage are described below. The IPF scheme has been designed to allow a degree of flexibility regarding the incorporation of additional features at a later stage and to adjust the terms of the scheme in the light of experience.

1. *Stage 1: registration*

-- Hungarian citizens 18 years of age and over, with a permanent address in Hungary, would be eligible to register to open an IPF.

The registration process is intended to avoid potential abuses of the scheme (for example, through exceeding the HUF 100 000 facility limit) and to benefit registrants from certain features of the scheme (for example, receiving information on all investment opportunities through the public offering programme).

-- There would be at least two registration periods, of up to four weeks each, per year throughout the life of the scheme.

-- Registration would be centrally managed, but would take place through up to 150 specially designated registration centres across the country, using identity cards for verification.

-- A special procedure has been designed to enable elderly or infirm citizens the opportunity to register.

-- A registration fee of HUF 2 000 (approximately US$2O) would be payable. Each registered citizen will receive a registration document or card with a unique registration number.

-- Each IPF investor would be granted an initial facility of HUF 100 000. Market research has confirmed this figure as an appropriate level. In the light of experience, however, this limit could be increased.

-- No credit-worthiness analysis would be conducted before a IPF is established for an investor.

-- IPFs would not be transferable, could not be drawn in cash and would only be available for specified privatisation investments.

2. *Stage 2: subscription*

-- Each IPF investor will receive a personalised subscription form in respect of each privatisation opportunity in which shares have been allocated to the IPF scheme. This feature will be in addition to the communication and marketing programme in support of each public offering.

-- The subscription form will indicate the minimum and maximum limits placed by the state on the amount that could be used by each IPF investor in each public offering.

-- Where appropriate, to encourage subscriptions, IPF investors may be offered incentives specific to each public offering (e.g. price discounts or bonus shares).

-- Completion of the subscription forms will be simple; completed forms can be sent back by post or handed in to any scheme registration centre.

3. *Stage 3: allocation*

-- The number of shares applied for are compared with the number of shares available for IPF investors and, in the event of over-subscription, a fair means of allocation will be applied as follows:

 • all applications will be scaled down, but to a level which is not lower than the minimum limit for subscriptions; and

 • if needed, a ballot will take place to allocate the minimum subscription limits.

The method of allocation set out above is intended to ensure equal treatment for all IPF investors, since alternative methods of allocation would be seen as unfair; for example, a "first come first served" approach would disadvantage investors living in rural areas.

-- IPF investors will be notified of the block of shares allocated to them and of the timetable of instalment payments required.

4. *Stage 4: instalment payments*

-- The amount due from IPF investors for each block of shares allocated to them would be paid in five annual instalments or ten half-yearly instalments, with each instalment representing payment for a whole number of shares. However, IPF investors may pre-pay any or all instalments, if they so wish.

-- Dividends on the block of shares would be credited to the IPF account to reduce IPF investors' instalment payments.

-- Compensation coupons could be used to pay the instalments or make prepayments.

144

-- There will be no interest charged on IPF balances if instalments are paid before the due dates.

-- IPF investors will receive regular statements of their outstanding instalment payments.

-- If the IPF investor were late in paying an instalment, he would receive a reminder and be charged interest.

-- If following a reminder, any instalment payment were not made, the citizen would forfeit the right to pay for any more shares from the relevant block of shares and the state would be free to dispose of the remaining shares in that block through the Budapest Stock Exchange or a private placement.

-- There would be no recourse to an investor's other assets. That is, the investor's personal wealth would not be at risk.

5. *Stage 5: custody and release of shares*

-- Shares acquired by IPF investors would not be transferable or saleable until they were paid for.

-- IPF investors would be required to enter into a contract offering the shares as security ("ovadek") to the state until the corresponding instalment payments or pre-payments were made.

-- Shares would be released to IPF investors for sale or transfer on a *pro rata* basis against instalment payments (see 5.1.7 Example) but IPF investors who wish to have physical delivery of share certificates will be required to pay for the cost of printing them.

-- Voting rights on the shares acquired through the IPF would be exercisable by the IPF investor.

6. *Stage 6: sale of shares*

-- To discourage short-term speculation, the incentives that may be offered to IPF investors would be designed to encourage investors to retain shares, although such incentives should not be of such a nature that they would prevent an active secondary market from developing.

-- Further work is taking place in conjunction with the Budapest Stock Exchange to ensure a cost effective means for IPF investors to sell their shares within a properly regulated market.

7.   Example

An IPF investor is allocated ten shares of HUF 1 000 each. The investor will be required to make instalment payments of HUF 2 000 per year in cash or compensation coupons. Following the payment of each year's instalment of HUF 2 000, two shares will be released from "ovadek" to the IPF investor. These shares will be freely available to the IPF investor to retain, sell or transfer as he wishes, as illustrated below.

8.   Risk for IPF investors

The IPF scheme has been specifically designed to minimise the risk of investing in quoted shares by small investors. However, unless the government is prepared to underwrite all losses, the risk cannot be entirely eliminated. The IPF investor will be at risk only to the extent that:

a)   he has paid for the shares in full; and

b)   the market price of the shares falls below the subscription price paid.

Table 2. **The IPF scheme**

	Instalment made (HUF)	Total instalment due (HUF)	Number of shares released to investor	Number of shares in "ovadek"
Original allocation: 10 shares of HUF 1 000 each	-	10 000	-	10
Instalments				
Year 1	2 000	8 000	2	8
Year 2	2 000	6 000	2	6
Year 3	2 000	4 000	2	4
Year 4	2 000	2 000	2	2
Year 5	2 000	-	2	-

B. Compensation coupon scheme

Many features of the IPF scheme could be extended to improve the current practices for dealing with compensation coupon holders and their participation in the programme of public offerings. Whilst a thorough investigation of the scheme for compensation coupon holders is not within the scope of this report, the following conceptual features, falling into four distinct stages, could be adopted for the benefit of the original holders of compensation coupons.

1. Stage 1: confirmation of participation

-- Original holders of compensation coupons would be contacted in writing to confirm whether they wish to participate.

-- There will be a number of confirmation periods throughout the life of the scheme.

-- Confirmation of participation would be centrally managed.

-- Each original compensation coupon holder will receive a registration document or card with a unique registration number.

-- Each original compensation coupon holder would be granted the opportunity to participate in the programme of public offerings up to the value and number of compensation coupons registered. The limit could be increased by registering additional compensation coupons.

2. Stage 2: subscription

-- Each confirmed original compensation coupon holder will receive a personalised subscription form in respect of each privatisation opportunity by means of a public offering in which shares have been allocated to compensation coupon holders.

-- The subscription form will indicate the minimum and, if appropriate, maximum limits placed by the state on the amount that could be used by each compensation coupon holder in each public offering.

-- Completion of the subscription forms will be simple; completed forms can be sent back by post or handed in to any designated collection point.

3. Stage 3: allocation

-- The number of shares applied for are compared with the number of shares available for compensation coupon holders and, in the event of over-subscription, a fair means of allocation will be applied as follows:

147

- if deemed desirable, original compensation coupon holders would be given priority over secondary holders of compensation coupons;

- all applications will be scaled down, but to a level which is not lower than the minimum limit for subscriptions; and

- if needed, a ballot will take place to allocate the minimum subscription limits.

-- A letter of allotment will be sent to the original compensation coupon holders, stating the amount owed, and requesting attendance at a designated collection point within a certain period to exchange compensation coupons for the shares allotted.

4. Stage 4: exchange

-- The amount owed for each block of shares must be settled in full in exchange for compensation coupons.

-- If the exchange is not made by the due date, the shares allotted will be sold by other methods.

V. Systems and logistics infrastructure

The timely implementation and successful operation of the KRP will require the development, within a very short time period, of substantial supporting systems and logistics.

A system has already been established for the issue and exchange of compensation coupons, albeit on a smaller scale than would be required to enable large-scale participation of compensation coupon holders in a programme of public offerings. Many aspects of the systems and logistics infrastructure required in support of the IPF scheme could be adapted to improve the existing system for compensation coupons to facilitate large-scale participation of compensation coupon holders in the programme of public offerings. A thorough investigation of the existing system for compensation coupons was not, however, within the scope of this report and further work would be required in this area.

A. Technical solution

In examining the technical options for an appropriate level of systems and logistics development to support the IPF scheme's requirements, a wide range of factors have been considered, including the:

-- capability of the existing national infrastructures (for example, in respect of telecommunications, the banking system and the Budapest Stock Exchange); and

-- different levels of systems sophistication and the related costs of development, implementation and operation.

On the basis of this investigation, the following technical solution is recommended the:

-- establishment of a nationwide network of up to 150 registration centres;

-- establishment of a central computer centre for maintaining the IPF accounts and processing all documents; and

-- development of an interface to the banking system (for handling payments) and to the Budapest Stock Exchange (for handling custodial systems, company registers and dividend distribution).

B. *The role of the Budapest Stock Exchange*

The close involvement of the Budapest Stock Exchange in the IPF scheme's development and administration will be essential.

In the short term, the systems currently being developed under the control of the Budapest Stock Exchange to handle custody of shares, company registers and dividend distribution will need to accommodate the IPF scheme's requirements.

The current paper-based approach of using physical share certificates is incompatible with the handling and trading of high volumes of small blocks of shares and is inconsistent with worldwide trends towards efficient capital market operation.

In the medium term, therefore, to enable a cost effective means of trading in small blocks of shares and to handle the high volume of shares being traded, the Securities Law (and possibly the Civil Code) will need to be amended to allow shares to be handled in paper-less ("immobilised" or "dematerialised") form.

VI. Implementation plan

All target dates are dependent on government approval of the IPF scheme and its financing in mid-September 1993. Any delay in the approval process will delay the successful implementation of the Programme and the IPF scheme. Subject to this, the main activities and key dates (from September 1993 to May 1994) are.

Table 3. **Timetable**

	Beginning	End
Communications programme, including research, public relations, educational broadcast, information materials	end of September 1993	end of April 1994
Development of the IPF registration system	mid-February 1994	mid-April 1994
Pre-registration advertising for the IPF scheme	early March 1994	early April 1994
Advertising in support of the first public offer	mid-March 1994	end of March 1994
First public offer	early April 1994	end of April 1994

Note

*   This Report was presented by Dr. György Lajtai (formerly Director, Economics Department, State Property Agency, currently Director with the Hungarian Credit Bank, Budapest) at the fifth meeting of the Advisory Group on Privatisation, Paris, 2-4 March 1994.

In June 1994, parliamentary elections were held in Hungary and the new coalition government has not yet decided its approach to the original description of the model. The implementation of the programme is presently suspended, but there are declarations that -- perhaps with some modifications -- the project will be relaunched early next year.

Mass Privatisation in Russia

Maxim Boycko, Andrei Shleifer, Robert W. Vishny*[1]

I.   Introduction

When Anatoly Chubais was put in charge of the State Committee on the Management of State Property (GKI) in October 1991, privatisation was not at the top of Russia's reform agenda. Price liberalisation and control of the budget were the top priorities. Politicians and the public debated whether Russia should be privatising at all before macroeconomic problems were solved.   No privatisation programme existed at the time.   In fact, the very name of Mr. Chubais' agency reflected the government's ambivalence about privatisation.

Two years later, privatisation has become the most successful reform in Russia. By January 1994, about 45 per cent of Russian industrial workers were employed by privatised firms. Privatisation has spread even wider in service firms. Over 60 per cent of the Russian people supported privatisation, and Chubais has become one of the better known politicians.

In this paper, we try to describe and evaluate the progress of Russian privatisation.   Doing so at this point raises the obvious timing problem. Privatisation in Russia is extremely young. What has been accomplished is largely a transfer of ownership of cash flow and control rights of firms from "the state" to "private parties." Real changes in the operations of enterprises have barely begun. We cannot, therefore, evaluate the progress of Russian privatisation based on the actual efficiency improvements it has delivered. Instead, we need to use a more subjective yardstick to evaluate the accomplishments of privatisation, namely our educated estimate of the likelihood that privatisation will lead to restructuring of privatised firms. We argue that the key prerequisite for restructuring is **depolitization** of firms, meaning a change in their conduct from meeting the wishes of politicians to maximising profits. In the paper, we try to evaluate whether privatisation in Russia is in fact depolitizing state firms.

Section II presents our case for looking at depolitization to predict restructuring success. We argue that, in most countries, politicians try to influence firms to pursue political objectives, such as excess employment or location in particular areas. Managers of firms extract subsidies from the Treasury in return for addressing these political goals. The inefficiency of public enterprises is the result of this politicisation of firms. We argue that privatisation is just one of several steps that make it more expensive for politicians to influence firms. As such, privatisation reduces the amount of inefficiency that firms accept to satisfy politicians, but it does not make firms fully efficient. Creating product market competition, improving corporate governance and eliminating political control of capital allocation are other important steps that make political influence more expensive. An important message of section II is that debates about whether privatisation, corporatisation, or any other single measure, is "sufficient" to make firms efficient miss the point: these are all partial depolitization measures.

Section III discusses the design of Russian privatisation in light of the objective of depolitization. In particular, we discuss why Russia opted for voucher privatisation rather than for a Polish-style mutual fund scheme. We also show that, quite aside from its objectives, the Russian programme was to a large extent shaped by the political constraints on what was feasible.

Section IV presents the basic facts about Russian privatisation, including some evidence on its extraordinary speed. We also address an important puzzle that the evidence raises, namely the remarkably low valuation of Russian firms in the marketplace. Sections V, VI, and VII look beyond privatisation and ask what other mechanisms can reduce political influence on firms. Section V briefly describes the state of product market competition in Russia. Section VI examines governance of firms through equity ownership. We present some survey evidence suggesting that privatisation in Russia is leading to very significant ownership by managers and workers, and some ownership by large outside shareholders. While some management and outsider ownership is a cause for optimism, the extent of insider entrenchment raises concerns about future restructuring. Section VII turns to depolitization of capital supply mechanisms as a step toward depolitization of firms. We first describe the current capital allocation mechanisms in Russia, which are still primarily political and dominated by the financing practices of the government and the Central Bank. Commercial banks are playing only a minor role in capital allocation. We also describe the role of macroeconomic stabilisation in depolitizing capital allocation in Russia. The evidence in sections VI and VII suggests that, in the near future, if capital allocation is to contribute to depolitization of firms, it should avoid the highly politicised commercial banks. Section VIII summarises our findings.

II. The goals of privatisation

A. *Restructuring and depolitization*

To focus on the goals of privatisation, it is useful to start with asking "what" is wrong with public enterprises and "why"? On the question of "what" there is much agreement: public enterprises are inefficient. They employ too many people, produce goods that consumers do not want, locate in economically wrong places, do not upgrade their capital stock and so on. While these problems are particularly severe in Eastern Europe, public enterprises throughout the world are conspicuous for their inefficiency as well[2]. This observation is no longer controversial.

The question of "why" public enterprises are inefficient is harder to answer. Standard public finance starts with the presumption that governments maximise social welfare, and views public enterprises from this vantage point. In particular, public enterprises are supposedly productively efficient, and in fact cure monopoly and externality problems caused by private firms[3]. As a positive theory of public enterprises, this one fails miserably. More recent work has stayed with the assumption of benevolent government, but argued that public enterprises are inefficient because the government is poorly informed about their efficiency, and so rationally subsidises them to pursue uncertain projects[4]. These theories might explain why governments subsidise highly uncertain R&D projects or defense contracts. It does not, however, make much sense as an explanation of dramatic inefficiency of public agriculture, coal mining and other relatively routine production. The high costs and inefficiencies of such firms are public knowledge, yet the government still does not insist on their restructuring.

An alternative theory of public enterprise argues that they are inefficient because they become the means by which politicians attain their political objectives[5]. Excess employment, location in economically inefficient places, production of wrong goods, and underpricing of output all help politicians to get votes or avoid riots. For example, it is plausible to argue that the principal objective of the Russian communists was to secure their own survival against (perceived) external and internal threats. Many features of the communist economy follow from this assumption. Russian state enterprises produced so many military goods because the politicians cared about security and not social welfare. The government lavished capital on the military firms at the expense of consumer product firms for the same reason. The communist government invested resources in public health, but not in health care for the elderly, because it needed healthy soldiers, not because it was humanitarian. The communist government asked firms to overemploy people because it insisted on full employment to prevent social unrest that would threaten its control. The government created large collective farms to control peasants and so avoid the perceived threat from them. State firms produced large farm machinery to ensure that only these large state farms could survive. Thus a simple view of political objectives can go some way toward explaining many of the inefficiencies of the Soviet economy. The examples can be multiplied, and extended around the world. Public enterprises are inefficient because their inefficiency serves the goals of politicians.

Except in a pure command economy, managers need not automatically do what politicians want them to do. Instead, managers and politicians bargain over what the firm does. Managers usually have objectives that are closer to profit maximisation than politicians do, if only because they want to maximise resources under their control. To convince managers to pursue political objectives, politicians subsidise firms. In return for the subsidies, managers hire extra people, locate in economically inefficient places and so on. Note that the relationship between politicians and managers is best described as a bargain: managers might be the ones who come to the politicians and beg for money threatening to lay off workers if they don't get it. But such begging by the managers only works when politicians themselves care about employment. Because politicians want something other than profits from firms, bargaining between managers and politicians results in payments from governments to firms (subsidies or soft budget constraints) in return for the inefficiency.

This framework has an obvious implication for privatisation and other restructuring policies. Specifically, the objective of these policies must be to change the terms of trade in the bargain between politicians and managers against the former, i.e. to make it more expensive for politicians to buy inefficiencies with subsidies. To do that, either the cost to the politician of finding a dollar of subsidies must increase, or the ability of that dollar to buy extra inefficiency must fall, or both. When subsidies become more expensive and less effective, managers will do less to cater to the objectives of the politicians, and the firm will begin to restructure. In this paper, we will consider privatisation and other policies from this perspective of depolitization.

The first question to ask is whether restructuring actually requires privatisation, i.e. change in the ownership of **cash flows** of state firms. It is sometimes argued that all that is really necessary is to change **control** from politicians to managers, i.e. to corporatise state firms[6]. Once control changes, cash flows can remain publicly owned as long as managers get some incentives to maximise profits. These incentives might come from incentive contracts for the managers, from product market competition, or from hard credit policies (these issues are discussed later). Indeed, many state enterprises in Poland have begun to restructure in the regime of product market competition and stricter oversight by banks without privatisation[7]. This evidence suggests that privatisation of cash flows is not necessary for restructuring when control is removed from politicians.

The depolitization model outlined above suggests that corporatisation is one of the key steps that make subsidies less effective. The reason for this is that, by turning control over from politicians to the managers, corporatisation enables the managers to extract more surplus in the bargain with politicians. Whereas before corporatisation politicians could order firms to, say, employ extra people, now they have to pay them to do it, which is more expensive. Because corporatisation raises the cost to politicians of getting firms to cater to their wishes, it stimulates restructuring. But how much restructuring it stimulates depends on the other determinants of the costs of political influence. For example, in Poland after stabilisation, the combination of corporatisation and tight budgets significantly reduced subsidies to firms and stimulated restructuring. In Russia, monetary policy is not as tight, and hence the effectiveness of corporatisation by itself would likely be much lower since politicians have too much money to influence firms. More generally, corporatisation has often failed to lead to significant restructuring because politicians have attempted to regain their control over firms[8]. In a country like Russia, where the mechanisms of political influence are numerous and the politicians' demand for influence is high, corporatisation by itself is a rather weak measure.

Of course, everywhere in the world politicians try to exert influence even over private, let alone state, firms by offering them procurement contracts, regulatory and tax breaks, and outright subsidies in return for meeting political objectives. So what does privatisation accomplish that corporatisation doesn't? How does privatisation depolitize firms? First, when managers and outsider shareholders receive substantial cash flow rights, the cost of convincing firms to be inefficient by pursuing political objectives rises, since they now care about the foregone profits from failing to restructure. This incentive effect makes it more expensive for politicians to get what they want, and hence presumably accelerates restructuring. Second, in many cases the mechanisms for political influence over firms are dismantled when firms are privatised. For example, after privatisation, ministries are abolished. This change both eliminates one political constituency that wants to control the firm (i.e., the ministry) and makes control by politicians operationally more difficult. Third, privatisation creates a political constituency of owners-taxpayers who oppose government interference in the economy because it raises their taxes and reduces their profits, and thus contributes to depolitization through a political rather than an economic mechanism. For all these reasons, privatisation by itself is a critical depolitization (and hence restructuring) strategy.

B. Beyond privatisation

Important as privatisation might be for depolitization, it is not sufficient. Politicians try and often succeed in getting private firms to pursue political objectives as well. For example, privatised Russian firms still receive subsidies in exchange for keeping up employment. Many private firms in Italy continue close relationships with politicians. Other measures promoting depolitization must complement privatisation. This paper will examine three critical strategies: product market competition, equity governance and capital allocation.

Throughout the world, product market competition plays a critical role in depoliticizing firms. When firms are facing efficient rivals, they have to be efficient themselves to survive in the market place or else get subsidies[9]. But keeping an inefficient firm in a competitive market from going bankrupt is much more expensive for a politician than keeping afloat an inefficient monopoly that can waste large monopoly rents before it begins to lose money. Unfortunately, politicians realise that competition raises the cost to them of exerting influence, and often restricts product market competition by political action. First, politicians often protect domestic firms from both foreign and domestic competition, which of course leaves them with rents that can be dissipated on politically desirable activities. Second, the bankruptcy procedures are often politicised, and hence inefficient firms are "rehabilitated" rather than allowed to go bankrupt. But when politicians fail to undermine competition, restructuring benefits come fast. By creating a competitive marketplace through both domestic competition and openness to trade, both Poland and Czechoslovakia have made great strides in depolitizing firms.

The second important depolitization mechanism is equity governance, which refers to giving equity ownership to active decision makers. Equity governance in the first place means significant management ownership, but it is also fostered by significant shareholdings by large investors, also referred to as core investors or active investors, who can put pressure on the managers to restructure and to resist pressures from politicians[10]. The reliance on core investors for governance has characterised privatisation programs in France, Mexico, and, more recently, Czechoslovakia. Unfortunately, politicians can disrupt the functioning of this governance mechanism as well by preventing outside shareholders from voting their shares or otherwise exercising their control rights. The third key depolitization mechanism is replacing political allocation of capital with private allocation. As long as the allocation of credit in the economy is politicised, it will be the firms who cater to politicians rather than shareholders that get credit. Bankrupt firms will simply seek debt relief from the politicians, and satisfy political objectives in return. Even managers incentivised through their own ownership or through pressure from large shareholders will cater to the politicians in exchange for credits and subsidies. The success of restructuring relies critically on depolitization of credit policies.

This means two things. First, it requires the elimination of soft credits and subsidies from the government, which have historically been the most effective mechanism of control by the politicians. But politicians cannot be controlled unless money is controlled. Hardening the budget constraints of firms requires macroeconomic stabilisation. Second, depolitization of capital requires the availability of capital on commercial terms. While some restructuring can take place without much new investment (firms can lay off some employees, change their product mix using the existing equipment, reduce waste in inventories and so on), substantial restructuring usually requires capital. Needless to say, such depolitization of capital allocation is usually opposed by politicians, who try to control credit policies through bankruptcy regulation, control of banks, and inflationary finance. But while getting private capital allocation to replace political capital allocation may be the hardest task, it is perhaps the most significant for eventual depolitization of firms.

To summarise, restructuring the Russian economy requires depolitization of firms. This strategy must be pursued on many fronts, including privatisation, competition policy, corporate governance and capital allocation. To assess the likely success of the Russian privatisation, we will need to look at the progress on all these fronts.

III. The Russian privatisation programme[11]

The Russian privatisation programme was designed to meet the objectives set out in the previous section. Yet it was also designed in an extremely hostile political environment. As a result, the programme had to accommodate the political and economic demands of various stakeholders in state firms, so as to get their support or at least preclude active opposition. The principal stakeholders included enterprise managers and employees, whose lobbies controlled the parliament and who themselves effectively controlled state firms in the transition, and local governments who gained much of the political influence over firms that the centre lost. The second part of this section explains how these constraints shaped the privatisation program.

A. *Description of the program*

As a first step, the programme divided firms into those that would be sold primarily for cash by the local governments, and those that would go into the mass privatisation program. In this way, most small shops and some smaller enterprises were immediately allocated to the local governments, who demanded the revenues from small scale privatisation as their major concession (although later small shops were sold for vouchers as well).

As a second step, the programme delineated larger firms into those subject to mandatory privatisation, those subject to privatisation with the permission of the Privatisation Ministry, those requiring government approval for privatisation, and those whose privatisation was prohibited. Mandatory privatisation included firms in the "light" industries, including textiles, food processing, furniture etc. Firms requiring GKI approval tended to be somewhat larger firms, yet not operating in any of the important strategic industries. Major firms in most strategic industries, such as natural resources and defense, could only be privatised with the agreement of the government. In practice, this restriction meant that these firms could not be fully privatised. Even if some part of their equity could be privately owned, control always remained with politicians. Finally, some firms including those involved in transport, space exploration, health, education, etc., could not be privatised at all.

As a third step, all large and medium-sized firms, except for those in the last list, were to be corporatised[12]. That is to say, they were to re-register as joint-stock companies with 100 per cent of equity owned by the government, a corporate charter, and a board of directors. Initially, the board would have representation by the Property Fund (the selling agency of the government), the management, and the workers. Boards of directors did not have any representation by outsiders. The corporatisation decree, signed by Yeltsin in May 1992, was correctly viewed as the first major step toward subsequent privatisation of state firms.

Parallel to corporatisation, divisions of state firms had the right to split off and become independent. This proved to be rather difficult because of resistance from the management of the parent company and the local officials. Nonetheless, such split-offs occurred in many cases.

Once a firm is corporatised, its managers and workers got to pick between three privatisation options. The first option gave workers 25 per cent of the shares of the enterprise for free, yet made these shares non-voting. In addition, workers got 10 per cent at a 30 per cent discount to book value. Top managers got 5 per cent at book value. The second option gave managers and workers together 51 per cent of the equity, all voting, at a nominal price of 1.7 times the book value of assets. This of course represented a very low price relative to the market value of these assets in a highly inflationary environment. Workers could pay for these shares in cash, with vouchers (to be discussed later), or through the retained earnings of the enterprise, and could pay over some relatively short period of time. Finally, a third option, imposed by the managerial lobby in the Parliament, allowed the managers to buy up to 40 per cent of the shares at very low prices if they promised to privatise the firm quickly and yet not to go bankrupt. For a variety of reasons, this option has hardly been used.

Once the managers and workers select their benefits option, they submit a privatisation plan that describes how the rest of the shares are to be sold. While some enterprises are subject to mandatory privatisation, in practice the filing of privatisation plans is almost always voluntary. The principal way in which the sale of shares takes place in Russia is through auctions of shares for vouchers. Every person in Russia was offered a privatisation voucher for a small fee, and most people picked them up. The voucher has a denomination of 10 000 roubles, is supposed to expire in mid-1994, and is freely tradable. This voucher is usable as the sole allowable means of payment in auctions of shares of privatising enterprises. Each privatising enterprise goes through its individual voucher auction in the city where it is headquartered (systems have been built to enable people to buy shares of firms located in other cities). Bidding in these auctions is very easy: the principal type of bid is to submit your voucher and to get however many shares it buys at the equilibrium price. Because vouchers are tradable, some investors acquire blocks of vouchers and bid for large blocks of shares. In a typical company, up to 30 per cent of the shares is sold in voucher auctions, although smaller stakes are sold in "strategic" enterprises that are privatised.

Voucher privatisation is clearly the defining feature of the Russian program. It was chosen over the alternative mass privatisation scheme using mutual funds for four reasons, listed in order of increasing importance[13]. First, a mutual fund scheme would be too difficult to implement in Russia technologically. Second, it was hoped that vouchers would involve people more actively in privatisation by giving them choice of what to invest in, and hence make privatisation more popular than a mutual fund scheme that does not involve choice. Third, a mutual fund scheme that imposes large shareholders on the managers would have created serious opposition from the managerial lobby, and so made implementation of the programme difficult. Fourth, there was a great concern in Russia that the large state-sponsored mutual funds owning large stakes in Russian companies would become politicised and hence be unable to enforce restructuring policies. For these four reasons, Russia gave up the instant large shareholder advantage of Polish-style mutual funds and opted for a voucher privatisation programme[14].

The fate of the shares neither allocated to the workers nor sold in voucher auctions remains uncertain. One strategy incorporated into the privatisation programme is to sell shares through investment tenders to domestic or foreign investors, where the means of payment would be investment commitments rather than vouchers or cash. In practice, this strategy has often amounted to a giveaway of shares to managers, their relatives and friends. In other cases, some shares can in principle be retained by the government for some period of time. In yet other cases, the government might contribute the shares toward industry associations and financial-industrial groups (to be discussed later). In most enterprises, the privatisation of the last 20 or so per cent of the shares was not fully specified by the privatisation plan, and hence shares remain in the government-controlled Property Funds.

B. The programme in light of the constraints it faced

The design of the programme clearly reflected the political constraints. As we show below, all important "stakeholders" got major concessions.

The local governments got control over small scale privatisation, as well as most revenues from it. They would have received revenues from large scale privatisation as well, except that the predominant means of payment was vouchers. Most important, voucher auctions were run locally, which gave local governments some limited opportunity to exclude undesirable outsiders from voucher auctions. Thanks to these concessions, local governments in most cases did not resist privatisation, although many would have preferred cash to voucher payments.

Enterprise workers received the most generous concessions of any privatisation in the world. They get either 25 per cent of the firm for free plus 10 per cent at below book, or 51 per cent at still very low price of 1.7 times book. Moreover, they get to choose the privatisation option for the firm in a vote. With the benefit of hindsight, workers benefits in the Russian privatisation appear very high, and may have adverse consequences for governance (see below). It is important to realise, however, that at the time the programme was proposed, the groups in the Parliament demanding 100 per cent worker ownership appeared to present the greatest threat to privatisation. It is only by making a coalition with those groups by offering high worker ownership that the reformers succeeded in defeating the managerial lobbies that opposed privatisation.

Concessions to the managers do not appear large on the surface, but in truth they are simply enormous. Direct ownership stakes of managers are only 5 per cent in variant 1 (perhaps more in variant 2), although in many cases managers buy more cheap shares in voucher auctions or in the aftermarket from the employees (more on this below). A much more important concession to the managers is that the privatisation programme does not impose large shareholders on the firm, so managerial independence in Russia at least *ex ante* is much greater than elsewhere in Eastern Europe. Recall that in Czechoslovakia firms got core investors as part of privatisation, and in Poland they are expected to get mutual funds as blockholders. The fact that forced introduction of major shareholders did not occur in Russia is a major concession to managers, reflecting their Parliamentary influence as well as their *de facto* control of enterprises. Insistence on core investors would have raised strong managerial opposition and made privatisation impossible, especially since privatisation in Russia is still effectively discretionary.

The Russian privatisation failed to address the wishes of the central bureaucracy, and the result has been that the bureaucracy has continued to fight privatisation every step of the way. As we mentioned, bribing the bureaucracy is one of the greatest challenges of economic reform.

In short, the Russian privatisation programme represents a political compromise reflecting the existing property rights and political influences in the country. The real question is whether privatisation is nonetheless likely to lead to restructuring. We turn to this question next.

IV. The progress of Russian privatisation

This section documents the pace of Russian privatisation and also discusses evidence on market value of assets sold in voucher auctions.

A. *Corporatisation*

Table 1 presents the results on corporatisation. By 31 December 1993 out of about 5 000 large enterprises slated for mandatory privatisation, 2 670 actually registered as joint-stock companies. In addition, 7 812 enterprises corporatised on a voluntary basis. The apparent enthusiasm for corporatisation among many medium-sized enterprises suggests that workers and managers concluded that corporatisation gives them more benefits and/or better opportunities to keep control over the enterprise as compared to small-scale privatisation[15]. Nine hundred and eighty-one joint-stock companies were formed on the basis of subdivisions of state enterprises that previously did not have the status of a juridical person. Overall, by 31 December 1993, 11 463 joint-stock companies were registered.

Table 1. **Corporatisation results by 31 December 1993**

	Mandatory	Voluntary	Subdivisions	Total
JSC registered	2 670	7 812	981	11 463
Var 1	34%	21%	14%	23%
Var 2	65%	77%	84%	75%
Var 3	1%	2%	2%	2%

In 75 per cent of the enterprises, workers chose variant 2 that gives them and the managers voting control, whereas in 23 per cent, they chose variant 1. In most cases, the ostensible reason for choosing variant 2 is that otherwise control might revert to the outsiders. Variant 1 is chosen in cases where the enterprise is too capital intensive for workers and their families to afford variant 2, or when the relationship between workers and managers is sufficiently tense that the managers fear giving workers voting shares. Interestingly, variant 3 is hardly ever chosen, even though it gives the largest ownership stake to the managers.

B.   Voucher distribution and use

Between October 1992 and January 1993, 150 million Russians could pick up their vouchers at their local Savings Banks. The fee for the voucher was only 25 roubles (5 cents at the prevailing exchange rate). Because, as we explained, privatisation in Russia was much more populist than privatisation in Czechoslovakia, the idea of charging a reasonable participation fee (US$35 in Czechoslovakia) to eliminate marginally interested citizens was rejected. By the end of January 1993 almost 97 per cent of vouchers were distributed.

Shortly after its introduction, the voucher became the first liquid security in Russia. It is actively traded on dozens of organised exchanges throughout the country. On the largest exchange in Moscow, the Russian Commodity and Raw Material Exchange, the volume of trade easily reaches 60-100 000 vouchers per day (US$600 000 - US$1 000 000 at prevailing prices). Apparently, investors willing to participate in voucher auctions do not experience major problems in assembling large blocks of vouchers.

Wide swings in the market price of the voucher, as exhibited in Figure 1, seem to be easily attributable to political developments in Russia[16]. The voucher rose briefly in the second half of November and early December 1992 anticipating demand for vouchers from investors in the upcoming closed subscriptions and voucher auctions. The fall of the Gaidar government in mid-December led to a collapse in the voucher market. In January through April 1993, the large amount of voucher auctions and closed subscriptions notwithstanding, the rouble voucher price stagnated, quickly falling in dollar terms. The voucher price doubled in just a few weeks shortly after President Yeltsin's victory in the referendum on 25 April 1993 that revealed strong public support for the economic reform. After the October 1993 coup in Moscow the price of the voucher almost tripled.

C.   The pace of voucher auctions

Tables 2 and 3 present some basic statistics on the pace of voucher auctions in Russia[17]. Voucher auctions began in December 1992, when 18 firms were sold in eight regions. By April, the pace of sales reached 613 enterprises in 58 regions. In June, sales reached almost 900 firms, which seems to be a sustainable monthly rate. Altogether, 8 292 firms have been privatised in voucher auctions by the end of 1993.

One way to look at the pace of sales is by focusing at the number of employees who work in privatised companies (See Table 3). By the end of 1994, almost 8.8 million employees worked in firms privatised in voucher auctions, which represents roughly 45 per cent of the manufacturing labour force in Russia. In June through December the privatisation rate averaged 900 000 employees per month, or about 4.5 per cent of industrial employment. If this rate continues to 1 July 1994, when vouchers are set to expire, another 5.4 million Russian industrial workers will end up in the private sector, so that the total will amount to over 70 per cent of manufacturing employment. This is rather fast for 18 months of mass privatisation in a country where no other reform has worked.

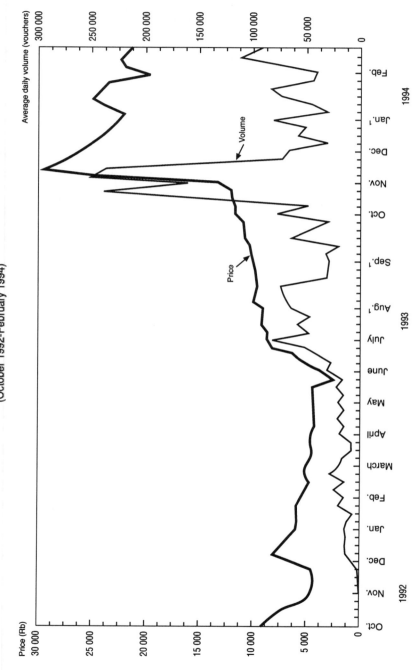

Figure 1. **Voucher weekly price and volume traded at RTSB**
(October 1992-February 1994)

1. Some months contain more than weekly observation.
Source: Russian Privatisation Center.

166

Table 2. Voucher auctions (December 1992 - December 1993)

	Dec.	Jan.	Feb.	Mar.	April	May	June	July	Aug.	Sept.	Oct.	Nov.	Dec.	Total
Number of enterprises sold	18	107	194	439	613	581	896	910	896	776	961	887	1 014	8 292
Number of employees (000)	44	189	192	548	844	598	811	753	924	833	923	1 040	1 096	8 797
Weighted average (% of charter capital sold)	16.9	11.6	22.9	23.5	23.4	19.3	20.9	23.2	20.6	20.3	18.6	18.3	19.4	20.3
Vouchers accepted (000)	158	229	544	2 268	4 217	3 745	4 440	6 664	4 279	4 847	4 672	2 874	4 541	43 478
Weighted average auction rate (1 000 rouble shares per voucher)	3.2	3.1	2.7	2.3	1.7	1.2	1.8	1.2	1.6	1.5	1.8	3.0	2.2	1.8

Table 3. Voucher auctions by size of the enterprise

Size class	Number of enterprises	Percentage of enterprises	Number of employees (millions)	Percentage of employees	Number of employees in the Russian industry (millions)	Percentage of employees in the Russian industry	Percentage privatised
<500	5 257	63.4	1.1	12.8	3.02	15.0	37.0
501-1 000	1 236	14.9	0.9	10.6	2.35	11.7	40.0
1 001-5 000	1 484	17.9	3.2	36.8	7.28	36.2	45.0
5 001-10 000	216	2.6	1.5	17.4	3.14	15.6	49.0
>10 001	99	1.2	2.0	22.5	4.32	21.5	46.0
Total	**8 292**	**100.0**	**8.8**	**100.0**	**2.11**	**100.0**	**44.0**

An average firm that goes through a voucher auction has about 1 100 employees and roughly 50 million roubles of charter capital. It sells about 21 per cent of its shares (11 million roubles of charter capital) in the auction in exchange for about 5 400 vouchers. In terms of numbers, medium-sized firms dominate: 78 per cent of firms privatised trough voucher auctions have less than 1 000 employees. However, large firms account for a very large share of privatised assets and employment. Firms with more than 1 000 employees account for 78 per cent of employment and 83 per cent of assets of enterprises privatised through voucher auctions. As Table 3 suggests, large firms on average privatise somewhat faster than medium and small firms.

D. Asset values

One of the most interesting aspects of voucher auctions is the prices at which assets sell. Table 2 shows that the number of shares with a book value of 1 000 roubles that a voucher with a face value of 10 000 roubles bought started out at around 3 at the turn of the year, and fell toward around 1.2 in May before recovering to 1.5 - 3.0 range towards the end of the year. Recall that the book value of shares is defined as of January 1992, and therefore is not adjusted for inflation. Moreover, the book value uses the depreciated value of capital stock, which is often artificially low. Russian companies in late spring were therefore selling at about 6 times the January 1992 book value of shares. The price level from January 1992 to May 1993 increased almost 70 fold.

A rough computation suggests what these numbers imply. Suppose that enterprises that were privatised by the end of 1993 are representative of the Russian industry. These enterprises constitute about 45 per cent of the Russian industry, and approximately 20 per cent of the value of these enterprises have been sold in voucher auctions. That is a total of 9 per cent of all equity was sold through June 1993. As Table 2 indicates, about 45 million vouchers were accepted for this equity. The dollar price per voucher fluctuated widely over the year with the average being at about US$10. Thus the estimate of the dollar value of accepted vouchers is US$450 million. That puts the total value of the Russian industry at about US$5 billion. It is possible to make these calculations differently, and to come up with numbers as high as US$10 billion. The point, however, is inescapable: the whole Russian industry is valued in voucher auctions at something like the value of a large Fortune 500 company.

Perhaps an even more dramatic way to look at the numbers is to examine the prices in some focal transactions. Tables 4a and b present the results of voucher auctions, and the implied dollar values of companies in the ten largest by employment and ten most valuable transactions. We see from this table that the market value of ZIL, the truck and limousine maker with 100 000 employees, a ready market for as much of its product as it can make, and a large chunk of Moscow real estate, is about US$16 million. The market values of Uralmash and

Permsky Motors, two household names in Russian manufacturing, are US$4 and US$6 million respectively. The Caterpillar and General Electric of Russian manufacturing thus appear to be virtually worthless.

Table 4*a*. **Ten largest enterprises sold in voucher auctions in descending order of employment (1 July 1993)**

Employees	Name of enterprise	Industry	Month of sale	Implied US$ value of enterprise
103 000	ZIL	Truck manufacturing	April	15 857 826
44 817	Preobrazhenskaya	Fishing	April	118 477
42 928	Rostselmash	Automobile manufacturing	April	771 477
35 000	Permsky Motors	Engine manufacturing	March	6 276 015
34 041	Uralmash	Machine production	April	3 908 214
32 769	Zapadno-Sibirsky Metallurgical Plant	Metal production	March	3 890 820
27 351	Ribinsky Motors	Aircraft engines	March	988 241
26 417	Volgograd Tractor Factory	Tractor manufacturing	March	570 747
24 198	Pervouralsky Novotrubny Factory	Metal production	April	2 548 514
17 942	Dalnevostochnoi Morskoi Parochodstvo	Shipping	April	

The list of most valuable companies contains some new names. Next to ZIL, the most valuable company is hotel Minsk in the centre of Moscow (with 154 employees), whose management made a futile attempt to keep the price of shares low by disguising the name of the company (presumably they wanted to buy more shares themselves). A chocolate factory with 1 500 employees is worth 50 per cent more than Uralmash with 34 000. Some businesses do have value, although the overall level of prices is quite low.

Table 4*b*. Ten largest enterprises sold in voucher auctions in descending order of implied US$ value (1 July 1993)

Implied US$ value of enterprise	Name of enterprise	Industry	Month of sale	Employees
15 857 826	ZIL	Truck manufacturing	April	103 000
8 412 378	Na Tverskoi	Hotels	May	154
6 716 613	Sayan Aluminum Plant	Aluminum production	Dec.	8 056
6 276 015	Permsky Motors	Engine manufacturing	March	35 000
5 724 558	Russian Chocolate Factory	Chocolate production	January	1 490
3 908 214	Uralmash	Machine production	April	34 041
3 890 820	Zapadno-Sibirsky Metallurgical Plant	Metal production	March	32 769
3 692 419	Vladimir Tractor Factory	Tractor manufacturing	March	16 500
3 597 752	Bratsky Aluminum Factory	Aluminum production	May	10 373
3 343 053	Koksokhim	Chemical production	May	4 940

One way to calibrate how low the prices of manufacturing companies are is to note that US manufacturing companies have market value of about US$100 000 per employee. Russian manufacturing companies, in contrast have market value of about US$100 per employee. The difference is 1 000 fold!

171

Indeed, a value of US$15 billion for an automobile company equivalent of Zil, or of US$4 billion for Caterpillar is not implausible.

What might explain such a low price level of Russian assets? The first hypothesis is that most of these firms are really worthless, since they have a very outdated capital stock. We submit, however, that this hypothesis goes only part of the way in explaining the pricing. Consider the following rough calculation. At the PPP value of the dollar, Russian manufacturing wages average about US$200 per month, which is about one tenth of western manufacturing wages. In fact, estimates of the Russian standard of living as about one-tenth the western standard are suggested by more detailed calculations. If the value of the Russian companies were in the same proportion to wages as it is in the West, then these companies should be worth about one-tenth of what their western counterparts are worth. On this calculation, the value ratio of 1 000 still seems implausible.

The low quality of Russian assets thus fails to explain their low market value by a factor of 100. Additional explanations are needed. One line of argument is that private wealth in Russia is limited, and hence the low value of assets are explained by this low value of private wealth, which translates into the low value of the voucher. This theory is implausible once it is realised that there was perhaps US$15 to US$20 billion of capital flight from Russia in 1992 and 1993. Moreover, foreigners can participate freely in voucher auctions, which again raises the available pool of capital. Why wouldn't a foreign investor buy 20 per cent of ZIL for US$3 million, when foreigners are paying billions for automobile and truck companies in Eastern Europe? The capital shortage story cannot plausibly explain the low valuation.

The plausible explanations fall under the general category of expropriation of shareholders by stakeholders. That is, while assets themselves have some value, the part of the return to these assets that is expected to accrue to outside shareholders after the stakeholders are done, is very small.

Three important types of stakeholders take a cut. The first is employees. As one very progressive Russian manager has put it, the goal of his privatised company is to raise its efficiency and make profits so that it can increase wages. Many Russian firms continue to pay for kindergartens, hospitals, schools and other services for their workers. There is little doubt that, particularly with the high levels of employee ownership that are obtaining in Russian companies, some of the profits will continue to be spent on wages and benefits to the workers. One sobering fact in this regard is that privatisation through sales of East German firms brought Treuhandanstalt a net negative revenue of US$200 billion. In part, this reflects the excessive wages that East German companies had to pay their workers after privatisation. Even so, the dramatic losses reflect the extraordinary value of workers claims even in a country like Germany, where, unlike in Russia, workers are not majority owners of firms.

The second important stakeholder is the managers, who are likely to expropriate shareholder wealth through asset sales to their own privately held businesses and other forms of dilution. This theft by managers is probably the principal reason for the remarkably high capital flight from Russia. Shareholder rights in Russia are not protected (more on this below), and few companies expect to pay dividends in the near future, leaving more for managers to take.

The last stakeholder responsible for reducing firm value to outside shareholders is the government, which expropriates them through taxes, regulations, restrictions on product mix and lay-offs, custom duties and many other interventions including potential nationalisation. The fear of government expropriation is often referred to as "political instability" and surely explains some of the low value to outside shareholders. Of course, expropriation of shareholders by the government is nothing other than continued politicisation of now privatised firms. Evidently, the Russian market estimates that such politicisation is likely to continue so that, between them, the three types of stakeholders will grab about 99 per cent of shareholder wealth.

In sum, voucher auctions have been a great success and have helped move a substantial part of the Russian industry into the private sector, even though the implied asset values have been very low. The next question is whether rapid privatisation is likely to lead to restructuring.

V. Product market competition[18]

In section II, we argued that privatisation is only one of several steps needed to depolitize Russian firms. In the next three sections, we discuss the other steps, beginning with product market competition. As we argued above, product market competition is extremely important in raising the cost to politicians of influencing firms. For this reason, competition strategy, including facilitation of entry and openness to imports, has been a critical reform strategy in Poland and Czechoslovakia. Unlike these countries, Russia has not had much success with competition as a depolitization strategy both because it started out with an extremely non-competitive economy and because policies failed to foster competition.

Russia inherited from central planning a highly uncompetitive economy. To facilitate central control, most industries were highly concentrated[19]. Import penetration in most sectors has been extremely low, and trade collapsed with the collapse of COMECON. Finally, central planners have established very rigid supply chains, and built a transportation and storage system to match these rigid supply chains. As a result, most firms in Russia, even if they were not unique producers of particular goods, bought their inputs from specifically designated suppliers only and sold their outputs to specifically designated customers only. No competition worked or could easily begin to work in most goods markets.

Competition policy could of course address these problems. Unfortunately, competition policy in Russia has done the reverse. Moscow bureaucrats -- whose personal financial concerns have not been allayed by privatisation -- have plotted to resurrect their ministries in the form of trade associations and financial-industrial groups, so as to facilitate both collusion and subsidised finance from the Central Bank. To this end, they have tried to consolidate rather than break up firms. Nor is there much talk about opening up foreign trade and stimulating competition in this way: existing firms rarely fail to get protection. Even at the local level, where competition could probably be the single most reliable strategy of depolitization, politicians have restricted it. Many local governments have already taken actions to protect incumbent firms from entry through licensing and other anti-competitive strategies. Finally, privatisation of transport, which may be the single most effective pro-competition strategy, has been slow in most regions.

Moreover, competition is most effective when companies that lose money actually go bankrupt. The Russian bankruptcy law, written under close supervision of the managerial lobby, allows for effectively permanent "rehabilitation" of bankrupt companies under existing management. In part as a response to this law, and in part as consequence of a long history of borrowing from the government, Russian companies rarely repay their debts. As long as debts and negative cash flows do not result in hardships for the management, but simply lead to help from the government, depolitization will remain an elusive goal.

This leaves us with somewhat pessimistic view of the role of product market competition in depolitizing Russian firms in the near future despite the fact that free trade, free entry and other competition promoting policies have been essential in depolitizing firms in Eastern Europe. While we argue below that other depolitization strategies have worked better in Russia, competition policy remains a gaping hole in the reforms.

VI. Corporate governance through equity ownership

In discussing equity governance, we will distinguish between management and outside shareholder ownership. As we argued in section II, management ownership works as a governance device when managers refuse to cater to the preferences of the politicians. Ideally, managers must have high ownership stakes, yet at the same time not be completely entrenched, so that outside investors can oust them when they fail to maximise profits. To begin, we briefly discuss the evolution of management ownership in Russia.

Systematic data on management and other shareholder ownership in Russia do not exist. Two researchers working at GKI, Joseph Blasi and Katarina Pistor, have conducted small surveys of firms that ask managers about the ownership structure of their firms. The surveys ask not just about the results of voucher auctions, but about the actual ownership structure that emerges after some trading of shares. Tables 5 and 6 present the preliminary results of the two surveys that together cover 55 firms. The data in these surveys are self-reported, and hence in some cases may be incorrect.

Nonetheless, the results present a very clear picture. In the Blasi sample (Table 5) managers and workers together end up owning an average of 70 per cent of the company. Of that, about 17 per cent on average is owned by the management team, of which about 7 per cent on average (and less than 3 per cent if we exclude one company) is owned by the CEO. The ownership of the additional shares is divided between outsiders and the Property Fund (the government), with the outsiders owning the average of 14 per cent and the Property Fund owning the average of 16 per cent. Note that in many cases a good chunk of the shares of the Property Fund is spoken for. In many companies, 10 per cent of the Property Fund shares are going to be transferred to the ESOP, and in a few cases, such as ZIL, an investment tender is planned. Thus the 70 per cent figure probably underestimates insider ownership.

Pistor's sample (Table 6) covers larger firms than Blasi's but also oversamples a few specialised regions. For example, she has six firms (observations 19-24) from the Ivanovo textile regions which had peculiar variant 1 privatisations with virtually no outside investors. Nonetheless, Pistor's results are surprisingly similar to Blasi's. On average, management and workers in her sample together own about 61 per cent of the equity. Her data do not allow us to divide this between managers and workers. Outsides on average own about 19 per cent, as does the Property Fund. Pistor's sample appears to have fewer completed ESOP transactions, so Property Fund ownership is likely to fall. Pistor's sample thus confirms the overwhelming insider ownership of Russian firms.

The evidence suggests that management teams end up owning considerably more than they get in the closed subscription. They usually get 5 to 10 per cent of the shares of their companies from the combination of the subsidised distribution and shares they get through the ESOPs. In Blasi's data, however, they end up with 17 per cent on average even though ESOPs have not yet been distributed in most companies. Managers usually try to enhance their ownership of shares by buying more in the voucher auctions as well as buying shares from workers. Sometimes the managers get loans from the company to supplement their stakes. In the end, managers end up with much higher ownership than they got in the closed subscription.

High as the managerial ownership of cash flows is, it probably underestimates their degree of control. Indeed, managers in most companies aggressively consolidated their control beyond that warranted by their ownership of shares by getting workers' voting support either informally or through formal "trust" arrangements. In several "takeover" situations, managers only succeeded in keeping their jobs because of worker support. In many companies, managers actually encourage workers to buy more shares to consolidate their own control.

This emerging picture of workers as allies of the managers, who not only fail to provide any monitoring of the managers, but actually contribute to their entrenchment, is quite unique in Russia. In Poland and elsewhere in Eastern Europe, workers collectives often counterbalance managers' control -- though not necessarily with the best results for restructuring. In Russia, in contrast, workers collectives appear to be passive, although of course this passivity might be a reciprocation for highly accommodating managerial practices. Thus, while worker passivity allayed the fears of many who worried about worker control, the price managers pay for worker support may well be the slowdown of restructuring. The greatest fear is that, when credit constraints begin to tighten, workers will become natural allies of politicians in preventing restructuring, and thus will disrupt depolitization of firms.

In sum, Russian managers are emerging from privatisation with often quite substantial ownership of cash flows. They are also emerging with a tremendous amount of control, particularly because of their influence over the workers' collectives. In smaller companies, this ownership structure may well be efficient because it provides managers with a strong incentive to maximise profits (as long as they do not get captured by the workers' collective). In the largest companies, however, some external checks on the managers are needed to prevent their entrenchment and capture by politicians.

Table 5 provides some data on large shareholders from the Blasi sample. On average, about 14 per cent of the shares is owned by outside investors. Of that, about 9.5 per cent is owned by blockholders whom managers were willing to identify to the interviewer. Thus, in this sample, blockholders acquire almost two-thirds of the shares that outsiders get in the voucher auctions (recall that managers and workers also participate actively). Pistor's data in Table 6 presents a similar picture. Of the 19 per cent of shares owned by outsiders in her companies, about 10.6 per cent on average is owned by blockholders. In Pistor's sample, investment tenders have been completed more frequently than in Blasi's, and so the blockholders have gotten their shares through those as well as through voucher auctions.

Evidence from the largest companies, where blockholders are particularly important for restructuring, suggests an even greater presence. In ZIL, the largest Russian enterprise privatised so far, out of the 30 per cent of shares offered in a voucher auction, 28 per cent were bought by seven large investors. Moreover, all of these investors appear to have business ties, so ZIL might end up with a 25-30 per cent shareholder. A private company holds an 18 per cent stake in Uralmash, another industrial giant. A Russian Harvard Business School graduate bought a 6 per cent stake and is now becoming the CEO of Vladimir Tractor

Table 5. **Workers, management and outsider ownership in the Blasi sample of privatised firms**

| Company | Employment | Management and workers | | | | Outsiders | | Property Fund | Option* |
| | | Workers | Management | | Total | Block-holders | Total | | |
			CEO	Total					
Zil	103 000	35	-	5	40	20	35	25	1
Machine tools	1 500	-	-	-	60	0	10	30	2
Radio	5 000	55	0	5	60	0	20	20	1
Trucking	-	90	1	3	93	4	7	0	1
Chalk	120	55	-	5	60	9	9	31	1
Trucking	80	-	-	-	80	0	0	20	lease
Steel	181	89	8	11	100	0	0	0	2
Steel	342	29	1.5	35	64	23	26	10	2
Metal	350	66	10	18	84	1.4	16	0	2
Furniture	1 200	46	10	5	51	-	-	-	2

* One of the three privatisation options (variants) available in the Russian privatisation law (See text).

Source: Blasi Sample.

Table 5. **Workers, management and outsider ownership in the Blasi sample of privatised firms** (cont'd.)

Company	Employment	Management and workers				Outsiders		Property Fund	Option*
		Workers	Management		Total	Block-holders	Total		
			CEO	Total					
Women's wear	2 300	90	0	0	90	0	0	10	1
Machine tools	3 500	33	small	18	51	17.5	19	30	2
Pasta	320	57	small	4	61	-	18	20	2
Wheat	2 000	28	2.5	45	73	1	9	18	2
Department store	1 100	10	-	30	40	28.4	40	20	1
Trucking	526	45	-	30	75	1	3	22	1
Trucking	1 300	58	3	5	63	1	7	30	2
Mean	**6 897.17**	**52.82**	**9.56**	**16.71**	**69.58**	**6.55**	**13.44**	**15.89**	-

Table 6. Workers, management and outsider ownership in the Pistor sample of privatised firms

Company	Employment	Managers and workers		Outsiders		Property Fund	Option*
		Management	Workers	Blockholders	Others		
1	1 161	18	65	2	15	0	2
2	479	0	0	100	0	0	2
3	479	25	26	24	0	20	2
4	915	-	-	0	30	0	2
5	772	-	-	3	24	20	2
6	568	10	52	12	6	20	2
7	812	-	-	19	9	0	2
8	-	15	47	16	2	20	2
9	>5 000	-	-	38	11	0	2
10	300	56		36	8	0	2
11	450	56		18	6	20	2
12	3 500	5	14	0	0	59	1
13	2 869	15	36	20	11	18	2
14	27 351	48		0	15	37	2
15	1 800	80		9	0	11	2
16	7 401	70		5	0	25	2
17	800	38	42	0	0	20	2
18	-	78		0	2	20	2
19	2 766	59		20	1	20	1
20	3 358	80		0	0	20	1
21	3 993	5	75	0	0	20	1
22	5 026	-	70	0	0	25	1
23	3 787	75		0	0	25	1
24	4 600	-	70	0	0	25	1
25	3 500	51		4	25	20	2
26	5 456	63		10	17	20	2
27	22 500	68		8	3	20	2
28	430	11	49	20	0	20	2
29	3 814	54		0	26	20	2
30	1 091	80		0	0	20	2
31	34 041	5	10	18	11	31	1
32	7 392	64		0	0	26	1
33	10 000	5	20	3	15	32	1
34	3 839	61		4	15	20	2
35	24 198	56		4	20	20	2
36	1 788	6	48	8	18	20	2
Average	-	61.4		19		19.3	-

*   One of the three privatisation options (variants) available in the Russian privatisation law (See text).

Source: Pistor sample.

Works, his former employer. First Voucher Investment Fund bought large stakes and has appointed Chairman of the Board in Krasny Octyabr, a famous chocolate factory in Moscow. A similar picture emerges in other well known privatisations.

This evidence underscores the importance of voucher tradability for the formation of blockholdings in Russia. Accumulating blocks of vouchers, and then bidding them in a voucher auction is the principal strategy by which potential large investors can get their blocks. Without voucher tradability, the only strategies for accumulating large blocks would be to start an investment fund, which some large blockholders are clearly doing, or to buy shares in the aftermarket, which is very difficult. The creation of a liquid market for vouchers has enabled the Russian privatisation to do what for political reasons it could not accomplish directly: to create core investors for many major companies.

Who are these large blockholders in Russia? They appear to be of three types. The first is private voucher investment funds which were created following the Czech model. These funds collect vouchers from the population in exchange for their own shares, and then invest them through voucher auctions. GKI evidence indicates that about 650 funds have been formed. They have over 30 million shareholders, and have collected about 50 million vouchers, or one-third of the total. The largest funds are located in Moscow: some of they claim to have over 3 million shareholders. While the Russian funds are more restrained than the Czech funds were in promising high returns, they surpass them in other forms of mismanagement -- some funds evidently spending some of their principal on expenses.

What do the funds do with the vouchers? Apparently, about 60 per cent of the vouchers have been invested in privatising companies. But funds are also actively speculating in vouchers, buying and selling them across Russia in an effort to take advantage of price differences across space and time. Many Russian funds appear disinterested in corporate governance. But some funds, led by First Voucher Fund and Alpha Capital (the two largest funds), have acquired large stakes in several companies and have actively challenged the management. This corporate governance role of investment funds is only likely to increase.

The second type of large investor is wealthy individuals and private firms, that made their fortunes in the last few years in trade and other commercial activities. These investors often have the financial and perhaps even the physical muscle to stand up to the managers. While managers try to discourage these investors, in some cases, their presence is clear: these investors, for example, got the largest share of ZIL and Uralmash, and Vladimir Tractor Works.

The third category of large investors is foreigners. To them, prices that obtain in voucher auctions present a major attraction. At the same time, they do not usually openly challenge the managers, for fear of a political reaction. Indeed, they usually acquire their stakes through Russian intermediaries. Foreign investors are still insignificant relative to other large shareholders, but they might come to play an important role in restructuring.

Anecdotal evidence suggests that large shareholders often try to use their votes to change company policies (though less often to change management). Alpha Capital, for example, has started campaigns to get firms it invested in to pay dividends. Other large investors want firms to sell some of their land holdings. In some cases, such as Vladimir Tractor Works, an outside investor offered his candidacy to run the company, but lost to the incumbent manager.

So far, corporate managers have resisted these challenges fiercely and rather successfully. They threaten the workers with dismissals if they do not support the incumbent, and appear to be getting the critical worker support. But managers also physically threaten challengers at shareholder meetings, rig shareholder votes, illegally change corporate charters (from one share one vote to one shareholder one vote, or something like that), refuse to record share trades in corporate share registers, etc. Most of these activities are not reported in the press. The current situation is best described as a stalemate: large outside shareholders are clearly posing a challenge to the existing management but management in turn, often with the support of the workers, has managed to repel most threats. The market for corporate control in Russia is very lively; it remains to be seen whether it is effective enough to get restructuring going.

The key question is whether the large shareholders will be able to play their role without being stopped by the political process. Many managers are appealing to the local governments (and to the Central government) to restrain large investors. The management of Bolshevik has unsuccessfully lobbied GKI to force Alpha Capital, their large investor, to sell its shares. The government of Primorsky Krai (the South Eastern seacoast region of Russia) has temporarily stopped privatisation after a couple of enterprise managers were sacked in a shareholder vote. And perhaps in the most extraordinary action so far, the head of ZIL, the ubiquitous truck maker, has appealed to President Yeltsin to keep the government's control of the company through the "golden share", thus eliminating the controlling influence of the outside investors.

VII. Summary

The transition from political to private governance is clearly very painful. Politicians do not give up their control over enterprises very easily. They have resisted privatisation from the start, and they are still trying to bring firms under the control of industry associations and financial industrial groups. Moreover, the residual equity stakes that remain in the hands of Property Funds may well be used in the future to reassert political control over enterprises.

As political governance recedes, it is replaced to a significant extent by managerial control. Such control is better than control by politicians, since managers with significant ownership stakes have more interest in value maximisation and restructuring. Nonetheless, in many cases managerial ownership needs to be supplemented by large outsider ownership to put pressure on the managers (and workers collectives) to restructure. As of now, large outside shareholders face tremendous resistance from both managers and politicians in exercising their control rights. Still, they remain the most effective source of external governance in Russia. In the future, their role will increase when they become a source of capital as well as oversight.

VIII. Capital

Effective restructuring is thwarted by political allocation of capital. When politicians lavish capital on some firms that they want to have high output and employment, these firms have no incentive to restructure, even if they have made headway in other dimensions of depolitization. Moreover, firms that do not get capital as part of the political allocation can achieve only limited restructuring, since substantial restructuring usually requires capital. In this section we show that capital allocation in Russia now is completely politicised, and suggest some strategies for improving this dismal situation.

A.   *Current capital allocation*

Most capital of Russian enterprises still comes from the state, which includes both subsidies from the budget and directed credits from the Central Bank. In 1992 total subsidies from the budget accounted for 21.6 per cent of GDP[20]. Most of these subsidies went to enterprises, and included import subsidies, energy subsidies, and subsidies for making interest payments on already subsidised credits. Directed credits from the Central Bank to enterprises added up to an additional 21 per cent of GDP. An expansion of credits became very rapid in the beginning of 1993, but slowed down by the middle of 1993[21].

The allocation of credits and subsidies is highly politicised, in terms of who benefits and how much. Agriculture and energy are the main beneficiaries of the government's and Central Bank's policies, as are very large manufacturing firms. Firms lucky to get credits through the Central Bank usually get them at negative real interest rates. In addition, the government often subsidises the interest payments to the Central Bank made by the enterprises from the budget. Finally, enterprises often do not repay the loans, except from proceeds from the new loans. Thus the combination of subsidies and loans reallocates massive resources to some sectors of the economy. It is not surprising, in this regard, that Russia has made no progress in privatising agriculture: what farmer would take the fat of the land over that of the Central Bank?

In its allocation of credit, the Central Bank does not discriminate between state-owned and privatised firms. All firms deemed worthy of credits get them[22]. This of course does not bode well for the effectiveness of privatisation in getting restructuring going.

The credits of the Central Bank are channelled through commercial banks. Many of them are descendants of former Soviet sectoral banks, in which case they simply allocate Central Bank credits to enterprises in their respective sectors. Such is the situation in Agriculture and Construction, for example. In addition, some enterprises have themselves formed commercial banks, that take credits from the Central Bank and then pass it through to the enterprises that founded them, their suppliers and customers. Commercial banks thus do not make credit allocation any less political, or any more conducive to restructuring.

While some selected sectors are getting credits, it appears that smaller firms in Russia have been substantially cut off from the public subsidies and credits. For example, the majority of firms in Blasi's sample did not report getting subsidies or subsidised credits from commercial banks, and complained about not having capital to restructure. The Central Bank explicitly denies credits to new firms on the grounds that lending to them is unsafe. The question is: can these firms find capital elsewhere if they want to restructure?

It appears that private capital markets do not meet this need. Some privatised firms are planning a public equity issue in 1994, although it is not entirely clear how much they can raise without promising investors dividends, restructuring, or at least a governance role. Some commercial banks are providing credit from their own resources, but that situation usually occurs only when there are non-commercial reasons for making loans or when debt contracts can be enforced by physical force. This is not surprising: lending as a practice does not make sense without a bankruptcy procedure that gives creditors access to the borrower's assets, but such a procedure does not exist in Russia. Without bankruptcy, debt contracts cannot really work. Rapid inflation is an additional factor that undermines long-term lending by banks of their own funds. Finally, many privatised, and even state, firms are forming joint ventures with private domestic and foreign investors, which gives them access to some capital and know-how[23]. Despite the success of joint ventures, they remain a trivial part of the Russian capital market. Political risk remains great and the exchange rate, tax, and bribe policies toward foreign investors are predatory. At least in the near future, then, private markets will not address the capital needs of restructuring Russian enterprises.

In sum, capital allocation in Russia is the main roadblock to restructuring. The Central Bank lending policies are highly politicised, whereas the rapid inflation undermines whatever private capital allocation might be emerging. Firms not benefitting from the Central Bank credits face a harder budget constraint and are beginning to restructure. However, substantial restructuring of these firms requires capital, which is not forthcoming from the commercial banks until inflation subsides. Stabilisation will obviously improve this situation greatly. In the meantime, the question of how to deliver capital to the private firms must be addressed.

B. Privatisation and stabilisation

An essential step to rationalising capital allocation in Russia is to control aggregate credits and subsidies, and thus to stabilise the rouble. Indeed, most western attention and aid have been focused on stabilisation. This attention raises the question of the relationship between privatisation and stabilisation. Some have argued that privatisation disrupts the existing economic structure, and so monetary stabilisation should take the first priority. Once the economy stabilises, privatisation and restructuring can take place. This position is best described as "stabilising socialism". An alternative position argues that privatisation should take the first precedence. Once the firms are private, stabilisation can work.

Both of these views are wrong. The main expense of the Russian government, and hence the main reason for money creation, is cheap credits to state industry and agriculture. As long as firms remain public, the basic demand for subsidies, and hence money creation and inflation will not go away. Foreign aid can temporarily plug the hole by replacing money creation with dollars in subsidies to state firms. But such stabilisation is only temporary. As long as the basic demand for politically driven credit remains, stabilisation cannot succeed without privatisation.

For a similar reason, privatisation cannot lead to restructuring if the government continues to print money and subsidise selected firms and sectors. Privatisation of agriculture in Russia has been subverted by the government's credit policies. Politicisation of capital allocation is made possible precisely by the ability of the government to print money. When this ability is limited, subsidising selected firms as long as they do not restructure will prove much costlier. This will allow private governance and capital supply mechanisms to begin to play a role, and hence create a hope of restructuring.

Privatisation and stabilisation policies are thus complementary. Privatisation allows the demand for state credits to fall, which in turn makes stabilisation possible. Stabilisation cripples the political credit mechanism, and in this way stimulates restructuring.

This section outlined the problems with political capital allocation in Russia, and showed how stabilisation can improve the allocation process. Given the pivotal role of capital allocation in depolitization, progress on this front will determine the success of restructuring in Russia.

IX. Conclusion

This paper presented a view of privatisation as a step in the depolitization of firms -- the severance of public influence on private enterprises. In this regard, we focused on four aspects of change in the way firms are run and financed that could influence the success of depolitization: privatisation itself, competition policy, equity governance, and capital allocation. We then evaluated Russian privatisation from this vantage point.

In some respects, Russian privatisation has been a great success. Firms are being privatised at a breathtaking pace. Equity governance mechanisms are emerging very rapidly, and some of them, particularly large shareholder activism, are beginning to shake up Russian firms. The population approves of privatisation, and actively participates in the process.

At the same time, large scale privatisation in Russia is just over one year old. Most firms remain state-owned and many have been legally prohibited from privatising at all. Politicians are not giving up their control of firms easily and are actively resisting depolitization. Competition policy has not been effective. And most importantly, the allocation of capital is still completely dominated by the Central Bank, with commercial banks playing a relatively passive role in financial markets. Nor is it likely that a responsible monetary policy will emerge in Russia in the near future.

Last, and most important, the political landscape in Russia is treacherous. Old line politicians -- in the government, in the newly elected Parliament and in the regions -- by and large continue undermining all reform, including privatisation. The reformers have failed to either destroy or win over these politicians and, with the prominent exception of Anatoli Chubais, have left the government. Without question, the greatest success of Russian privatisation has been to limit the influence of the old line politicians. The fundamental open question about the success of privatisation and other reforms in Russia is how to finally overcome their resistance.

Notes

*   Based on a presentation made by one of the authors (Maxim Boycko, Russian Privatisation Center, Moscow) at the fifth meeting of the Advisory Group on Privatisation, Paris, 2-4 March 1994.

1.   This paper is largely based on a paper originally published in *The Brookings Papers on Economic Activity, 2: 1993,* p. 139 - 192. The authors are, respectively, from the Russian Privatisation Centre, Harvard University, and the University of Chicago. David Fischer and Florencio Lopez-de-Silanes provided excellent research assistance. Some of the results reported in this paper use surveys conducted by Joseph Blasi and Katarina Pistor for the GKI.

2.   Mueller (1989) and Vining and Boardman (1992) survey the evidence on the relative efficiency of public and private firms.

3.   Atkinson and Stiglitz (1981).

4.   Laffont and Tirole (1993), Dewatripont and Maskin (1991).

5.   A version of this theory is presented in Boycko, Shleifer and Vishny (1993).

6.   For a discussion of distinction between cash flow rights and control rights in the characterisation of ownership see Grossman and Hart (1986).

7.   See Pinto et al (1993) and Blanchard and Dambrowski (1993).

8.   Nellis (1988) presents evidence that incentive contracts of managers of public enterprises are often repealed when managers begin to restructure in earnest and thus violate the goals of the politicians. After their contracts are repealed, managers are told explicitly not to lay off workers, to continue building plants where politicians want them, etc. Nellis' examples illustrate the fragility of corporatisation as a depolitization strategy.

9.   A formal model is Hart (1983).

10.   Shleifer and Vishny (1986) stress the role of large shareholders in governing firms in the West. Frydman and Rapaczynski (1991), Lipton and Sachs (1990), and Blanchard et al (1990) present privatisation schemes that turn on

the pivotal role of large shareholders in delivering governance to privatising firms.

11. Shleifer and Vishny (1992) and Boycko and Shleifer (1993) present some ideas that went into the program. A legal description is Earle, Frydman and Rapaczynski (1993).

12. Sachs (1992) makes the arguments for corporatisation.

13. The case for the mutual fund scheme is presented by Lipton and Sachs (1990). In the context of Russia, Sachs (1992) suggests that the choice of a mass privatisation programme is not important as long as that programme is actually implemented.

14. A more detailed discussion of voucher schemes versus mutual fund schemes is contained in Frydman and Rapaczynski (1991) and Boycko, Shleifer and Vishny (1993b).

15. In small scale privatisation in Russia, the main benefit provided to workers is a cash payment equalling 30 per cent of the price obtained in the auction. If the workers' collective happens to win the auction, workers receive a 30 per cent discount.

16. The more puzzling fact that the voucher price is so **low** is discussed below.

17. Voucher auctions are the best documented part of the large scale privatisation in Russia. Little aggregate information exists about the actual pace of closed subscriptions, in which workers and managers buy shares according to the chosen variant. In the vast majority of cases a closed subscription precedes a voucher auction for a given company. Thus, before a voucher auction, some 40-51 per cent of shares of a typical company have already been sold.

18. Joscow et al (1994) provide a comprehensive discussion of competition policy in Russia. They also present a more optimistic view of the efficacy of competition.

19. IMF et al, "A Study of the Soviet Economy" presents some evidence on industrial concentration in the Russian economy. Brown, Ickes and Ryterman (1993) and Joscow et al (1994), however, argue that the Russian economy is no more concentrated than the US economy, and simply does not have as many small firms.

20. Data in this section comes from two World Bank studies: "Subsidies and Directed Credits to Enterprises in Russia: a Strategy for Reform," and "Russia: the Banking System in Transition."

21. Sachs (1993) discusses recent Russian monetary policies.

22. According to a senior official at the Central Bank, the question of public versus private ownership does not come up in the decisions to allocate

credits by the Credit Commission. The same official, when asked whether the Central Bank would always give credit to a firm on the verge of shutting down, said that "the Bank would never let things go that far, and would lend at a much earlier stage."

23. Foreign investors prefer joint ventures over outright ownership of Russian companies because they can focus on the part of the Russian company's business that actually has some promise, do not inherit the liabilities from the remaining businesses and allow the incumbent management to retain control over the rest of the firm. Moreover, the firm can usually still draw on state credits to support non-viable businesses.

References

AGHION, Philippe and Olivier J. BLANCHARD, "On the Speed of Transition in Central Europe", mimeo, 1993.

ATKINSON, Anthony B. and Joseph E. STIGLITZ (1980), *Lectures on Public Economics,* McGraw-Hill, London.

BLANCHARD, Olivier J. and Marek DABROWSKI, "The Progress of Restructuring in Poland", in *Post-Communist Reform: Pain and Progress,* MIT Press, 1993.

BLANCHARD, O. J., R. DORNBUSCH, P. R. KRUGMAN, R. LAYARD, and L. H. SUMMERS (1991), *Reform in Eastern Europe,* MIT Press, Cambridge, MA.

BOYCKO, Maxim and Andrei SHLEIFER, "The Politics of Russian Privatization", in *Post-Communist Reform: Pain and Progress,* MIT Press, 1993.

BOYCKO, Maxim, Andrei SHLEIFER, and Robert W. VISHNY, "Voucher Privatization", *Journal of Financial Economics,* forthcoming, 1993b.

BOYCKO, Maxim, Andrei SHLEIFER, and Robert W. VISHNY, "A Theory of Privatization", mimeo, 1993.

BROWN, Annette N., Barry ICKES and Randi RYTERMAN, "The Myth of Monopoly: A New View of Industrial Structure in Russia", mimeo, 1993.

DEWATRIPONT, Mathias and Eric MASKIN, "Credit and Efficiency in Centralized and Decentralized Economies", mimeo, 1991.

FRYDMAN, Roman and Andrzej RAPACZYNSKI, "Markets and Institutions in Large Scale Privatization", in V. Corbo, F. Coricelli, and J. Bossak, eds., *Reforming Central and Eastern European Economies,* World Bank, Washington, D. C., 1991.

FRYDMAN, Roman, Andrzej RAPACZYNSKI and John EARLE (1993), *Privatization in the Transition to a Market Economy,* Pinter Publishers, London.

GROSSMAN, Sanford J. and Oliver D. HART, "The Costs and Benefits of Ownership: a Theory of Vertical and Lateral Integration", *Journal of Political Economy,* 1986.

HART, Oliver D., "The Market Mechanism as an Incentive Scheme", *Bell Journal of Economics,* 1983.

INTERNATIONAL MONETARY FUND ET AL (1991), *A Study of the Soviet Economy.*

JOSCOW, Paul, Richard SCHMALENSEE and Natasha TSUKANOVA, "Competition Policy in Russia During and After Privatization", *Brookings Papers on Economic Activity,* 1994, forthcoming.

KIKERI, Sunita, John NELLIS and Mary SHIRLEY (1992), *Privatization: the Lessons of Experience,* World Bank, Washington, D. C.

LAFFONT, Jean Jacques and Jean TIROLE (1993), *A Theory of Incentives in Regulation and Procurement,* MIT Press.

LIPTON, David and Jeffrey D. SACHS, "Privatization in Eastern Europe: the Case of Poland", *Brookings Papers on Economic Activity,* 1990.

MUELLER, Dennis (1989), *Public Choice II,* University Press, Cambridge.

NELLIS, John, "Contract Plans and Public Enterprise Performance", World Bank Staff Working Paper No. 118, 1988.

PHELPS, Edmund S., Roman FRYDMAN, Andrzej RAPACZYNSKI and Andrei SHLEIFER, "Needed Mechanisms for Corporate Governance and Finance in Eastern Europe", *Economics of Transition,* 1993.

PINTO, Brian, M. BELKA, and S. KRAJAEWSKI, "Transforming State Enterprises in Poland: Evidence on Adjustment by Manufacturing Firms", *Brookings Papers on Economic Activity.*

SACHS, Jeffrey D., "Privatization in Russia: Lessons from Eastern Europe", *American Economic Review Papers and Proceedings,* 1992.

SACHS, Jeffrey D., "Prospects for Monetary Stabilization in Russia", mimeo, 1993.

SHLEIFER, Andrei and Robert W. VISHNY, "Large Shareholders and Corporate Control", *Journal of Political Economy,* 1986.

SHLEIFER, Andrei and Robert W. VISHNY, "Privatization in Russia: First Steps", mimeo, 1992.

VINING, Aiden and Anthondy BOARDMAN, "Onwership vs. Competition: Efficiency in Public Enterprise", *Public Choice,* 1992.

WORLD BANK (1993), "Subsidies and Directed Credits to Enterprises in Russia: a Strategy for Reform", Working Paper.

WORLD BANK (1993), "Russia: the Banking System in Transition", Working Paper.

Mass Privatisation: A First Assessment of the Results in the Republic of Kazakhstan

James B. Varanese*

I. Introduction

The State Property Committee (GKI) of the Republic of Kazakhstan is charged with the administration of the Kazakh National Privatisation Programme 1993-95 (Second Stage)[1]. The Kazakh National Privatisation Programme includes four components: (a) the Small-Scale Privatisation Programme, (b) the Mass Privatisation Programme, (c) the Case-By-Case Privatisation Programme, and (d) the Agriculture Privatisation Programme[2,3]. The scope of all four privatisation methods in Kazakhstan include virtually all sectors. See Table 1 at Annex I[4]. This paper primarily focuses on the Mass Privatisation Programme of Kazakhstan (MPP).

The MPP, developed by the GKI and its advisors, is a "state-of-the-art" voucher distribution and share auction scheme[5]. The MPP blends successful features of other mass privatisation schemes currently undergoing implementation in various countries.

State-owned enterprises (SOEs) with employees numbering between 200 and 5 000 are eligible for privatisation via the MPP. Ultimately, the number of SOEs corporatised under the MPP might total 8 000 to 12 000, each to be privatised through auctions in several waves. It is anticipated that the first wave will include approximately 1 150 SOEs, although the precise number is not yet final.

The MPP mandates that voucher coupons representing symbolic (non-monetary) investment points be distributed to eligible Kazakh citizens. These voucher coupons are not tradeable, but must be allocated to one or more licensed investment funds (IFs). It is anticipated that the investment points will be allocated by participating Kazakh citizens, prior to each of the several waves of privatisation, to one or more licensed IFs.

The voucher-based privatisation component of the MPP is organised through auctions of the shares of former SOEs. It is anticipated that, as a general rule, 51 per cent of the shares of each SOE included will be sold via auction. Only licensed IFs and their fund managers (FMs) may participate in these auctions. Outside of the auction process, certain shares of former SOEs may be reserved (up to 10 per cent) for direct subscription by employees and management.

II. Preliminary results

The implementation of the MPP in Kazakhstan is only partial, although the speed of the implementation is impressive. Thus far, thousands of Kazakh SOEs have initiated the process of "corporatisation", meaning their transformation into joint-stock companies with shares. The distribution of voucher coupons to eligible citizens is approximately 70 per cent + complete, with virtually all eligible citizens participating. Approximately 89 IFs have been licensed as of January 1994. The sale of the newly corporatised enterprises to IFs via auctions is anticipated to begin in mid-1994. See Table 1 below.

Table 1. **Mass privatisation: leading indicators**

SOE corporatisation	Voucher coupon distribution (Percentage of eligible citizens receiving coupon book.)	Investment fund licensing	Share auctions
Founding documents approved for 83% of 3 015 SOEs targeted as of January 1994	Jan. 1994: 33% Feb. 1994: 60% Mar. 1994: +70%	103 IF applications received: 89 IF licenses granted as of January 1994	None to date: first wave auction scheduled for mid-1994

These preliminary indicators for the MPP set forth above demonstrate that -- by comparison with the Small-Scale Privatisation Programme and the Case-By-Case Privatisation Programme -- concrete privatisation results under the MPP have yet to be achieved. Overall, privatisation outside the MPP (by standard means) was achieved in virtually all of the GKI's regional (or Oblast) administrative centres in a variety of forms, including privatisation via (a) sale or lease to worker's collectives, (b) property leases, (c) sale of shares in newly formed joint stock companies, and (d) by other methods. See Table 1 (categorized by region or Oblast) and Table 2 (categorized by sector) in Annex II.

The Small-Scale Privatisation Programme conducted a pilot programme in August and September of 1993 to sell or lease 153 separate small-scale enterprises via auctions. This programme is scheduled to continue to achieve further results in the first quarter of 1994.

The Case-By-Case Privatisation Programme had a notable success in the sale via international tender of the shares of the Almaty Tobacco Factory in 1993. This programme also continues to gain momentum in the first quarter of 1994 as some 38 enterprises in various sectors -- including minerals, petrochemicals, and retail -- have been scheduled for privatisation via similar international tenders.

III. Methods and objectives of the Kazakh MPP

Although the first auctions of the shares of SOEs have not yet been held, the methods used have been considerably refined and important MPP objectives have been substantially achieved.

Corporatisation

SOE corporatisation and preparation for privatisation occurs at regional GKI administrative centres under the direction of the central GKI located in Almaty. In Kazakhstan, the relevant unit of regional government administration is the Oblast. The 21 Oblast GKI have achieved substantial results. See Table 1 at Annex III. Nonetheless, many enterprises that may be auctioned in the first wave have yet to be corporatised.

The primary method of corporatisation is through the use of uniform incorporation/foundation documents developed by the central GKI in Almaty. One roadblock to speedy corporatisation is the lack of effective institutional infrastructure and leadership at the Oblast level. One remedy for non-performing SOEs and Oblast administrators is that their mandates may be cancelled and outside experts appointed at the cost of the relevant SOE. This remedy does not appear to have been widely enforced against non-performing SOEs and Oblast administrators.

Distribution of voucher coupon books

The distribution of voucher coupon books has achieved substantial penetration to most regions of Kazakhstan. The task is enormous: Kazakhstan is one of the world's largest countries in land mass and its population is dispersed. The administrative machinery for voucher coupon book distribution are the branches of the State Savings Banks; to supplement this machinery, SOEs have been enlisted to also distribute voucher coupon books.

The cost to each citizen for the voucher coupon book is nominal (approximately US$.10) to achieve the greatest public participation. Voucher coupon books are registered in the name of the recipient and are not tradeable. Only Kazakh nationals are eligible to receive voucher coupon books. Not all citizens receive an equal number of investment points; citizens in rural areas will receive 120 per cent of the normal allotment. Investment points may be only allocated to a licensed IF; there is no other permitted use. The Kazakh voucher coupon book distribution scheme is tightly controlled to prevent fraud; to date, there have been few reports of abuses.

Investment fund licensing

IFs and FMs are licensed and their operations overseen by an Inter-Departmental Commission on Licensing Investment Funds and Fund Managers (the "Inter-Departmental Commission"). Approximately 89 IFs have been licensed. The Inter-Departmental Commission also has the authority to audit IFs and has already undertaken an audit of newly licensed funds, correcting a number of errors, including (a) insufficient evidence of paid-up Charter Capital, (b) failure to pay licensing fee, and (c) Founding Agreement and Charter either lacking or not in accordance with the applicable law and regulations.

Unlike other Central-East European countries with mass privatisation programmes permitting investment funds to act as intermediaries -- most notably the Czech Republic -- Kazakh chartered banking institutions may not found IFs in accordance with applicable Kazakh banking laws and regulations. Likewise, Kazakh institutions in which the state holds an ownership share in excess of 30 per cent may not found IFs.

Foreign entities are also prohibited from founding IFs. This does not rule out the role of foreign investment company expertise. A foreign investment company may elect to establish a Kazakh subsidiary that would be eligible to retain or become a licensed FM, and thereby enter into an investment advisory contract manage an IF.

In all cases, each IF and its affiliated FM must compete in the market to persuade citizens to allocate their investment points to that IF. Citizens will be initially restricted to allocating no more than 25 per cent of their investment points, and will be subsequently permitted to allocating the remaining investment points as more knowledge and experience is gained with the conduct and performance of the various IFs and FMs.

The number of investment points obtained by an IF directly correlates to the buying power of that IF at the share auctions. Importantly, the GKI and the Inter-

Departmental Commission plan to issue anti-fraud and truth-in-advertising regulations to control the advertising campaigns of IFs.

Share auctions

As a general rule, the share auctions for SOEs will typically offer the majority of shares to IFs. The one notable exception to the general rule that the majority of shares will be offered at auction is in the case of those SOEs that have been grouped into strategic or sectoral "holding companies". In these holding companies the Kazakh Government will retain -- at least at the outset -- a controlling interest[6]. There is no reliable estimate of the book value of the SOEs to be offered for sale at the auctions.

SOEs are auctioned for symbolic (non-monetary) investment points to the highest bidding IFs. As a result of the applicable diversification rules, no IF may invest more that 5 per cent of its capital (meaning its total investment points) to any one SOE. As a result of the applicable share dispersion rules, it is anticipated that no IF will be permitted to acquire in excess of 10 per cent of any one SOE at any one share auction and not in excess of 20 per cent through all available means.

Central depositary system

The GKI intends to establish a central depositary system (CDS) for the holding of IF-owned securities in Kazakh issuers. To date this CDS is not yet operational, but is in the planning stage. The GKI, with funding from multi-lateral funding institutions, has acquired the necessary computers and is now building the necessary database that would be the platform for the CDS.

IV. Post-privatisation securities market

IFs are subject to licensing and diversification rules that will substantially affect the post-privatisation securities market. The shares of former SOEs acquired by IFs at the auctions are, following the auction, freely tradable. Thus, the essential precondition for an infant securities market is satisfied. The following analysis sets forth some preliminary observations regarding the anticipated role of the IF in the post-privatisation securities market.

Concentration of ownership

As a consequence of licensing and capital requirements, there will be a limited number of IFs. The number of licensed IFs that are expected to be significant participants in the auctions for former SOEs cannot now be estimated because voucher holders have not yet allocated their investment points among these IFs. The dispersion of the investment points among the IFs will be one factor affecting the concentration of IF ownership in the market.

Restructuring SOE operations

IFs will initially hold a maximum of 20 per cent in any single SOE. Accordingly, IFs will need to cooperate to achieve the leadership necessary to restructure. Unlike certain other countries, IFs will not fear restructuring proposals based solely on concerns about the security of SOE loans held by credit institutions. Specifically, IFs are not permitted to be affiliated with chartered financial institutions holding debt (such as banks). Consequently, it is anticipated that this infant securities market will be divorced from debt-side influences that appear to have surfaced in countries where major banks and insurance institutions control the IFs.

Restructuring SOEs via sale of control block to foreign investors

If diversification rules will require some degree of cooperation among IFs to assemble control blocks of shares for sale to strategic investors, but will be less of an impediment than would be the case were the shares in former SOEs widely held among the populace.

Integrity of securities market

IFs will need to be managed in a fairly transparent manner; both IFs and FMs are licensed and their operations overseen by an Inter-Departmental Commission on Licensing Investment Funds and Fund Managers. Among other regulations, disclosure rules, anti-fraud protections, and prohibitions on conflict-of-interest are in place. This oversight will be accompanied by fairly broad regulatory powers to audit IFs and terminate the licenses of non-complying FMs. The IFs will be the major players in the securities markets. All of the foregoing should discipline IF operations and, accordingly, strengthen the integrity of the securities markets.

V. Final observations

Many mass privatisation programmes seek to optimise speed, stability, and SOE restructuring. The optimal blend will depend on the economic, political and cultural context in which privatisation takes place. As a departure point, mass privatisation programmes may be analysed along the following two dimensions:

--   the control dimension, i.e. whether privatisation is controlled from the top down by a central governmental agency, or from the bottom up by SOE management and employees;

--   the sequencing dimension, i.e. whether SOE restructuring is attempted prior to the transfer of ownership to private owners, or is deferred until after the transfer of ownership to private owners.

Top-down versus Bottom-up

The top-down model of mass privatisation reserves initial privatisation responsibility to the regulating authority for privatisation, i.e. the Ministry of Privatisation or the GKI.   The top-down approach emphasises stability (programme implementation) and centralisation.   By contrast, the bottom-up model of mass privatisation delegates initial responsibility to the SOE itself to formulate a unique privatisation project. These unique privatisation projects may, and often do, allocate a percentage of the shares of the SOE for voucher distribution to citizen-participants who hold investment points.   The bottom-up approach emphasises enterprise restructuring (unique projects) and decentralisation.

We see that the Kazakh MPP -- adapting to the unique needs of the Kazakh context -- uses an accelerated top-down approach.   Speed of privatisation is provided by the inclusion of large numbers of SOEs in auctions (similar to the Czech model and others).   Stability of privatisation is provided by licensing and regulating the IFs and FMs (similar to the Polish model and others).   The implementation of the MPP requires that both the SOEs be quickly corporatised and prepared for a mass auction, and that the IFs and FMs be carefully licensed and equipped to fulfil their role as portfolio managers.

Restructure first versus privatise first

The essential conflict is an issue of speed and control.   Privatisation can be most speedily accomplished if difficult issues of restructuring are deferred until after privatisation;   however, this transfers restructuring decisions to private owners.   In the view of many, sequencing privatisation before restructuring is beneficial if one adopts the position that restructuring is most effectively accomplished by private owners.

We see that the Kazakh MPP -- again adapting to the unique needs of the Kazakh context -- uses the privatise first and restructure later approach.   As a general rule, the GKI does not actively intervene to restructure SOEs privatised via the share auctions. These restructuring decisions are deferred to the IFs who will control the SOE following the share auctions.

Notes

*   Based on a presentation made by the author (James Varanese, White & Case, Prague) at the fifth meeting of the Advisory Group on Privatisation, Paris, 2-4 March 1994.

1.   Presidential Decree on the National Privatisation Programme (No. 695-XII, approved 21 June 1991; 1993-95 Second Stage approved 5 March 1993).

2.   The Small-Scale Privatisation Programme is reserved for small (200 employees or less) enterprises and assets.

3.   The Case-By-Case Privatisation Programme is reserved for the privatization of very large (5 000 employees or more) or unique enterprises.

4.   Unless otherwise indicated, the information contained in Tables 1-6 are based on information provided by the GKI and other Kazakh Government agencies.

5.   The MPP implements the directives set forth in the Law on Denationalisation and Privatisation (No. 696-XII, 22 June 1993, and amended on 18 January 1992 and 12 April 1993).

6.   These holding company structures are outside the scope of this paper. However, it is sufficient to note that they contain a significant number of valuable enterprises and represent a significant portion of the total capital to be privatised under the MPP.

Table 1. **Distribution of privatised enterprises by branch of economy as of 1 January 1994**

Name of branch	1991-1992		1993	
	Number of enterprises	Percentage	Number of enterprises	Percentage
Total	8 693	100.0	2 495	100.0
Industry	965	11.1	422	16.9
Construction	550	6.3	237	9.5
Agriculture	972	11.2	344	13.8
Transport and road maintenance	559	6.4	469	18.8
Trade	2 226	25.8	392	15.7
Cafes and restaurants	614	7.1	79	3.2
Everyday services	1 806	20.8	210	8.4
Public utilities	241	2.8	46	1.8
Others	760	8.7	296	11.9

Table 1. **Report on results of privatisation of state property as of 1 January 1994**

Name of oblast region	Enterprise (objects) privatised as of 1 January 1994			
	By worker collectives	By non-public legal entities	On lease terms	Transferred free of charge
Akmolinsk	37	54	32	-
Aktyubinsk	27	16	2	-
Almaty	18	23	-	-
Atyrau	8	7	-	-
East Kazakhstan	40	14	-	-
Zhambyl	39	99	1	-
Zhezkazgan	8	2	-	-
West Kazakhstan	4	13	-	-
Karaganda	20	3	7	1
Kzyl-Orda	17	6	-	-
Kokshetau	9	1	-	-
Kostanai	31	36	-	-
Mangistau	7	4	-	-
Pavlodar	9	34	8	6
North Kazakhstan	8	5	1	-
Semipalatinsk	33	15	-	2
Taldy-Korgan	15	27	-	-
Torgai	2	1	-	1
South Kazakhstan	10	9	1	-
City of Almaty	52	17	-	-
City of Leninsk	1	-	1	-
Total	**386**	**586**	**51**	**10**

Table 1. **Report on results of privatisation of state property as of 1 January 1994** (cont'd.)

Name of oblast (region)	Enterprise (objects) privatised as of 1 January 1994			
	By joint-stock companies	Otherwise	Total	Since 1991 (for reference)
Akmolinsk	140	-	263	610
Aktyubinsk	21	23	89	272
Almaty	33	-	74	379
Atyrau	90	-	103	292
East Kazakhstan	82	29	165	526
Zhambyl	94	4	337	628
Zhezkazgan	33	4	37	191
West Kazakhstan	134	-	151	387
Karaganda	25	-	56	457
Kzyl-Orda	74	1	98	387
Kokshetau	1	4	15	187
Kostanai	21	-	91	343
Mangistau	4	3	24	115
Pavlodar	25	19	199	597
North Kazakhstan	162	-	176	473
Semipalatinsk	93	20	153	423
Taldy-Korgan	90	6	138	527
Torgai	-	-	4	133
South Kazakhstan	150	5	175	1 177
City of Almaty	75	-	144	608
City of Leninsk	1	-	3	31
Total	**1 338**	**124**	**2 495**	**8 693**

Table 2a. Number of enterprises and objects privatised in 1993 as of 1 January 1994

Enterprises and objects, including	Methods of privatisation				Since 1991 (all methods)
	By worker collectives	By non-public legal entities	On lease terms	Trans-ferred free of charge	
Trade	118	92	15	-	2 226
Cafes and restaurants	30	27	2	-	614
Everyday services	89	74	2	3	1 806
Public utilities	2	34	2	-	241
Industry	23	45	2	-	965
Construction	20	60	-	-	550
Agriculture	52	35	-	7	972
Transport	8	109	-	-	559
Others	44	110	28	-	760
Total	**386**	**586**	**51**	**10**	**8 693**

Table 2*b*. **Number of enterprises and objects privatised in 1993 as of 1 January 1994**

Enterprises and objects, including	Type of company		Total	Since 1991 (all)
	As joint-stock companies	Other		
Trade	125	42	392	2 226
Cafes and restaurants	11	9	79	614
Everyday services	33	9	210	1 806
Public utilities	7	1	46	241
Industry	337	18	422	965
Construction	142	15	237	550
Agriculture	239	11	344	972
Transport	345	7	469	559
Others	99	15	296	760
Total	**1 338**	**124**	**2 495**	**8 693**

Table 1*a*. **Progress report on transformation of state enterprises subject to incorporation**

No.	Name of oblast	No. of enterprises subject to incorporation (oblast total)	No. of enterprises with documents approved by territorial committees		No. of enterprises with state-registered documents	
		Total	Total	Per cent	Total	Per cent
1.	Aktyubinsk	273	273	2 100	189	89
2.	Almaty	83	70	84	70	100
3.	Akmolinsk	125	96	76	24	25
4.	Atyrau	78	78	100	78	100
5.	East Kazakhstan	187	154	92	83	54
6.	Zhezkazagan	100	95	95	95	100
7.	Zhambyl	219	194	81	175	90
8.	Karaganda	275	175	76	77	43
9.	Kokshetau	147	144	93	77	53
10.	Kostanai	260	221	85	204	92
11.	Kzyl-Orda	62	62	100	14	23
12.	Mangistau	54	58	91	53	100
13.	Pavlodar	148	145	91	43	30
14.	Semipalatinsk	86	82	25	82	100
15.	North Kazakhstan	141	135	96	80	22
16.	Taldy-Korgan	94	89	98	30	34
17.	Torgai	71	48	89	6	13
18.	West Kazakhstan	155	162	98	49	30
19.	South Kazakhstan	141	141	100	138	96
20.	City of Almaty	301	77	26	77	100
21.	City of Leninsk	9	9	100	9	100

Table 1*b*. Progress report on transformation of state enterprises subject to incorporation

No.	Name of oblast	No. of enterprises with documents submitted to territorial committee		No. of enterprises engaged in preparatory work	
		Total	Per cent	Total	Per cent
1.	Aktyubinsk	3	1	2	1
2.	Almaty	13	16	-	-
3.	Akmolinsk	-	-	30	24
4.	Atyrau	-	-	-	-
5.	East Kazakhstan	3	2	10	6
6.	Zhezkazagan	5	5	-	-
7.	Zhambyl	-	-	25	11
8.	Karaganda	76	27	22	8
9.	Kokshetau	-	-	3	2
10.	Kostanai	39	15	-	-
11.	Kzyl-Orda	-	-	-	-
12.	Mangistau	-	-	6	9
13.	Pavlodar	-	-	1	1
14.	Semipalatinsk	4	5	-	-
15.	North Kazakhstan	2	-	3	2
16.	Taldy-Korgan	5	5	-	-
17.	Torgai	-	-	23	32
18.	West Kazakhstan	3	3	1	1
19.	South Kazakhstan	-	-	-	-
20.	City of Almaty	101	34	123	41
21.	City of Leninsk	-	-	-	-

MAIN SALES OUTLETS OF OECD PUBLICATIONS
PRINCIPAUX POINTS DE VENTE DES PUBLICATIONS DE L'OCDE

ARGENTINA – ARGENTINE
Carlos Hirsch S.R.L.
Galería Güemes, Florida 165, 4° Piso
1333 Buenos Aires   Tel. (1) 331.1787 y 331.2391
Telefax: (1) 331.1787

AUSTRALIA – AUSTRALIE
D.A. Information Services
648 Whitehorse Road, P.O.B 163
Mitcham, Victoria 3132   Tel. (03) 873.4411
Telefax: (03) 873.5679

AUSTRIA – AUTRICHE
Gerold & Co.
Graben 31
Wien I   Tel. (0222) 533.50.14

BELGIUM – BELGIQUE
Jean De Lannoy
Avenue du Roi 202
B-1060 Bruxelles   Tel. (02) 538.51.69/538.08.41
Telefax: (02) 538.08.41

CANADA
Renouf Publishing Company Ltd.
1294 Algoma Road
Ottawa, ON K1B 3W8   Tel. (613) 741.4333
Telefax: (613) 741.5439
Stores:
61 Sparks Street
Ottawa, ON K1P 5R1   Tel. (613) 238.8985
211 Yonge Street
Toronto, ON M5B 1M4   Tel. (416) 363.3171
Telefax: (416)363.59.63
Les Éditions La Liberté Inc.
3020 Chemin Sainte-Foy
Sainte-Foy, PQ G1X 3V6   Tel. (418) 658.3763
Telefax: (418) 658.3763

Federal Publications Inc.
165 University Avenue, Suite 701
Toronto, ON M5H 3B8   Tel. (416) 860.1611
Telefax: (416) 860.1608
Les Publications Fédérales
1185 Université
Montréal, QC H3B 3A7   Tel. (514) 954.1633
Telefax : (514) 954.1635

CHINA – CHINE
China National Publications Import
Export Corporation (CNPIEC)
16 Gongti E. Road, Chaoyang District
P.O. Box 88 or 50
Beijing 100704 PR   Tel. (01) 506.6688
Telefax: (01) 506.3101

**CZECH REPUBLIC – RÉPUBLIQUE
TCHÈQUE**
Artia Pegas Press Ltd.
Narodni Trida 25
POB 825
111 21 Praha 1   Tel. 26.65.68
Telefax: 26.20.81

DENMARK – DANEMARK
Munksgaard Book and Subscription Service
35, Nørre Søgade, P.O. Box 2148
DK-1016 København K   Tel. (33) 12.85.70
Telefax: (33) 12.93.87

EGYPT – ÉGYPTE
Middle East Observer
41 Sherif Street
Cairo   Tel. 392.6919
Telefax: 360-6804

FINLAND – FINLANDE
Akateeminen Kirjakauppa
Keskuskatu 1, P.O. Box 128
00100 Helsinki
Subscription Services/Agence d'abonnements :
P.O. Box 23
00371 Helsinki   Tel. (358 0) 12141
Telefax: (358 0) 121.4450

FRANCE
OECD/OCDE
Mail Orders/Commandes par correspondance:
2, rue André-Pascal
75775 Paris Cedex 16   Tel. (33-1) 45.24.82.00
Telefax: (33-1) 49.10.42.76
Telex: 640048 OCDE
Orders via Minitel, France only/
Commandes par Minitel, France exclusivement :
36 15 OCDE

OECD Bookshop/Librairie de l'OCDE :
33, rue Octave-Feuillet
75016 Paris   Tel. (33-1) 45.24.81.67
(33-1) 45.24.81.81

Documentation Française
29, quai Voltaire
75007 Paris   Tel. 40.15.70.00
Gibert Jeune (Droit-Économie)
6, place Saint-Michel
75006 Paris   Tel. 43.25.91.19
Librairie du Commerce International
10, avenue d'Iéna
75016 Paris   Tel. 40.73.34.60
Librairie Dunod
Université Paris-Dauphine
Place du Maréchal de Lattre de Tassigny
75016 Paris   Tel. (1) 44.05.40.13
Librairie Lavoisier
11, rue Lavoisier
75008 Paris   Tel. 42.65.39.95
Librairie L.G.D.J. - Montchrestien
20, rue Soufflot
75005 Paris   Tel. 46.33.89.85
Librairie des Sciences Politiques
30, rue Saint-Guillaume
75007 Paris   Tel. 45.48.36.02
P.U.F.
49, boulevard Saint-Michel
75005 Paris   Tel. 43.25.83.40
Librairie de l'Université
12a, rue Nazareth
13100 Aix-en-Provence   Tel. (16) 42.26.18.08
Documentation Française
165, rue Garibaldi
69003 Lyon   Tel. (16) 78.63.32.23
Librairie Decitre
29, place Bellecour
69002 Lyon   Tel. (16) 72.40.54.54

GERMANY – ALLEMAGNE
OECD Publications and Information Centre
August-Bebel-Allee 6
D-53175 Bonn   Tel. (0228) 959.120
Telefax: (0228) 959.12.17

GREECE – GRÈCE
Librairie Kauffmann
Mavrokordatou 9
106 78 Athens   Tel. (01) 32.55.321
Telefax: (01) 36.33.967

HONG-KONG
Swindon Book Co. Ltd.
13–15 Lock Road
Kowloon, Hong Kong   Tel. 2376.2062
Telefax: 2376.0685

HUNGARY – HONGRIE
Euro Info Service
Margitsziget, Európa Ház
1138 Budapest   Tel. (1) 111.62.16
Telefax : (1) 111.60.61

ICELAND – ISLANDE
Mál Mog Menning
Laugavegi 18, Pósthólf 392
121 Reykjavik   Tel. 162.35.23

INDIA – INDE
Oxford Book and Stationery Co.
Scindia House
New Delhi 110001   Tel.(11) 331.5896/5308
Telefax: (11) 332.5993
17 Park Street
Calcutta 700016   Tel. 240832

INDONESIA – INDONÉSIE
Pdii-Lipi
P.O. Box 4298
Jakarta 12042   Tel. (21) 573.34.67
Telefax: (21) 573.34.67

IRELAND – IRLANDE
Government Supplies Agency
Publications Section
4/5 Harcourt Road
Dublin 2   Tel. 661.31.11
Telefax: 478.06.45

ISRAEL
Praedicta
5 Shatner Street
P.O. Box 34030
Jerusalem 91430   Tel. (2) 52.84.90/1/2
Telefax: (2) 52.84.93
R.O.Y.
P.O. Box 13056
Tel Aviv 61130   Tel. (3) 49.61.08
Telefax (3) 544.60.39

ITALY – ITALIE
Libreria Commissionaria Sansoni
Via Duca di Calabria 1/1
50125 Firenze   Tel. (055) 64.54.15
Telefax: (055) 64.12.57
Via Bartolini 29
20155 Milano   Tel. (02) 36.50.83
Editrice e Libreria Herder
Piazza Montecitorio 120
00186 Roma   Tel. 679.46.28
Telefax: 678.47.51
Libreria Hoepli
Via Hoepli 5
20121 Milano   Tel. (02) 86.54.46
Telefax: (02) 805.28.86
Libreria Scientifica
Dott. Lucio de Biasio 'Aeiou'
Via Coronelli, 6
20146 Milano   Tel. (02) 48.95.45.52
Telefax: (02) 48.95.45.48

JAPAN – JAPON
OECD Publications and Information Centre
Landic Akasaka Building
2-3-4 Akasaka, Minato-ku
Tokyo 107   Tel. (81.3) 3586.2016
Telefax: (81.3) 3584.7929

KOREA – CORÉE
Kyobo Book Centre Co. Ltd.
P.O. Box 1658, Kwang Hwa Moon
Seoul   Tel. 730.78.91
Telefax: 735.00.30

MALAYSIA – MALAISIE
University of Malaya Bookshop
University of Malaya
P.O. Box 1127, Jalan Pantai Baru
59700 Kuala Lumpur
Malaysia   Tel. 756.5000/756.5425
Telefax: 756.3246

MEXICO – MEXIQUE
Revistas y Periodicos Internacionales S.A. de C.V.
Florencia 57 - 1004
Mexico, D.F. 06600   Tel. 207.81.00
Telefax : 208.39.79

NETHERLANDS – PAYS-BAS
SDU Uitgeverij Plantijnstraat
Externe Fondsen
Postbus 20014
2500 EA's-Gravenhage   Tel. (070) 37.89.880
Voor bestellingen: Telefax: (070) 34.75.778

NEW ZEALAND
NOUVELLE-ZÉLANDE
Legislation Services
P.O. Box 12418
Thorndon, Wellington   Tel. (04) 496.5652
          Telefax: (04) 496.5698

NORWAY – NORVÈGE
Narvesen Info Center – NIC
Bertrand Narvesens vei 2
P.O. Box 6125 Etterstad
0602 Oslo 6   Tel. (022) 57.33.00
          Telefax: (022) 68.19.01

PAKISTAN
Mirza Book Agency
65 Shahrah Quaid-E-Azam
Lahore 54000   Tel. (42) 353.601
          Telefax: (42) 231.730

PHILIPPINE – PHILIPPINES
International Book Center
5th Floor, Filipinas Life Bldg.
Ayala Avenue
Metro Manila   Tel. 81.96.76
          Telex 23312 RHP PH

PORTUGAL
Livraria Portugal
Rua do Carmo 70-74
Apart. 2681
1200 Lisboa   Tel.: (01) 347.49.82/5
          Telefax: (01) 347.02.64

SINGAPORE – SINGAPOUR
Gower Asia Pacific Pte Ltd.
Golden Wheel Building
41, Kallang Pudding Road, No. 04-03
Singapore 1334   Tel. 741.5166
          Telefax: 742.9356

SPAIN – ESPAGNE
Mundi-Prensa Libros S.A.
Castelló 37, Apartado 1223
Madrid 28001   Tel. (91) 431.33.99
          Telefax: (91) 575.39.98

Libreria Internacional AEDOS
Consejo de Ciento 391
08009 – Barcelona   Tel. (93) 488.30.09
          Telefax: (93) 487.76.59

Llibreria de la Generalitat
Palau Moja
Rambla dels Estudis, 118
08002 – Barcelona
          (Subscripcions) Tel. (93) 318.80.12
          (Publicacions) Tel. (93) 302.67.23
          Telefax: (93) 412.18.54

SRI LANKA
Centre for Policy Research
c/o Colombo Agencies Ltd.
No. 300-304, Galle Road
Colombo 3   Tel. (1) 574240, 573551-2
          Telefax: (1) 575394, 510711

SWEDEN – SUÈDE
Fritzes Information Center
Box 16356
Regeringsgatan 12
106 47 Stockholm   Tel. (08) 690.90.90
          Tel. (08) 20.50.21

Subscription Agency/Agence d'abonnements :
Wennergren-Williams Info AB
P.O. Box 1305
171 25 Solna   Tel. (08) 705.97.50
          Téléfax : (08) 27.00.71

SWITZERLAND – SUISSE
Maditec S.A. (Books and Periodicals - Livres
et périodiques)
Chemin des Palettes 4
Case postale 266
1020 Renens VD 1   Tel. (021) 635.08.65
          Telefax: (021) 635.07.80

Librairie Payot S.A.
4, place Pépinet
CP 3212
1002 Lausanne   Tel. (021) 341.33.47
          Telefax: (021) 341.33.45

Librairie Unilivres
6, rue de Candolle
1205 Genève   Tel. (022) 320.26.23
          Telefax: (022) 329.73.18

Subscription Agency/Agence d'abonnements :
Dynapresse Marketing S.A.
38 avenue Vibert
1227 Carouge   Tel.: (022) 308.07.89
          Telefax : (022) 308.07.99

See also – Voir aussi :
OECD Publications and Information Centre
August-Bebel-Allee 6
D-53175 Bonn (Germany)   Tel. (0228) 959.120
          Telefax: (0228) 959.12.17

TAIWAN – FORMOSE
Good Faith Worldwide Int'l. Co. Ltd.
9th Floor, No. 118, Sec. 2
Chung Hsiao E. Road
Taipei   Tel. (02) 391.7396/391.7397
          Telefax: (02) 394.9176

THAILAND – THAÏLANDE
Suksit Siam Co. Ltd.
113, 115 Fuang Nakhon Rd.
Opp. Wat Rajbopith
Bangkok 10200   Tel. (662) 225.9531/2
          Telefax: (662) 222.5188

TURKEY – TURQUIE
Kültür Yayinlari Is-Türk Ltd. Sti.
Atatürk Bulvari No. 191/Kat 13
Kavaklidere/Ankara   Tel. 428.11.40 Ext. 2458
Dolmabahce Cad. No. 29
Besiktas/Istanbul   Tel. 260.71.88
          Telex: 43482B

UNITED KINGDOM – ROYAUME-UNI
HMSO
Gen. enquiries   Tel. (071) 873 0011
Postal orders only:
P.O. Box 276, London SW8 5DT
Personal Callers HMSO Bookshop
49 High Holborn, London WC1V 6HB
          Telefax: (071) 873 8200
Branches at: Belfast, Birmingham, Bristol, Edin-
burgh, Manchester

UNITED STATES – ÉTATS-UNIS
OECD Publications and Information Centre
2001 L Street N.W., Suite 700
Washington, D.C. 20036-4910 Tel. (202) 785.6323
          Telefax: (202) 785.0350

VENEZUELA
Libreria del Este
Avda F. Miranda 52, Aptdo. 60337
Edificio Galipán
Caracas 106   Tel. 951.1705/951.2307/951.1297
          Telegram: Libreste Caracas

Subscription to OECD periodicals may also be
placed through main subscription agencies.

Les abonnements aux publications périodiques de
l'OCDE peuvent être souscrits auprès des
principales agences d'abonnement.

Orders and inquiries from countries where Distribu-
tors have not yet been appointed should be sent to:
OECD Publications Service, 2 rue André-Pascal,
75775 Paris Cedex 16, France.

Les commandes provenant de pays où l'OCDE n'a
pas encore désigné de distributeur peuvent être
adressées à : OCDE, Service des Publications,
2, rue André-Pascal, 75775 Paris Cedex 16, France.

1-1995

OECD PUBLICATIONS, 2 rue André-Pascal, 75775 PARIS CEDEX 16
PRINTED IN FRANCE
(14 95 03 1) ISBN 92-64-14381-5 - No. 47747 1995